Recipes for Resilience

Common Sense Cooking for the 21st Century

Elizabeth J Walker

Published by New Generation Publishing in 2019

Copyright © Elizabeth J. Walker 2019

First Edition

The author asserts the moral right under the Copyright, Designs and Patents Act 1988 to be identified as the author of this work.

All Rights reserved. No part of this publication may be reproduced, stored in a retrieval system or transmitted, in any form or by any means without the prior consent of the author, nor be otherwise circulated in any form of binding or cover other than that in which it is published and without a similar condition being imposed on the subsequent purchaser.

www.newgeneration-publishing.com

CONTENTS

Preface *1*

Chapter One   Introducing Food Resilience *3*
   Lessons from the past 4
   The Little Ice Age 4
   Bringing food resilience onto the agenda 5
   The story of the Resilience Garden 6
   Emergency stores 7
   Welcome to the adventure! 8

Chapter Two   Food Stores *9*
   The history of stores 9
   Where to store food 10
   Storing water 11
   Cooking in an emergency 12
      Chickpea curry a la camping stove 12
      Fruit crumble in a pan 12
   Planning a food store 13

Chapter Three   Cooking *15*
   Using recipes 15
   Cooking from stores 16
   A resilient diet 18
   Measuring 18
      Some useful conversions: - 20
   Cooking methods 21

Chapter Four   The Resilience Garden *23*
   Tyre Gardening 23
      Potato Stacks 25
   Organic methods 25
   Seeds 26
   The five main aims of resilience gardening 26

    Growing spaces 27

Interlude The Seasons *28*

Chapter Five November..*29*

    Planning 29

    Raised beds 30

    Pruning 31

    Some seasonal foods available in November 32

    Preserving meat 32

    Eggs..33

    Milk..33

    Potatoes 34

    Apples 35

    Nuts and seeds..36

    Recipes for November..36
        Twice baked potatoes... 36
        Potato wedges... 37
        Mince and onions... 37
        Potato scones 38
        Bread.. 38
        Scrambled eggs.. 40
        Apple Crumble.. 40

Chapter Six December *42*

    Soil 42

    Compost 43

    Liquid plant feeds..43

    Some seasonal foods available in December 44

    Feasting 44

    Dreaming..45

    Onions..45

    Recipes for December 46
        Roast chicken... 46
        Roast potatoes.. 49
        Baked squash 50
        Glazed carrots 50

Brussel sprouts with onion and bacon	50
Steamed cabbage, leeks and mustard	51
Leftover stew	51
Chicken and lentil soup with stock	52
Baked apple	52
Carrot cake	53

Chapter Seven   January 54

Wild forage 54

Famine foods 55

Some seasonal foods available in January 56

The importance of grain 57

Recipes for January 58

Rabbit stew	58
Dumplings	59
Mince and barley broth	60
Lentil soup	61
Leek and potato soup	62
War soup – a modern famine recipe	63
Savoury crumble	63
Marmalade	64
Frothy jelly	65

Interlude   Imbolc 67

Chapter Eight   February 69

Greenhouses and cold frames..69

Fresh greens 71

Some seasonal foods available in February 71

A history of dairy products..72

Hard cheese...73

Recipes for February 74

Pancakes	74
Yorkshire puddings	75
Cheese sauce	76
Nut roast	77
Mashed swede and carrot	78
Simmered nettles	78
Cakes	78
Cake flavourings, icings and fillings	81

Chapter Nine   March 83

Preparing to grow 83

Slugs and other pests 84

Deciding when to sow 85

Some seasonal foods available in March 86

Stored produce 87

Animal welfare and Lent 87

Fishing 88

Recipes for March 88
    Wild garlic pesto 88
    Pasta bolognaise 89
    Sorrel sauce 90
    Pilau rice 91
    Sweet and sour sauce 91
    Pakoras 92
    Beer battered fish 93
    Chicken nuggets 93
    Rice pudding 94
    Upside down cake 95

Chapter Ten   April 96

Sowing 96

Plant identification 97

Cultivating mushrooms 98

Some seasonal foods available in April 98

Grinding grains 99

Bread and the Industrial Revolution 100

Recipes for April 101
    Scones 101
    Apple scone 101
    Drop scones 102
    Soda bread 102
    Kedgeree 103
    Pasta bake 104
    Purple sprouting broccoli 105
    Burdock root 105
    Urban survival oyster mushroom broth 106
    Noodles with shitake mushrooms 107
    Mock knotweed crumble 107
    Impossible pie 108
    Nettle beer 108

Technical terms used in brewing 109

Interlude   Beltane *110*

Chapter Eleven   May *112*

Planting Out **112**

The Dangers of Stakes **113**

Protecting your plants **113**

Liquid plant feeds **114**

Some seasonal foods available in May **115**

Checking your stores **116**

Adapting recipes **117**

Recipes for May **118**
   Pastry 118
   Quiche 119
   Vegetable pie with cheese pastry 120
   Pastry shapes, tarts and pasties 121
   Chilli con carne 122
   Bean and pasta salad 123
   Banana bread 123
   Elderflower cordial 124

Chapter Twelve   June *125*

Selective weeding **125**

Water and the garden **126**

Some seasonal foods available in June **127**

Strawberries, cream and haymaking **127**

Water supplies **128**

Emergency drinking water **128**

Recipes for June **130**
   Barley water 130
   Lemonade 130
   Herb teas 130
   Iced tea 131
   Raspberry syrup 131
   Seasonal salads 132
   Smoked trout and orange salad 132
   Red cabbage salad 133
   Spinach, bacon and avocado salad 133
   Tuna pasta salad 133

 Falafels.. 134
 Braised broad beans 134
 Asparagus 135
 Gooseberry and blackcurrant tart with sweet pastry 135
 Whipped cream 136
 Cheesecake 136

Chapter Thirteen July...*138*

Permaculture **138**

Annuals, perennials and self-seeding..**139**

'No Dig' gardening and fungal networks **140**

Forest Gardening..**141**

Some seasonal foods available in July **141**

Hydroponics **141**

Aquaponics..**142**

Urban food production **142**

Recipes for July **143**
 Chicken curry... 143
 Mushroom curry 144
 Spiced potatoes 145
 Cucumber raita.. 145
 Potato salad 146
 Coleslaw 146
 Thousand Island dressing... 146
 Pork steak with pepper.. 147
 Strawberry trifle.. 147
 Creme fraiche tarts.. 148
 Blackcurrant syrup... 148
 Raspberry jam... 149
 Dehydrating fruit 151

Interlude Lammas..*152*

Chapter Fourteen August..*154*

Preparing to harvest..**154**

Pests **155**

Pleasure **156**

Some seasonal foods available in August..**156**

Foraging **156**

Survival skills...**158**

Fire safety 158

Recipes for August 159
   Beans and sardines 159
   Gipsy toast 159
   Gammon and pineapple 159
   Hash brown potatoes 160
   Burgers 160
   Tomato ketchup 161
   Mustard sauce 162
   Guacamole 162
   Ratatouille 162
   Beef Bourguignon 163
   Pigeon casserole 163
   Cobblers 164
   Dauphinoise potatoes 164
   Green tomato chutney 165
   Lemon ginger crunch pie 166
   Damson jelly 166

Chapter Fifteen   September *168*

Harvesting root vegetables 168

Collecting seeds 169

Gathering fruit 170

Some seasonal foods available in September 170

Freezers 171

Preserving 172

Recipes for September 173
   Tomato passata 173
   Pizza 174
   Lasagne 175
   Waldorf salad 175
   Himalayan balsam curry 176
   Goulash 177
   Rissoles 177
   Fish and cheese pie 178
   Flapjacks 178
   Fruit leathers 179
   Elderberry wine 179

Chapter Sixteen   October *182*

Feeding the soil 182

Crop rotation 183

Summing up the year	**184**
Some seasonal foods available on October	**185**
Wild fungi	**185**
Winter is coming	**186**
Recipes for October	**186**
Stuffed marrow	186
Pumpkin soup	187
Tangy braised beef	188
Devilled kidneys	189
Liver and onions	190
Corned beef shepherd's pie	190
Braised celery	191
Brownies	191
Gingerbread people	192
Plain biscuits for decorating	193
The Xmas cake	193

Interlude   Samhain *196*

Conclusion *197*

Afterword *198*

Appendix One   Food Types *199*

Proteins	**199**
Carbohydrates and sugar	**200**
Fats and oils	**201**
Vitamins	**202**
Fat soluble	202
Water soluble	203
Minerals and trace elements	**204**
Potassium	204
Sodium Chloride	204
Calcium	205
Phosphorus	205
Magnesium	205
Iron	206
Zinc	206
Copper	207
Iodine	207
Trace elements	208

Appendix Two   Fourteen days on stored food *210*

Why keep stores?	**210**

A reminder about water 211
Suggested recipe list 212
A sample checklist for this fourteen day store 215
Customising your food store 215
    Some other useful supplies 216

Recommended Reading... *217*
About the Author.. *219*

Preface

'Recipes for Resilience' takes you on the journey towards your personal food security, starting from wherever you are right now. Even if you live in a city block, where access to growing space seems impossible, you are still at the centre of a huge sea of information on the internet.

There are recipes for everything, the collected gardening lore of centuries, whole websites devoted to survival skills. You could wander among these for days – and still be unable to cook a stew or raise a carrot. To be useful, this knowledge needs to be applied to practical matters.

'Recipes for Resilience' provides you with a framework on which you can assemble facts, tips and hints into an action plan. Use search engines to discover more about growing peas, cooking kale, making your own dehydrated survival meals. Take notes, try things out. You learn more thoroughly when you actually do something, rather than just read about it.

You can avoid the hazards of panic buying, or sit out a flood which blocks local roads, by having an emergency food store. Do you really want this to be five kilos of dried beans? Do you even eat beans? Use this book to design a store which caters for your own preferences. A fortnight's worth of supplies can fit in a box which goes under an average bed.

Get to know food – buy raw vegetables, cook from ingredients. Understand how food types go together. There are over a hundred recipes here. Most can be adapted to use only preserved stores; most can also make use of fresh garden produce. It depends what you have available at the time.

Learn about small growing spaces and how to manage them. Raise some edible plants just to see how it's done. A few leaves from windowsill herbs can supply essential vitamins. Work with the seasons when planning meals; think what could be growing in your area at each time of year.

Read this book, practise these recipes, and you'll know how to make the best use of the resources around you. Hunt for bargains, explore new strategies! As you make useful preparations for an emergency – which may never happen – you'll start eating better food at a cost far lower than you might imagine.

'Recipes for Resilience' is your guide book to a whole new landscape.

Chapter One

Introducing Food Resilience

This book is the second in the Resilience series, following on from 'The Resilience Handbook – How to Survive in the 21st Century' which outlines the full spectrum of modern survival skills. As the title suggests, here we're looking at what we eat.

Without enough food, you'd soon become exhausted. After three weeks, you might not survive at all. Programmes such as 'The Island' – created by resilience trainer Bear Grylls – demonstrate how a lack of energy can make finding solutions to your lack of food much more difficult, and even put you in danger.

We live in a civilisation which, like most others, depends upon an abundance of food. The people who benefit most from this are often the furthest away from the process of providing it. Food is on display everywhere in towns and cities – supermarkets, restaurants, cafes, advertising hoardings. Many people don't grow any food at all. Techniques for not eating too much are more popular than gardening lore.

Out in the countryside where it is actually grown, all that can be seen is green stuff and animals wandering around fields. If the average city dweller was suddenly pitched into this landscape, they would struggle to recognise anything edible. To be fair, this is not where most food comes from. It's raised in those long low sheds up the lane with the locked gates, in the rows of polytunnels on soil saturated with chemicals, or produced out of sight in distant countries.

The whole process of supplying an urban centre has always been dependent on an organised transport network. All this food is at the end of a long supply chain, which is currently based around fossil fuel. Much of it is produced in those intensive units, hungry for electricity and fertiliser. Guess where these come from?

Take fossil fuel out of the equation and start to worry. This is not a resilient position to be in. You are vulnerable to events far outside your control.

Should you flee to the countryside and start a small holding? Uproot yourself from your community and live among strangers with little chance of employment? Even if you have land, in a massive social upheaval, just when it would become really useful, you may not be able to hang onto it.

So what can you do?

Lessons from the past

Fortunately, civilisations are quite tough. As the resources on which they depend gradually run out – and they always do – their fall is often slow, spanning generations. It's even possible to reach a stable, sustainable equilibrium. For many early civilisations, the limiting resource was wood, for fuel and for building. They cut down all the trees around their cities until the landscape was bare.

Deprived of its protective cover, the fertile soil washed away; no food could be grown. Supply lines were stretched until they broke. Cities withered and died. There are many examples of this historical process described in 'Collapse' by Jared Diamond. Success stories are fewer, but a relevant one is Japan.

The Tokugawa era, from 1603, was one of peace and prosperity. Population grew; there was more building. Trees were cut down for houses, for living space, to clear croplands. Wood became scarce, farmland eroded. A huge fire, which consumed half of the capital city, highlighted the desperate shortage of timber. In 1666, nine years later, a series of proclamations ushered in a new age of woodland management. Japanese civilisation adapted; it found resilient solutions.

It took Japan nearly 40 years – a working lifetime – to get its forest management strategy fully in place back in the seventeen hundreds. The stabilisation of population numbers followed on from ground level, from individual choices backed up by a society aware of its vulnerabilities. The national diet began to include more seafood to exploit its island coast rather than burning forest to make fields. Cooking techniques adapted to conserve valuable wood. Japan still has extensive forests, which protect the densely populated coastal areas from flooding.

The Little Ice Age

Iceland was first settled by the Norse in 874 AD. They felled trees for houses, building and for smelting iron; these were slow to grow back in the cold climate. When the Little Ice Age hit in the 1300s, even barley couldn't survive; there followed nearly six centuries of famine.

Mainland Scandinavia was having its own problems with the climate change; the Icelanders were thrown on their own resources. They ate seaweeds and lichens, kept farm animals alive on the nutritious wild grasses. Firewood was so scarce that they couldn't even boil seawater for salt. They got inventive with fermented whey when it came to preserving meat; made use of hot springs for cooking. A third of the population survived.

This spell of cold weather ended around 1870. As the pack ice receded, trade with Iceland opened up again. With the income from fine woollen goods, they built up their fishing fleet and regained some prosperity. Electricity arrived, the huge potential of geothermal energy tapped, and the population soared to 300,000. Today, Iceland is self-sufficient in meat and dairy produce. Renewable energy heats greenhouses which grow enough vegetables for domestic consumption.

Although both Japan and Iceland attach a high priority to food production, this is under pressure from the modern world. As in Britain, the average age of farmers is rising and their overall numbers are falling. Island nations have limited space and are unable to accommodate the acreages needed to produce huge amounts of chemically supported crops. Cheap food imported from these sources further undermines the domestic farming sector.

Bringing food resilience onto the agenda

In Britain, we currently produce only 60% of the food we need to survive. If you take imported animal feed into consideration, as the Japanese do, this figure could be even less. Few people see this as an issue. Food production is so undervalued that we build more and more houses over high quality agricultural land.

Russia, even with its vast farmlands, still provides nearly half its own food from individual gardens. That's very resilient. We could aim to do something like that. Not by next year, or even in the next decade, but at a reasoned, steady pace. Target your consumer choices and pay attention to what you eat; cultivate pots of herbs, a vegetable garden, an allotment. Rediscover your ancient relationship with plants, learn to look after them. Bring home grown food into your diet, a few leaves at a time.

This is a long process and encounters some surprising barriers. Near where I live, some villagers banded together, fought fiercely and successfully to establish a community garden. They tilled the land, chose their favourite vegetables to grow, nurtured them to maturity – and then didn't get around to eating them!

Was this a waste of time, then? Certainly not!

Skills were learned. These are more portable than land. Food was growing where previously there had been none. People discovered that they had to begin changing their core lifestyle to exploit this new resource.

When I was a child in the Sixties, gardening was part of life. The new food affluence following the healthy but dull rationed diet, which persisted long after the war was over, simply meant that people indulged in growing flowers instead of dinner. Times were changing though.

The story of the Resilience Garden

Traditional gardening techniques involved a lot of hard work, and people were starting to spend more of their working lives in offices or retail outlets, getting unfit. There were more leisure options, television being the most influential. And, as the global economy picked up full steam, there was plenty of cheap food. Gardening slowly faded into a hobby, even an unwelcome chore separating one from the allure of the home screen.

Many modern children, when asked where milk comes from, will say 'the supermarket'. They'll help to tend vegetables, but view the unpackaged green leaves with suspicion. In just a couple of generations, we have forgotten essential knowledge which took thousands of years to accumulate.

What can we do about it? We're just coming to understand, through a science which once taught the opposite, that species diversity can be more productive than monoculture. That the agricultural chemicals responsible for high crop yields may be quite poisonous to us. That, taken over the long term, traditional methods might have previously undetected value.

Let's bypass the fossil fuel revolution. For our Resilience Gardens, we'll draw inspiration from modern pioneers of edible landscapes, dedicated to organic growing in every sense of the word. The techniques of permaculture and of forest gardening can be applied to the tiniest of spaces to grow food with little effort and no fossil fuel derived chemicals. The garden described in the following chapters is based on these.

To harvest enough vegetables to keep me going for a year, I'd need a whole acre. Adding meat, grain and wood for fuel – about seven acres. This is a lot of land to manage, hence agriculture was a community endeavour. Common pasture and woodland were important resources, the latter being an important reserve of wild food in a bad year.

Including the house, my whole patch of land is less than a twelfth of an acre. There's no way I can feed my family from that, and I expect the same applies to most of you. Self-sufficiency isn't what inspired me to start growing. It was emergency planning.

Emergency stores

The tale of how I came to be involved with this, through a career in outdoor event management, is a long and complicated one which ended up with the Resilience Handbook. Along the way, I discovered that most resources would be concentrated in the cities given a major disaster. Rural areas could be left to fend for themselves for up to a fortnight. There simply isn't enough help to go around.

A snowfall in Somerset disrupted supermarket deliveries for three days. Alarmed to see how quickly the shelves of fresh food emptied, I started to see the practical implications of this policy. I dug up the lawn to create a resilience garden. The initial aim was to provide enough fresh greens, at any time of year, to add a tiny amount to each meal should I ever be obliged to live off stores for a short while.

Having established the vegetable patch, I thought about what these stores should consist of. To be really useful in a crisis, they would have to be tinned or dried. Freezers are useful to preserve a surplus, but they depend on electricity. Even with a full scale domestic solar array, you'd struggle to keep them powered if the mains went down, though energy storage technology improves every year.

A fortnight's worth of supplies didn't take up much room. Put carefully away in the loft, out of casual reach, it began to go out of date. I had to build in rotation of supplies. I learned which foods would be really handy come the Zombie Apocalypse but pretty useless in everyday life, which is what mostly goes on. I adapted recipes to use up the stores, included my garden produce.

Now, I have enough food in a dedicated store to keep my household going for at least a fortnight, plus whatever is in the kitchen. I can grow a variety of vegetables – and know which ones won't thrive round here. There's enough edible greenery all year round in my garden patch to keep myself and my neighbours in essential nutrients until we can grow some more. I know where the nearest well is, and how to save rainwater.

Welcome to the adventure!

None of this took very much effort, and all of it is useful. Faced with an unexpected bill, I can switch to reserve and eat well on no budget. Having vegetables to hand means less trips to the supermarkets and when I do go, I take full advantage of bargain offers to restock the stores. Not only am I equipped to sit back and assess the situation in a national emergency rather than having to dash off panic buying, but my lifestyle as a whole is far more resilient.

From the 'The Resilience Handbook – How to Survive in the 21st Century':

'Resilience is often associated with sustainability. The two concepts are closely linked. An unsustainable practice is doomed to eventual failure, so it is not resilient either. Sustainability tends to start at the luxury end of the market and work downwards while resilience focusses on need and works upwards.

Sustainability asks "could you involve less air miles when choosing which food to buy?"
Resilience asks less comfortable questions such as "how much food can you access within walking distance of your home?"'

Not much, you might think, eyeing up the odd dandelion pushing its way through the pavement, but it's a trick question. Your own stores are the best place to start, followed by a growing space as near to home as possible. Although you should know about edible wild plants, there aren't enough around to forage on.

If you've got the time and energy to go for self-sufficiency, then do so by all means. You'll be contributing to a dangerously neglected skills reserve. Otherwise, an achievable goal is having enough to eat and drink during those two weeks before normal services are resumed. The more people who can keep themselves going, the faster this will happen.

On the way, you'll need to pick up cooking skills, stop eating hand to mouth with ready meals and takeaways, plan your living. Learn to hunt in the modern world, seize opportunities to gather food, to preserve it for later. Work with the seasons, the weather, the rhythm of the landscape. Let's bring some meaning back into the food we eat.

The quest for resilience is an adventure!

Chapter Two

Food Stores

There's a lot to say about gardening and its contribution to your diet, but storage is just as important. In an industrialised country, very little of your food supply is fresh. Most of it has been stored, sometimes for years. Even in our hunter-gatherer days, survival in northern winters depended upon preserved foods.

Certain berries – elder, for example – can dry out on the tree rather than fall and rot away. These are available as food for a lot longer. Perhaps someone made the conceptual leap and started drying berries on purpose. The tribe who had stores survived the winter in better shape, had more energy to go hunting in spring, thrived and expanded.

Having stores means having somewhere to keep them. A nomadic tribe needs hundreds of acres of wilderness to forage from. Staying in one place to hoard winter food soon depleted the surrounding area of other essentials. While agriculture may or may not have evolved from these opposing pressures, it was certainly a popular solution. Learning to grow your food plants instead of searching for them was a valuable skill. Taming animals who could provide you with milk, meat and eggs was another.

The history of stores

Stores probably came before gardening. From these small beginnings in the remote past, we have developed such advanced techniques that we can preserve nearly every foodstuff for a long time. We can even unfold entire meals out of a packet. The long supply chains on which we depend require such storage; the journey from field to shelf can take weeks.

Just because we are able to do something doesn't mean that we ought to. Our diet is ruled by what is convenient for transport systems and supermarkets. Once we would have preferred fresh food; now many people hardly recognise it. Cafes can't serve fresh dairy milk because small globules of cream give their customers the impression the milk has gone off.

Stored food loses vitamins and taste, which are often replaced by dubious chemicals. Its main virtue is being there when other food isn't.

During the second world war, from 1939–1945, Britain was cut off from its trading partners; it was difficult and dangerous to import food. Rationing was imposed and everyone was encouraged to grow vegetables. The population got hungry, but didn't starve. Back then, thousands of people were still living with the seasons. They were accustomed to store garden surpluses or allotment produce. Home grown food was an important part of the household budget.

Many houses had a walk-in pantry built on the north facing wall. These are surprisingly cool, even in summer. People knew how to make jams and pickles, how to use salt, sugar and vinegar for preserving. They had strategies to see them through to the next harvest season. More food could be grown in response to circumstances before stores ran out. Even so, the concentrated campaign to grow more didn't fully pay off until 1946, when we could finally have survived on our own resources.

That's the last time we could. Things have changed. Now we have half again as many people in Britain and less growing land. We've lost many key skills and acquired different tastes. Food resilience is a long way off.

We're not without resources though. The gardeners of old were applying techniques which were passed down from peasant farmers. Not all of these transferred well to a garden space. We have developed more intensive organic systems for tiny growing areas, which can provide spectacular yields.

Where to store food

The most important resource you can access right now is stored food. It's currently widely available, relatively cheap and has a long shelf life. To make the best use of this abundance in your resilience plan, view these stores as ingredients, not end products. A tin of corned beef, expanded with fresh vegetables, can feed more people than a can of ready-made stew for the same storage space.

What storage space? You're unlikely to have the walk-in pantry, but you might have a loft. This is probably full of insulating material. Access this space with an appropriate ladder and be careful when walking about. Loft floors are usually made of thin plaster between the rafters and won't hold anything, including you. Use plastic boxes with fitted lids to keep off dust and possible rodents. Lay some boards across the rafters to keep these on, and to keep itchy fibreglass away from your skin. Change your clothes and wash thoroughly after touching this.

These stores will be secure and accessible. Conditions are far from ideal though. A loft becomes stifling hot in summer and close to freezing in winter. Faced with such a wide temperature range, you can't keep butter up there. Tinned and dried foods, syrups, commercially pasteurised preserves; these can stand it. Remember to pay attention to the sell by dates.

A garden shed is another option. Not so hot in summer, it tends to be colder than a loft in winter. If plastic boxes aren't enough to keep off mice, obtain some metal trunks and use wooden battens to lift them off the floor a little. This will prevent damp gathering underneath and causing rust.

None of the above? Find a place for a cupboard – try to avoid using the kitchen as your stores tend to get mixed up with shopping. The game is to know they are always there as a back up. One of those 32 litre flat stack boxes can go under your bed or in a wardrobe. You can store enough emergency food for one person in these, as described in Appendix Two.

Storing water

Consider your water supply. Would you be able to access fresh water if the mains supply went down? I could walk to a functioning well; can you? Count water tanks, a bath filled with clean water, rainwater, water which may need to be boiled.

You need about two litres per person per day for drinking, before you get around to preparing food. Dried foods require quite a lot; beans must be soaked and the water thrown away even before cooking. You may be better off keeping tins, which come with their own water. Buy ones with no added salt.

If you depended upon the authorities bringing in drinking water, they'd probably act fast. You should design your emergency stores with your potential water supplies in mind though. Keep some bottled water in unopened containers. You will need to rotate these occasionally. The five litre (one gallon) ones provide useful vessels when a bowser or outside tap turns up. Ten of these should keep a couple going for the fortnight, on careful rations.

The trouble with water is its weight. These containers will be too heavy for most shelves and you will need boards to keep them on up in the attic. If you're confident of being able to access a source of water, keep a couple of larger plastic containers, the 25 litre (five gallons) ones sold in caravan shops. Store them clean, dry and empty. These are bulky, but very light. Fill them up as soon as possible should the mains supply threaten to fail.

Cooking in an emergency

Think about how you might be able to cook if there were no mains services... no gas, no electricity. In rural areas it's possible to keep caravan stoves of a decent size which use the larger gas bottles. A couple of the seven kilo ones should be enough for a fortnight, even with boiling kettles. You're unlikely to be allowed to store these in a city flat. Your options are far more limited. This is why assistance will be targeted at urban areas in the event of a serious emergency.

The smaller gas stoves, the sort suitable for camping on foot, can get you through if you're very careful. You should go on an adventure to find out how they perform, how much gas they use. Live in a tent for the weekend! It's a splendid way to test your resilience. Try out these recipes: -

Chickpea curry a la camping stove

One tin of chickpeas
One jar of curry sauce
One tin of new potatoes

Drain the tins and save the water, as long as it's unsalted. Cut the potatoes into quarters. Put everything in a saucepan. Using some of the water from the tins, rinse the curry jar out into the mix. Heat it up and cook it as per the instructions. Add edible green leaves, washed and shredded, towards the end of the cooking time.

Fruit crumble in a pan

Rub one spoon of coconut oil into two spoons of plain flour until the mixture looks like breadcrumbs. Stir in a spoonful of sugar. Use the same spoon for all the measuring.

Open and drain a tin of fruit, keeping the juice. Chop it up into large chunks if necessary. Toss it in the crumble mix until the fruit is well coated. You don't want the mix too wet. Tip the lot into a clean warmed frying pan and cook for about ten minutes, stirring the whole time. Add a little juice if it starts to stick.

Both recipes are made from stores. These stores can be used in more inventive meals when you're rotating them, as you'll have your normal cooking facilities then.

DANGER!

Barbecues and other charcoal burners are dangerous indoors. They give off poisonous carbon monoxide. You can only risk relying on them if you have a balcony or garden to use them in. If you can access wood, even fencing, a patch of soil away from buildings can host a small cooking fire.

Don't light fires directly onto concrete as it's liable to explode; tarmac can melt or catch fire. Use a metal sheet or container, propped up on bricks. Most of these solutions will involve your neighbours; working together in advance, you could have a better plan ready.

Planning a food store

Take into account how much room you have, your water supply and your cooking equipment. Dried foods take up less space and are lighter, but tinned ones can be eaten straight from the can. A balanced diet is important, and so is having enough energy. There's an example of a fourteen-day menu at the end of this book, along with a list of the stores you'd need for it.

This is based on what I like to eat, however. You'll need to adapt the plan for your own tastes. Remember that, most of the time, you'll be rotating your supplies in ordinary meals. It's important to be able to cook, but you also need to understand how various foods combine in recipes, and what you could use instead.

Coconut oil can replace butter in cakes; dried peas can form the basis of a curry instead of beef. You can build up personal stores designed to support your individual diet preferences, or food allergies, during an emergency.

Most meals contain protein, carbohydrates and fats. Fresh vegetables are an important addition, with their vitamins and minerals. Cakes and puddings have sugar, carbohydrates and fats. When planning your stores, you need to have enough of each food type on board. There's more information about this in Appendix One.

Factors to consider when creating a food store to last you a fortnight

Storage space – its location, size, security from rodents, insects and damp

The cooking facilities you're likely to have if mains services go down

Your emergency water supply

Planning a series of balanced meals

Your personal preferences – add some small luxury foods!

Now you have a good idea of how much food there is within walking distance of your home, because it's safe in your stores! Keep this topped up, change things as you get used to rotating supplies. What else might you need? Can you grow it? Buy it from a local producer?

Chapter Three

Cooking

At some point, we discovered fire and began to cook. This gave us the power to digest certain starches and doubled our ability to live from the land. We were able to use more root vegetables, eat dried beans, invent bread. Harmful bacteria and parasites in meat could be destroyed. It really gave us an edge.

Over untold centuries, we learned about nutrition through trial and error. Traditional cooking lore is often backed up by modern science. Vitamins and minerals interact in complex ways. Too much iron in your diet will interfere with your ability to make use of copper. Some foods contain phytic acid which binds to important minerals so our bodies can't use them.

Whole grain flour is one of these, but it's such a valuable food source that people worked out how to use it. By making sourdough bread, the enzyme phytase is able to break down the phytic acid and release the minerals. Enzymes are delicate things and the heat of baking quickly destroys them. Allowing bread to rise slowly gives this process time to work. It wasn't just about having a nice fluffy loaf.

In the future, science may well announce – with great excitement – that it is good for you to eat foods which grow in your locality, during their appropriate season. Your ancestors had to; you don't. I'm not suggesting you live on mashed swede and bacon, or give up bamboo shoots and quinoa. However, choosing to explore this path connects you to the landscape and improves your food resilience skills.

Using recipes

To be inventive with cooking, adapting recipes to reflect what is available, there's some basic principles to learn. Practice is the best way. You can find a recipe for bread on the side of yeast packets. It'll tell you how much of everything to use, how to mix it and how long to cook it for, but you have to knead the dough yourself. Everyone has their own style. Find out what's right for you.

Did your grandmother keep a recipe notebook? Start one of your own!

Some recipes in this book are indulgent, using the vast range of foods available today to jazz up your stored foods. Some can be put together in an emergency. Most will go either way. Resilience cooking combines storage with forage, which is added ingredients from anywhere. Your garden, the supermarket, a local farm; it all counts as forage. Growing, buying, gleaning – hunting takes many forms these days!

You can make an edible pasta dish, using a packet of tomato passata and a dash of Parmesan cheese, on your camping stove in a power cut. In normal times, you can add mince to make a bolognaise. Onions, leeks, shredded greens and peas are good in the mix too. Serve with grated cheddar and use the leftovers to make a lasagne the next day.

If the world brings you root vegetables and a rabbit, a traditional stew is a better bet. You need to make a stock from the carcasses of small game; there isn't much meat on them. Slow cooking in a tomato base is tricky; simmering bones in water with herbs isn't. Roots always take longer to cook than you'd think, unless you're roasting them in which case they will carbonise without careful attention. A user-friendly vegetable like the potato is rare and valuable!

An abundance of cheese combines with eggs and milk to form a range of dishes once popular in spring and summer. Other foods – apart from fresh leaves – were harder to come by then. Root vegetables would have sprouted; stored grain would be our main source of carbohydrates. The starch in grain is more digestible when powdered but it keeps better if left whole; once ground, the wheatgerm begins to spoil. A home grinding stone, or quern, was an important feature of Neolithic households. The 'daily grind' had a very real place in ancient domestic life!

There's a lot you can do with flour, especially when you've discovered ovens. Depending what you mix it with, you can make bread, pastry, crumbles, cakes or scones. Biscuits are a bit more advanced and require startling amounts of butter. Dumplings are easy and excellent with stew. With a single egg and some milk, you can make pancakes. Flour is good to thicken sauces and firm up burger mixes.

Cooking from stores

Flour is an important part of your emergency stores. Compared to tinned food, it has quite a short shelf life – less than a year – so you'll need to replace it regularly and use up your supplies in everyday life. This can be harder than it sounds.

Supermarkets are crammed with tempting cakes – meringues, custard slices, eclairs. Unless you're a food artist with plenty of spare time, you can't make these at home. If you want to use up those packets of flour, you have to leave these goodies in the supermarket from time to time, and eat home-made pastries.

Resilient living involves hard choices!

Pasta and rice store longer than flour. Although they're imported, they feature in the emergency stores box for that reason, and hence in a contemporary resilient lifestyle. Flour is the key staple in a northern climate, so it's important in the seasonal recipes. We make use of wheat today, but our ancestors were keen on barley.

Solid fats are rarely available in tins; liquid oils begin to spoil as soon as the bottle is opened. Where a recipe requires fats, my default is butter. I live surrounded by dairy cows. However, butter is hard to store, especially in hot weather without a fridge.

Working at off-grid events in summer, I had to find alternatives. There's a whole range of oils and fats available to suit all dietary choices. Experiment with the recipes... does coconut butter work well in pastry? There are organic vegan spreads which substitute exactly for butter, but can you make a crumble using hemp oil?

When supplies were particularly low, I've made a cake from cooking oil, oats, honey and an egg! It's a question of identifying the food types in a recipe, and learning what they do for the whole. In an emergency, being able to carry on with a diet similar to your normal one maintains your comfort zone and boosts morale. If you're accustomed to make your own pies, it's a small step to use corned beef instead of stewing steak.

Fresh meat and milk don't last long without refrigeration. Eggs in their shells last well, but use them up quickly once broken – don't buy cracked eggs! Dried, tinned and UHT milk feature in the stores. As with the flour, it requires a small lifestyle change to use these up in rotation. The UHT milk has the shortest shelf life, but substitutes easily for fresh milk in all the recipes. I prefer the taste of the semi-skimmed version; because I use it that's what I buy, even though the full fat milk may have more nutritional value.

You may prefer one of the many non-dairy milks. Again, note its shelf life. Store some and practise the rhythm of rotation. Does it work in these recipes? Could it be sourced locally?

Resilience often involves compromise.

A resilient diet

If your community was cut off without power, fresh meat would go off the menu within a week. Many peoples' diets rely on this food to add essential vitamins. A resilient lifestyle involves exploring alternatives in advance. Eat less meat in general, familiarise yourself with other sources of key minerals, especially garden vegetables.

Try replacing meat with canned chickpeas in a curry; use extra vegetables. Venture into using nuts, lentils and dried beans. These store well, but it's difficult to grow such crops in a cool, wet climate. In northern lands eggs, processed milk and hard cheeses formed the staple protein in the lean months of early spring. This was so important to survival that there was actually a mutation in our basic genes which allowed us to digest animal milk. Many people may not have this adaptation; it's less use in warmer countries where protein rich seeds grow more easily.

Once you understand the structures behind cooking, the various classes of ingredients and how they fit together, you can apply them to any food you come across. Your recipe notebook becomes your reference of choice.

Measuring

It's all very well weighing to the nearest gram on digital scales, but do you plan to carry them in your grab bag? We're talking resilience here – learn to measure by eye!

Since this requires starting with the right amounts as you practise, I've translated most of the recipes here into grams or ounces. Stick with one set. I know 25 grams isn't an ounce, but it works relative to 225 grams of something else and with limiting factors like the number of eggs.

I was brought up to consider a tablespoon to be roughly an ounce. Heaped for light, fluffy flour, or rounded for denser things like sugar. In the meantime, it seems to have diminished in size, from containing a fluid ounce of liquid to just over half that – the modern standard tablespoon holds 15 millilitres in most countries. Dry ingredients can still be heaped or rounded though; estimate an amount with your tablespoon, then weigh it.

Those nested plastic measuring cups? Fine, but a simple spoon can be found anywhere. You can even carve one yourself. The resilient cook needs to be able to estimate an ounce, or 25 grams, using any means available!

Officially, a tablespoon only holds half an ounce dry weight, but that's when levelled off with a knife. Learn to judge the larger amount by eye, and you can weigh things out a lot faster.

Three dessert spoons equalled two tablespoons, and still do. Originally, four teaspoons – not the smaller egg spoons – made a tablespoon. Australian tablespoons are still defined as 20 millilitres, but everyone else has downsized. Now three teaspoons make a tablespoon, unless they are the fashionably oversize ones deplored by the dispensers of medicine.

An official tablespoon holds just over half a fluid ounce. For anything larger than an ounce or 50 ml, this is an awkward way of measuring liquids. Get a marked jug. You soon get a feel for how much to add, once you're used to a recipe. A North American fluid ounce is slightly less than the UK Imperial one; consider them as equivalent for liquids here.

When you measure dry ingredients by eye with a tablespoon, you're judging them by volume rather than weight. You're expected to know that flour should be heaped but sugar rounded to get the same amount.

Some countries use a volume measure called a cup. This can be confusing if you're not used to it. People in these countries buy special baking cups and use them as you would a tablespoon. Flour takes up more space than sugar; a cup of flour is only four ounces, while a cup of sugar is eight.

For liquids, most cup measures you'll find refer to a standard of around eight US fluid ounces (237 ml). The rarely used British cup is larger at ten fluid ounces, or half an Imperial pint.

Theoretically, the measuring cup is used for butter as well. In practice, butter often comes in blocks. It's easier just to divide these up. A cubic inch of butter weighs about an ounce. Cut a half pound block into eight pieces, or a 250 gram one into ten for the metric recipes. (Which was easier? Dividing the block into eight, or ten? Just saying.)

These cubes are the sizes you're looking for in hard cheese and margarines as well, which are roughly the same density as butter.

One egg is a limiting minimum for a recipe; remember an unused half won't keep long. Raw egg is a breeding ground for bacteria.

Some useful conversions: -

1 ounce = 28.4 grams
16 ounces = 1 pound

25 grams = 0.9 ounces
1000 grams = 1 kilogram
1 kilogram = 2.2 pounds

1 fluid ounce (UK) = 0.97 fluid ounces (US) = 28.4 ml (millilitres)
1 fluid ounce (US) = 1.04 fluid ounces (UK) = 29.6 ml
1 cup = 8 fluid ounces (US); dry weight equivalent varies

1 teaspoon = 5 ml
1 dessert spoon = 10 ml
1 tablespoon = 15 ml (except Australia)
1 level tablespoon = about half an ounce dry weight
1 heaped or rounded tablespoon = a good guess at 25 grams, or an ounce.

You can search online for the whole range of weight and volume conversions. Type your query exactly (e.g. '5 fluid ounces UK in millilitres') and the answer may come up without your having to open any of the suggested links. There is often a lot of advertising on cookery sites. Bookmark a couple of reliable ones.

Don't worry too much about the complexities of non-standard measures. Most countries use the metric system for recipes, but people still cook by the handful at home. Some recipes need digital precision; you won't find them here. Pay more attention to the relative amounts of each ingredient.

The quantities given in this book will generally provide a meal for two; try doubling or halving them. Take notes in your kitchen diary as you adjust recipes to your own tastes.

Judging the exact amount of dried foods to use with a meal is tricky and depends on your personal appetite. I find pasta packets overestimate the measure for a single serving, but it may be a skimpy portion for a large man working hard. Have a strategy to use up leftovers.

If you didn't make enough, add more carbohydrates to the meal. Packaged nan bread is a good standby to boost rice dishes; it's a handy addition to the emergency stores, though it has a relatively short shelf life.

Cooking methods

I've kept to simple recipes in this book. You'll need a mixing bowl – a large pan will do – various heatproof containers to cook in, and some basic utensils. There's no fancy gadgets or complex techniques. You can replicate many of these meals on a camping stove or even an open fire.

There aren't any heat controls on a bonfire. It's quite an art to cook food without either burning it or letting the fire go out. A camping stove will only have low, medium or high settings. The evacuation centre may have an electric cooker when you're used to gas.

Certain general rules apply to any cooking device. Boiling needs a high heat, and plenty of liquid in the pan. When the liquid evaporates, the food will start to burn. Keep an eye on it, stir if necessary, and turn the heat down to simmer once it's boiling. Stir from time to time to make sure it's not sticking; it should be occasionally bubbling in a leisurely fashion.

Frying also needs a high heat, and constant attention. Only use enough oil to stop the food from sticking, and don't overheat it so that it smokes. Deep fat frying shouldn't be done over an open fire. It's easy to burn fried food. Try cooking sausages in the oven if you're readily distracted – they'll take longer, so set an alarm!

Melting is done on a very low heat, often over a bowl of hot water rather than a flame, and stops when the mixture is liquid. Don't add eggs to a hot mix.

Observe strict hygiene when handling raw meat or eggs. Wash your hands frequently during cooking; wipe down surfaces, and clean utensils as you go.

Baking is a very useful cooking method, but difficult to achieve without an oven. In field conditions, you can improvise using a metal box, by wrapping food in tinfoil, or even building a clay oven. Low, medium and hot are the settings you can expect to achieve, here roughly translated into common cooker temperatures.

Gas Mark 1 = cool = 140 C = 275 F
Gas Mark 2 = very low = 150 C = 300 F
Gas Mark 3 = low = 170 C = 325 F
Gas Mark 4 = low medium = 180 C = 350 F
Gas Mark 5 = medium = 190 C = 375 F
Gas Mark 6 = medium hot = 200 C = 400 F

Gas Mark 7 = hot = 220 C = 425 F
Gas Mark 8 = very hot = 230 C = 450 F
Gas Mark 9 = extremely hot = 240 C = 475 F

Even when a stove has no numbered settings, you can still estimate these from the controls. If using an unfamiliar gas oven make sure it stays lit when on a very low setting. With most, but not all, ovens, the top shelf is the hottest because heat rises. A fan assisted oven disperses the heat evenly; you can lower the temperature setting by 20 C.

How inventive can you get? Can you build a clay oven, use a haybox? Create a communal stew from thawing freezer food in the evacuation centre? Build useful skills up as you gradually explore resilience cooking. You have to eat – make it interesting!

Chapter Four

The Resilience Garden

Inspired by the possibility of a local emergency, the initial aim of the garden was to provide a fairly large number of people with a small amount of fresh food for a limited time. Unlike preserved stores, real vegetables can't be kept in the attic; they have to be growing already. Fresh greens contain many essential vitamins and minerals. You're unlikely to contract a deficiency disease in a couple of weeks, but you don't want your immune system to be weakened.

As with the stores, this proved to be quite involved. The Resilience Garden began to evolve as a concept, a gradual lifestyle change. It wasn't till I tried to explain it that I realised how intricate it had become. Growing a substantial amount of food had merged seamlessly with the rest of my to-do list.

I'm not a natural gardener. Until I realised something had to be done, the garden was a managed wildlife habitat with lawns for the children to play on, grazed by the guinea pigs rescued from the tip. I'd eradicated the brambles and encouraged native herbs to grow. There were tangled borders a metre wide as wildlife corridors. Small animals can move between feeding areas along these, out of sight of domestic predators.

Tyre Gardening

Since I wasn't going to displace the wildlife, I had to site the new vegetable patch in the lawn. My house is on the edge of former marshlands, only just above the old water level. The soil is a heavy unproductive clay, which sets like concrete in hot weather. A raised bed was called for, to contain a better quality growing medium.

I collected some old tyres and circled these around a small piece of ground, about two metres by six. I dug this over and finally gathered enough ingredients to fill it to the level of the surrounding tyres. Soil is everywhere, but although you are walking over it all the time, acquiring some more is difficult. If you don't want to scavenge, you can just buy some.

However, another aim of the Resilience Garden project was to minimise cost and make the techniques available to people on low budgets. I used a pile of soil dumped at the roadside by the farmer, combined with horse manure from a friend's stable. This was serviceable, though not ideal. I collected fallen leaves, composted kitchen waste, added coffee grounds.

It takes years to build up a good soil and resilience needs to take this into account. Once you have the framework you can build on it. A second layer of tyres was added, and the soil layer gradually became deeper. I cleared another area with the same method, then a third, and finally merged all three into a single vegetable patch about twenty feet square.

Tyre gardening has many advantages. There's a lot of used tyres. Currently any garage will let you take them away free of charge. Unfortunately, now you have to pay to dispose of them, which wasn't the case when I started this project. Even so, they are versatile. They're easily moved if you decide your new vegetable patch is in the wrong place. You can vary the height of the stack, taking your food plants out of reach of marauding rabbits or peeing dogs. My colleague built her neighbour a tyre garden he could reach from his wheelchair.

They are hard to beat for creating emergency growing spaces on tarmac or concrete. You can pad out the lower layers with sand, gravel, even kitchen waste. Top off with a few inches of good soil and sow a fast growing, above ground crop like rocket or cress. In all but the very depths of winter, you'll have edible leaves within a few weeks.

Tyres do contain cadmium and zinc, but since they take a thousand years to break down, this isn't leaching out in any great hurry. It can be a problem when tyre powder is created, thus dramatically increasing the surface area exposed. It takes a very long time for an intact tyre to get that crumbling, weathered look.

I experimented with different soil types inside my tyres. Root vegetables – parsnip and carrot – thrived in a sandier mix. I used builders' sand; it worked. I'm very fond of swedes, but they'd like their own spacious raised bed with a loose soil and a lot of sun. I don't have enough room for that; they don't grow strong enough to fend off the molluscs, so I have to do without them.

I gradually phased my tyres out and replaced them with a low wall of reclaimed brick which contains a bed of enriched soil about a foot deep. Most of the tyres were passed on to other garden projects. I keep a few for odd jobs because they are so useful – and for the annual potato stacks!

Potato Stacks

This is fun, and you hardly need any room. Start with a couple of tyres, fill them with soil to about two inches from the top and plant one large seed potato. As it grows, top up the stack, covering the stem and lower leaves. Always let the plant keep enough leaf clear to make itself plenty of food from the sunshine. Add a third tyre when it's large enough, and a fourth if it looks like a good strong one. Experts can raise this to six tyres!

The potato plant will grow underground and form its tubers in the loosely packed spaces of the tyres. The important thing is to keep the potato well-watered and given a liquid feed as often as possible. Spectacular harvests can be achieved, but it isn't quite as easy as it sounds.

If you have a clay soil, you can't use it to fill in, as it will set hard. Straw is the traditional material, but now comes in round bales the size of a small car. I found excellent results with scrap wool, but you'd need to know a sheep farmer.

For the experimental resilience gardener, buying in compost to fill up your potato stack is one answer. It's more expensive, but you can reuse it for different plants the next year, or add it to your raised beds. Buy a few exotic seed potatoes at a local Potato Day and raise them as a feature; the flowers are often quite pretty.

Organic methods

To create a resilience garden, you need to observe the way sun, rain and wind affect your growing area. You should work with the natural resources you have, not impose your own ideas of what ought to grow and where. Experiment, try different crops, read up about permaculture and forest gardening.

If your emergency food supply is addicted to chemicals, that's not resilient. It takes time to build up a miniature eco-system, so resist the temptation to go for short term gain. If you use weed killers, you will destroy the reserve of common edible plants which grow well in your garden. You can eat bittercress, shepherd's purse and groundsel; they are easily weeded out by hand or hoe where they get in the way. Stronger plants like nettles, dandelion and dock are best kept out in the wild areas, as they will compete fiercely with your vegetables and are hard to dig up.

Pesticides will kill both the insect pests and their natural predators. The pests will recover sooner, in the same way that rabbits breed faster than foxes, and redouble their attacks. Rather than get trapped in this cycle, try different crops. A good soil and plenty of feed also helps by strengthening plants to resist. Chemical fertilisers aren't necessary. Get a plastic bin, with a lid, and make your own plant feed. I use chopped comfrey and nettle leaves, with seaweed when I can get it from the beach.

Some vegetables just won't thrive where you happen to be. In Radstock, further inland, I was able to grow lettuces and onions. The poorer soil here won't support these, so I've turned to rocket and leeks. Adapt your gardening to the surrounding conditions; remember the aim of minimising cost. Your time is a valuable resource as well.

Seeds

The first seeds you buy will probably be commercially produced. Unless you buy specific types, these will be designed to depend upon chemicals. Many are 'F1 hybrids' which means that they will not breed true. At most, only half of their seeds can have the same qualities as their parents.

You're not going into plant genetics here, nor going for the biggest marrow prize. You need resilient food plants, adapted to the particular microclimate and eco-systems of your immediate area. When you find a vegetable which works for you, keep a couple of the healthiest looking ones and let them go to seed. See if you can get decent plants from them next year. I found that brassicas, such as rocket, were easy to keep going like this, but I'm still working on the leeks.

Most plants produce far more seed than you can use. As a resilience gardener, this is an important resource. It means that new gardens can be set up in your area very quickly, growing tried and tested varieties. Keep extra seed until the next harvest, then discard what wasn't needed. You can sprout some types if you know how, and eat the shoots in salads.

The five main aims of resilience gardening

To provide a small amount of fresh food for several households for a limited period at any time of year, should an emergency occur.

To work with wildlife in the area, including edible weeds.

To create and maintain the garden with the least possible cost and effort; to set it up to produce plenty of edible plants even if totally neglected at key times of year.

To cultivate using organic methods, not relying on any materials brought in from outside the immediate area.

To save seed and breed varieties fully adapted to the local microclimate and soil; to keep a surplus of this seed to establish more growing areas quickly if required.

There are collateral benefits too. The householder hosting a Resilience Garden has a continual supply of fresh organic vegetables. As the gardener, you are keeping an important craft alive and developing new techniques. The garden has more butterflies and birds, maybe even some rarer wildlife to enjoy.

Growing spaces

Suppose you haven't got a garden?

Use the Resilience Wheel to overcome barriers, as outlined in 'The Resilience Handbook – How to Survive in the 21st Century'. Look to the Community Quadrant. There may be allotments available. Ask your local Council. They're not ideal for your personal emergency growing, but better than nothing. You can practise your skills, involve other people, prove your abilities. There may be large untended gardens near your house. See if you can form an alliance with the owner, and share the produce.

What about joining a gardening club? Growing for resilience is a community asset, not just a hobby. You can tackle more ambitious projects in a group. Ours can source large amounts of spent mushroom compost from commercial growers; we are negotiating for used scaffold planks from builders. We began with a small piece of land formerly destined to become a car park. Now it's incorporated into the arts centre next door as an edible exhibit, and we have just been given a wildflower meadow to manage as well!

Take a look online at some of the Incredible Edible movement's achievements. The famous police station vegetable beds in Todmorden have been duplicated all over town. Fresh food is available freely to everyone; these groups are working to bring about the lifestyle changes needed to appreciate this. Other places, such as Bristol, are doing the same. Living in an urban area is no barrier to growing vegetables!

Interlude

The Seasons

The northern temperate zone of Earth has four seasons, ruled by day length and weather– autumn, winter, spring and summer. Each has its own nature. Our ancestors marked the central points of each season by celebrating the solstices and equinoxes. The transition between seasons was described by traditional cross-quarter days – Imbolc, Beltane, Lammas and Samhain (Hallowe'en).

Even today, when you can buy raspberries in January, this rhythm is still there to be accessed through the food you choose to eat. As the leaves turn in autumn, they mean apples, celery, bacon. Seeing the first green shoots of spring, you can look forward to eggs and fresh milk again. The warmth of summer brings salads, soft fruit and cream. Winter is a time of rest and contemplation, living on the fruits of your labour and planning ahead.

Yule – Xmas – held around the Winter Solstice, marked the darkest part of the year, the middle of winter. Imbolc, or Candlemas, some six weeks later, heralded the beginning of spring. The Equinox was the high part of this season, followed by the transition into summer at Beltane.

Winter Solstice	Mid-winter	December 21st
Imbolc	beginning of Spring	around February 1st
Spring Equinox	Middle of Spring	March 21st
Beltane (May Day)	beginning of Summer	around May 1st
Summer Solstice	Mid-summer	June 21st
Lammas	beginning of Autumn	around August 1st
Autumn Equinox	Middle of Autumn	September 21st
Samhain (Hallowe'en)	beginning of Winter	around November 1st

The quarter days can be predicted exactly, as they are astronomical phenomena. They're always within a day of the above dates. The cross-quarter days are linked to community life and natural conditions, so the exact dates were less certain. People often celebrate these on the nearest full moon, a relic from the days before street lights, or even roads between villages.

Join me now in November, as we begin the journey through these seasons!

Chapter Five

November

The ancient Celts began their year in this cold, wet, dull month, after Hallowe'en (Samhain) around the first of November. By then, all the harvest was gathered and preserved; the hard work was finished. It was a good time for a feast to use up the last odds and ends of fresh food, followed by long months indoors planning for the next season.

Much the same applies today. The bare bones of the land emerge. All but the hardiest of weeds are reduced to dry stems and mud-spattered leaves. The weather gets colder, the days shorter.

A low maintenance Resilience Garden continues to produce food with little effort on your part. Plants harvest the summer sunshine and store its energy to see them through the hostile conditions of the winter. We can eat some of the roots, bulbs and seeds they produce. Over thousands of years, we've bred our favourite food plants into the vegetables we recognise today. Given the right conditions, they know just what to do.

Your job is to provide those conditions!

Planning

Begin by planning your prospective vegetable garden. Spend some time observing how the sunshine, winds and rain affect your chosen area. Draw sketch maps. The sun will be higher in the sky during the growing season, so areas with good light now will get quite hot in summer. Save them for the sort of plants that need a head start in a greenhouse. You don't need your own, though they're a fun accessory; you can buy in seedlings raised by someone else.

None of your plants will like that windy corner where the gales howl in straight from the flat marshlands or down from the icy hills. Put something solid and cheap there, which will break up the wind. Potatoes fit the bill, or let a couple of spinach go to seed. These can grow up to two metres tall – tie them to stakes to stop them bending over. If the wind is really bad, put up a bit of open-work fencing; you want the light to get through.

If tall walls and fences keep your garden in total shade, read up on the sort of food plants which are happy with that. You could always grow exotic mushrooms, such as shitake and oyster – a useful source of protein which can fetch a good price. It's quite possible.

Check your growing area for established edibles which you might want to keep. My garden came equipped with a blackthorn, some elders, a rose hip and an apple tree. I added, among others, the wild garlic, comfrey, sorrel, lovage, wild strawberries, blackcurrants and raspberries, gradually editing out the non-edible weeds and legacy plants.

The garden was infested with brambles when I arrived. I tried to keep a token plant for the edible berries, but it grew long spiky tentacles and attacked me every time I went near it, so it had to go. The birds bring it in occasionally; I catch it young and pull it up by the roots, wearing gloves.

Docks, dandelions and nettles are confined to the edges and corners, where I maintained the wildlife corridor. This is particularly valuable for the slug-eating frogs. Less robust edible weeds such as plantain, groundsel and the harmless little bittercress live among the vegetables.

Once you've identified a good place for a vegetable patch, mark it out and dig it over. There's no rush. You've got until May to plant certain varieties. If the ground is thick with weeds or grass, lay a plastic tarpaulin or large sheets of card over it. Weigh these down well against the wind. The vegetation underneath will start to weaken and be dug up more easily later.

This technique gives you time to change your mind about the site of your patch. Using card, which rots away eventually, you could try a no-dig method, though this can look untidy in a ground level garden.

Raised beds

Should you build a raised bed? The soil in my garden is a thick, heavy clay. The sort of plants I want to grow struggle in it. I had to create a layer of good topsoil, and needed to contain it. My colleague in town has a much better soil; her house is built on an old market garden. She can grow directly into it.

The decision isn't just based on your soil type. Some areas of Somerset are poisoned with lead from the ancient mines; a raised bed is vital there, with a protective underlayer. If you find it difficult to bend, you can raise a bed to waist height. A stack of four tyres is ideal for this.

Assuming you need a raised bed, what else can you use? Bricks and mortar are a bit too permanent to begin with. It's better not to make your first bed set in stone, especially if you've no experience of gardening. Later, if you're happy with its situation, consider making a brick wall around it. Do this before you take away the original frame and it could be so much easier. You can leave space for possible expansion in your plan.

Wooden planks are a good material. They won't last forever as soil is wet and wood will rot. A raised bed made from thin planks, or dismantled pallets will last a year or three. Don't use railway sleepers drenched in creosote, but old scaffold planks are ideal. Use square lengths to hold the corners together. Screws make a stronger join than nails; the latter may split the wood as you hammer them in.

You may have no experience of joining bits of wood together. Ask your neighbours for advice. Have a look for how-to videos online. Buy a book. Here in Glastonbury, our gardening clubs hold regular workshops teaching simple woodworking techniques. Often, these can attract grant funding. If you're working on your own resilience plan, as outlined in the Resilience Handbook, this could be one of your community projects.

There's a few important basics. Read safety advice and follow it. Don't use power tools in the rain – always have a circuit breaker – or leave other tools lying around outside when you're done. Try not to let nails and screws escape into the long grass where they may ambush you later. You'll probably need a hand to hold a corner in place while you fix it. Don't leave nail points sticking out.

Plastic is resistant to rot, but might look ugly. Bricks or rocks can hold soil in, laid dry. If you've really got nothing else, make a low bank of the turf you just dug up. Lay it soil side up and the birds will pick out all the grubs.

The wall of your bed will shade the area underneath it unless it's filled to the top. Build it up in stages if you can't fill it all at once, but remember to cut any corner posts with the final size in mind. A bit of extra height here allows you to drape nets over the crops.

Clear the ground and build your frame. Once it's complete, live with it for a couple of weeks. Is there room to get past it? With a wheelbarrow? Is it far enough away from the stone wall? Avoid narrow gaps which gather damp and slugs.

Pruning

As you plan your garden, consider the shade cast by trees or bushes. November is a good time for pruning trees. Leave it too late and frost may get into the cuts; wait till spring and the tree will bleed sap. Most of the leaves have fallen to enrich the ground. Bare branches are easier to reach and less trouble to dispose of.

Identify your trees; do some online research. Some ornamental berries are edible, some most emphatically not. Certain woods, such as laurel, can give off toxic fumes when burned. Take these to the tip; allow other trimmings to dry out, and have a bonfire. The wood ash is a good fertiliser.

You can prune most trees at any time of year, but don't remove more than 25% in any one year. Learn which part of the tree carries the fruit – old growth or new? Climbing ladders and dealing with large branches is best left to professionals who know what they're doing. Wood is quite heavy, as you will find if a piece falls on you.

Some seasonal foods available in November

Spinach, broccoli leaves, rocket and cress – many badly chewed leafy vegetables recover as the slugs perish in the cold!
The last of the windfall apples; the main crop is already in storage.
Stored potatoes and root vegetables.
Leeks in the garden; onions and garlic in stores.
Nuts; dried peas and beans.
Jams, pickles and chutneys made from the autumn harvest.
An abundance of meat, lard and suet.
Fresh eggs would be getting scarce in the olden days; hens stop laying as the days get shorter. Milk would also be in short supply, but there would still be butter, cheeses and other dairy products.

Preserving meat

Every landscape has its key foods, which affect the history and very nature of the peoples living within them. Olive trees and tomatoes are important around the Mediterranean, fish in the icy north, coconuts in the tropical south. In the temperate zones, with their pronounced seasons, domestic animals were crucial to early communities.

The resilient farmers of old used every resource available to them. They didn't depend on hay for animal fodder over the winter, but harvested other crops as well, such as vetch. Acorns and beech nuts from the forest were important food for pigs; leafy branches carried back for cattle.

Despite this range of solutions, there was rarely enough winter feed to accommodate all the animals born over the year. Some had to be slaughtered, and the meat preserved. This is quite difficult, and can be dangerous if not done properly. It's one of those skills that could be very valuable to a resilient community.

Where electricity is easily available, freezing meat is the easiest and most useful preserving method. In some countries, winters were cold enough for this option; there you would be struggling to find enough firewood to thaw it out!

Otherwise, meat was kept edible by salting, smoking, drying or pickling. You can try making bacon from pork yourself; there are instructions online, even kits you can buy. Smoking your own meat is more complicated, unless you live in a remote rural area with the right sort of trees. Here, the online devices are concerned with imparting flavour rather than preserving in any real sense.

Drying any food is difficult in the unpredictable island climate of Britain. Special racks and shelters have to be built. Warmer countries with less rain use a lot of dried meats. Sample some biltong or jerky – could you use it in a stew?

Eggs

Chickens are small and easy to feed. However, unless they're kept under artificial lighting, they've stopped laying by November. Fresh eggs keep well on a cool shelf – not a fridge – but would probably run out before the winter solstice.

Eggs are an important binding ingredient in many recipes, such as cake. They're also a valuable source of protein and vitamins, so it was worth preserving a few even if they'd be no good for cooking with. Pickled eggs are quite easy to make, but their sharp taste isn't very popular nowadays.

Milk

Cows need a lot of feeding to make milk; a reduced winter diet causes them to stop producing. During the summer, the abundance of fresh milk would be turned into butter and cheeses. Soft cheese doesn't keep well, and butter only a few weeks, so the mainstay of winter dairy foods would be hard cheese. The recipes involving fresh milk and cream would have to be shelved until spring.

Many peasant farmers kept sheep for milk. These are hardier than cows and need less food, though don't give as much milk. It has a different fat content to cow's milk, but can still be used for butter and cheeses. With sheep, you could feed your family; with a cow, you had surplus produce to trade. Cows are an important symbol of wealth in many folk tales; their living quarters were often shared with those of the people.

Potatoes

Root vegetables such as turnips and swedes store well and provide valuable carbohydrates over the winter. The potato only came to Britain at the end of the 1500s, first officially planted in Ireland by the explorer Sir Walter Raleigh.

Potatoes were a staple crop in the Americas, so many other visitors had stocked up on them for their return voyages. Left over tubers grew easily, and were soon established in the Canary Islands and Spain on a more casual basis. Spanish armies carried them as provision, and local peasant farmers soon caught on to their value as winter food, despite initial suspicion of their bitter, poisonous berries.

Widespread cultivation was delayed by rules governing the use of open fields, but the potato can produce a harvest even in cold weather. As the second part of the Little Ice Age affected European climate, they became more widely accepted; traditional crops becoming less reliable.

Potatoes yield at least twice the calories per acre than grains do, requiring no threshing or grinding. One acre, and the milk from a single cow, could feed an entire family for a year. Unlike grains, they could be grown in the backyard plots of the Industrial Revolution. Populations rose in Europe due to this new food source.

However, in the 1800s a new strain of potato blight (Phytophthora infestans) spread throughout the Americas, and soon arrived in Europe. The lack of genetic diversity – most farmers grew the 'Lumper' variety – made potato crops there especially vulnerable. The blight turned the tubers into a slimy mush, completely inedible, and the soil remained infected for many years. Catastrophic famines followed, especially in Ireland where the population fell by half. In 1882, about forty years after the blight first struck, it was discovered that a solution of copper sulphate and slaked lime ('Bordeaux mixture') could prevent it becoming established.

Potato plants are still relatively new to Europe and are quite vulnerable to native diseases. Commercially grown seed potatoes are raised in sterile soil and regularly inspected. They're produced from seed not tubers, so don't transmit soil-based parasites, and are grown in higher lands where there are less disease-carrying aphids around. Planting supermarket potatoes, which don't have these safeguards, risks introducing long lived pathogens into your vegetable patch.

Apples

The native wild apples of Europe and North America (Malus sylvestris) are small, bushy trees and their fruit is the rather bitter crab apple. Although these were an important food in Neolithic times, the sweeter apples from Central Asia (Malus sieversii) were welcome, and spread rapidly across the continents. Modern trees (Malus pumila) are a mixture of these two types.

Apples may be the first cultivated fruit trees. The ancient Egyptians, Greeks and Celts all understood the techniques of grafting. Small orchards have been commonplace throughout history; apples feature in many folk tales. Later, monasteries engaged in selective breeding; a popular variety of the day was the 'Costard'. Someone who sells fruit from a barrow is still called a 'costermonger'.

The Victorian era saw the development of many modern apples, including Cox's Orange Pippin and the Bramley Seedling. In the nineteen fifties, new rootstocks were introduced, which led to smaller trees and commercial mass production. The British climate, with moderate temperatures and reliable rainfall, is ideal for apple growing. Picked in late autumn and stored in a cool – not freezing – place over winter, apples keep well. A modern store uses a controlled atmosphere with low oxygen levels, but high humidity and carbon dioxide.

If you have a shed, you can try this simple technique. Take a five gallon plastic bin with a tight fitting lid and fill it with apples picked from the tree. Windfalls or damaged fruit don't keep well. Close the lid and leave the tub somewhere cool and dark, away from wind or frost. The ambient temperature is important; it's too warm inside a house.

The apples generate a small amount of carbon dioxide, which is heavier than air and gradually fills up the container. This reduces the production of ethylene by the fruit; the chemical which hastens decay. Apples can be kept like this for several months, but need to be used up quickly once the tub is opened. With a very basic home store, you can keep going in fresh apples right up till the rhubarb is ready!

Whole apples can be used in many recipes; pies, fritters, chutneys, even stews and other meat dishes. They can be preserved by drying in slices, making into jams, jellies or juice – and by fermenting into cider. This popular alcoholic drink needed no extra sugar or yeast, and quite brown apples could be thrown into the mix! Some parts of Britain even grow special cider apples.

Nuts and seeds

Nuts and large oil rich seeds are generally crops found in warm climates. Only walnuts and hazel really thrive in the north. Sweet chestnuts and almond can be grown in mild areas, and some exotic nut trees look promising. Grey squirrels can be a real pest to growers, but the monkey puzzle tree should keep them off!

Nuts travel well, so were often imported from the south. Almond milk was surprisingly popular in Tudor times, around the 1500s; marzipan was another almond-based product. Most ordinary people had to make do with native nuts and a few oil seeds, such as hemp. Vegetable proteins were obtained from peas and beans which, unlike nuts, had to be cooked.

Recipes for November

Twice baked potatoes

Baked potatoes take quite a while to cook. Choose large ones, all about the same size, with skins that scrub up well; you need to keep them on for this recipe. A fist-sized potato can take up to two hours in a low medium oven (Gas Mark 4; 180C; 350F) on the middle shelf. They're ready when they feel soft, but cut one in half just to check it's cooked right through before serving.

It's worth putting extra in to use the next day in this recipe.

Take some leftover baked potatoes, cut in half longways. Scoop the insides out into a bowl, being careful not to break the skin. Mix in a little butter, grated cheese, cooked bacon, fried onions or mushrooms; you don't need much of each. Spoon the filling back into the potato skins and stand them upright on a baking tray.

Sprinkle with grated cheese and cook in a medium oven (Gas Mark 5; 190C; 375F) for about half an hour, or until the cheese has browned. I prefer the middle shelf, but you can move them to the top. If the skins got too badly torn, wrap the whole thing in silver foil and cook as above.

Serve with a winter salad, baked beans and chutney.

Baked sweet potatoes are much the same, but have a shorter cooking time and you don't eat the skin.

Potato wedges

Wash enough potatoes, depending on your appetite. One medium-sized spud per person should be enough. You can leave the peel on if it's clean enough. Cut the potatoes into pieces about the size and shape of orange segments, and parboil for 8 minutes in water which is already boiling.

Drain at once and leave to settle in the sieve for a couple of minutes. They should still be quite hard; if you've accidentally cooked them soft, consider mashed potatoes instead. Preheat the oven to a hot medium (Gas Mark 6; 200 C; 400F). Drizzle the potato wedges with olive oil, sprinkle with salt and shake in the sieve to make sure they're all coated. You can add ground pepper and Italian style cheese powder at this stage too.

Arrange them in a single layer on a large baking tray or two. Cook for 40–45 minutes near the top of the oven. Check them after half an hour, turn them over with a spatula. If you're using two trays, swap them around; they may need a little longer to get well browned.

These are a good substitute for deep fried chips, with less fat and a safer cooking method. You can skip the boiling stage if you don't have a sieve, but they'll take a bit longer in the oven and need watching more at the end.

Where a recipe calls for adding things to boiling water, it's more energy efficient to boil this water in an electric kettle. Heating water up in a pan is slower, especially if you don't put a lid on it.

Mince and onions

200 grams (8 ounces) of raw beef mince
1 large onion, chopped
2 cloves garlic, finely chopped
2 teaspoons of gravy granules
1 tablespoon of cooking oil

Lightly fry the mince, onions and garlic in the pan, until the meat is just brown and the onions are going transparent. Stir in 200 ml (half a pint) of hot water and simmer gently for 20 minutes, stirring occasionally. After about 10 minutes, sprinkle the gravy granules over the top and mix them in. Stir a bit more often as the mince thickens.

This is traditionally served with mashed potatoes; again, it's worth making extra to use in other recipes.

Much the same recipe will serve for larger pieces of meat; the cooking times increase. Stews made with chunks of meat take about 30 minutes of simmering, casseroles using slices or chops need an hour or so, a pot roast even longer. Long slow cooking is best done in an oven, or a very thick pan; the food may burn in a thin walled utensil.

Potato scones

200 grams (8 ounces) mashed potatoes
50 grams (2 ounces) self-raising flour, plus a half teaspoon of baking powder if you have it
25 grams (1 ounce) butter
a pinch of salt

Using a large bowl, mix the flour and potatoes together, then add the salt and butter. Mash together with a fork to make a stiff mix without lumps. Knead this lightly and roll the dough out on a floured board. Just under half an inch (one centimetre) thick is about right.

Cut into triangles and cook for 5 minutes on each side. Use a hot griddle, or thick frying pan, lightly greased.
Serve with a savoury dish, or spread with jam. These quantities make about eight scones.

Left over mashed potatoes can also be used to make potato cakes. For each four ounces of potato, stir in one egg and two tablespoons of plain flour. This will make a sticky dough; have more flour handy to coat your hands, and also the plate you put the uncooked cakes on.

Divide this dough into four thin burger shapes; fry in hot, shallow oil for a few minutes on each side. Potato cakes go well with a fried breakfast, or spread with tomato ketchup for a quick snack. They're best eaten hot.

Bread

500 grams (16 ounces) strong wheat flour
1 teaspoon of salt
1 teaspoon of dried yeast, or one of those little packets you can empty straight into the mix
325 ml (10 fluid ounces) of warm water; this amount may vary with the type of flour you use

Optional extras : -
1 teaspoon of sugar
15 grams (half an ounce) of soft butter, or a tablespoon of oil

A large bowl for mixing
A loaf tin or similar for baking, ready greased and floured. Bread cooks better in a tin with thin metal sides; if you don't have one, you can try making rolls.

Start with this recipe, using the individual packets of yeast which are so handy in your resilience stores. Get a feel for when the texture of the dough is right, then you can experiment with using more flour, which will require adjusting the amount of water. A bread mix should be slightly wet before the kneading stage. This recipe makes one small loaf.

If you're using dried yeast from a tin, follow the instructions to make it up. It'll take about fifteen minutes in a warm place to start frothing. Remember to subtract any liquid used for this from the total; starting with the right amount of water is quite important in making bread as the texture changes while you work it.

Put the flour into a large bowl, stir in the salt and sugar, rub in the fat. Add the yeast, then slowly mix in the rest of the water. The dough needs to hold together, but not be too sticky. Have the water jug and a small bowl of flour handy when you start to knead the dough with your hands in case you need to adjust the amounts. If it feels dry, try kneading for a bit before adding any more water.

Bread needs a good pummelling, lots of turning over, folding and squishing down. Ten minutes is a good time to spend doing this. If you skimp on it, the finished loaf may be too solid. By the end, the dough shouldn't be sticking to your hands at all, but have become more elastic. Only practice will show you how this translates into the sort of loaf you prefer.

Mould the dough roughly to shape and drop it into the loaf tin, trying not to disturb the flour coating. Push it out to fill the corners, cover the whole with a clean damp cloth and leave it in a warm place to rise. It should achieve at least an inch above the lip of a one pound loaf tin. How long this takes depends on how well you kneaded it and the warmth it's rising in. A couple of hours ought to be enough.

Bake on the middle shelf in a preheated hot medium oven (Gas Mark 6; 200C; 400F) for 30 minutes. The loaf should have come away from the sides of the tin now; if not, slide a knife in to loosen it. If you tip the bread out and tap on the bottom of the loaf, there should be a hollow sound. Give it another 10 minutes if you're not sure, unless it's starting to burn. Once you've decided it's done, put the loaf on a wire rack to cool.

Strong flour is specially processed for bread making, from 'hard' wheat, which is high in gluten. The protein strands of the gluten trap a lot of the carbon dioxide gas released by the yeast. This gas expands as the loaf bakes, and the mesh of strands sets around these bubbles, giving a light texture to the bread.

Other flours can be used, but the bread may be heavier. Wholemeal flour rises a little less readily in general, but you can add texture with nuts, seeds or raisins. Try the basic recipe a few times to get the idea, then experiment!

Scrambled eggs

One or two eggs per person
Milk – measure out one half eggshell per egg used
A knob of butter

Stir the eggs and milk together, being sure to break the yolks. Using a thick bottomed pan, melt the butter but don't let it brown. Pour the mixture into the pan, and stir gently but firmly with a wooden spoon as it begins to set. Cook to taste, and serve on toast.

Scrambled egg only takes minutes to cook, so if you want to add fried onions, chopped chives, grated cheese or bacon bits, you need to prepare these in advance. The main disadvantage to this quick, low calorie meal is that the pan is really quite difficult to wash afterwards.

In the days when one had to outwit a chicken to get eggs, it was customary to check them before adding to other valuable ingredients. Some birds would hide their eggs, so you weren't sure how old they were! You'd always break them into a cup first, to see if they'd gone off.

Apple Crumble

100 grams (4 ounces) butter, or coconut oil
200 grams (8 ounces) plain flour
100 grams (4 ounces) sugar
3–4 large apples

Rub the butter into the flour until the whole mix is like largish breadcrumbs. If it's too greasy, add a bit more flour, but on the whole, stick to the recipe. Stir in the sugar. Your fruit crumble mix is now ready.

Peel, core and chop the apples. Stew them gently, with a few tablespoons of water, for about ten minutes. Spare tins of fruit, raisins and left over jams can all be added. You're aiming for a fruit layer at least an inch deep in your baking dish, and not too wet. Strain off the fruit juice and save it to drink later.

You'll need a deep baking dish; don't fill it all the way to the top. It doesn't rise, since you're using plain flour, but the fruit juices can bubble up through the crumble and burn into a sticky mess. Spoon the crumble mix over the fruit, covering to a depth of nearly an inch.

How much mix you make depends on how big your dish is; these are sample quantities for a medium-sized one. Keep the proportions the same to make more or less. If you misjudge it dramatically, crumble is a very forgiving recipe and will sit quietly on the fruit while you quickly make some more. It'll also keep in the fridge till the next day.

Pop it in the middle of a preheated medium oven Gas Mark 5, 190C; 375F) for about half an hour. It'll be turning light brown when it's ready; leave it for longer if it's not, checking often. An hour is more than enough.

Serve with custard, ice cream, or a sauce made from the fruit juice.

Chapter Six

December

Winter has come. The light fades out before afternoon has even got properly started, the ground is rock solid with frost or thick with mud. Even the weeds and the molluscs have given up for the time being. The only garden chores are cleaning your tools, maybe sorting out the shed and responsibly disposing of the weed killers that you have now forsworn.

It's pleasant to walk around on the occasional sunny morning, with frost sparkling on bare twigs, and admire your work so far. Go for a walk and see how much food there isn't everywhere else. Storage, followed by agriculture, was the key to human survival in the northern winter landscape.

Put a bird feeder up, mindful of local cats, and return to your armchair reading. Although the internet is a fabulous resource, there's nothing like a good gardening book. It's more accessible when your hands are muddy, and it doesn't run out of batteries or signal in the allotment.

There are thousands of these books but you only need two. One as your main guide and one for a second opinion. Investigate your local library; they can order books for you. Read a few before choosing the style you like best and buying your own. Consider starting a garden diary. You could include recipes, photos, pressed flowers.

I began with 'The Allotment Handbook' by Caroline Foley which is an excellent month by month beginners' guide to cultivation. The iconic 'Grow your own vegetables' by Joy Larkcom supplies greater detail, especially useful if something is giving me problems. The really adventurous should take a look at 'Plants for a Future' by Ken Fern, and be inspired into experiment!

Soil

How do you tell if soil is any good? Dig up a trowel full. Rub it between wet fingers. If it turns into a ball and goes slippery, it's clay. If it powders and trickles away, it's sand.

The best soil combines these properties into a loam. This has enough structure to retain water and nutrients, but is lighter than clay. Loams crumble without powdering, and are quite dark in colour. Any base soil can be converted into a loam, but if yours is particularly unpromising, a raised bed will concentrate your efforts.

Most organic materials can be pressed into service to create a growing medium. Contained against blowing away, straw or cardboard can provide cheap bulk. Layer these with manure or fallen leaves and finish with a good layer of potting compost. A deep bed will settle; use growbags laid on top for the first year. Stick to surface crops rather than root vegetables till your soil is well mixed. Earthworms will do this job for you.

Once you have a basic soil structure to work with, consider its quality. Plants need nutrients to build up healthy roots and leaves. You have to make sure they have plenty of these available. It's difficult to tell if you have a fertile soil until things actually start growing. Fortunately, it's easy to add these essential elements as you go.

Compost

As you pull up weeds, or harvest vegetables, you're removing the nutrients they used. Other plants can only access them once they've returned to a soluble form, through the process of decay. You can recapture these important chemicals and return them to the soil, using a compost heap.

It's quite an art to create a good one, as opposed to a heap of rotting weeds. Correctly done, they generate a lot of heat which kills off weed seeds and persistent roots. The bacteria responsible for this controlled decay need oxygen; the material in a compost heap has to be turned over from time to time to keep air in the mix. It takes at least a couple of months to finish the process; longer in cold weather.

Unlike commercial compost, yours will be full of twiggy bits. Shovel some into a sieve and give the worms half an hour to escape. Throw the lumps back into the heap, or into a new one beside it. Many gardeners keep two going at once, one ready to use and the other accepting new material. Use the sieved compost as a mulch around your vegetables.

Liquid plant feeds

If you don't want a compost heap, send your garden waste off to the local recycling company. You can make compost teas or liquid feed instead, though these don't do much to improve soil structure. For a compost tea, throw a few handfuls of chopped weeds into one of those useful large lidded plastic bins. Cover with water and leave for a couple of days, stirring into a froth daily. Then strain out the plants and water the soil with the liquid.

As with a compost heap, this is an aerobic process, but compost teas don't get hot enough to kill off seeds or pathogens. They're a quick fix for plants which are struggling. You can make a stronger liquid feed using an anaerobic process, which takes a lot longer.

Fill your bin one quarter full of comfrey, one quarter full of nettles and finish with a quarter bin of seaweed. Add water to the top. Put the lid on tight and leave it to rot down. This process is smelly; keep the bin in your wild patch!

Poke the material back under the water every week or so. After a few months – again, longer in cold weather – an aerobic stage will begin. The liquid clears somewhat, the smell decreases, and the plants will have rotted down to a sludge. Bale this concentrated feed out into a clean bin – one cupful of it is enough to add to a watering can – and apply to the soil around your vegetables. Top it up with rainwater to make it last longer. The sludge is too rich for direct application; bury it where you want a hungry crop to grow.

Some seasonal foods available in December

Stores are at their fullest and most varied.
There isn't much fresh food to be foraged, only wild roots and hardy edible weeds.
You can use the leaves of some biannual and perennial vegetables from your own garden, such as brassicas and tree onions.
Small game and fish are back on the traditional menu now there's less farm work.

Feasting

The harvest was well and truly gathered in by December, and the storehouses overflowing. The Yuletide celebrations were a good excuse to get this food eaten; much of it wouldn't keep for long.

> "Beef, mutton and pork, shred pies of the best,
> pig, veal, goose and capon, and turkey well drest;
> Cheese, apples and nuts, jolly carols to hear,
> as then in the country is counted good cheer."
>
> Thomas Tusser, 1573.

This verse celebrates a typical Christmas in Elizabethan England. Even though agriculture was still quite primitive, there were times of great plenty for all.

These were only possible due to the attention paid to farming during the rest of the year. Even the rights to gather moss from certain trees to feed hungry winter cattle were a subject of community discussion. The appearance of a troupe of travelling entertainers must have been a welcome relief from this rather oppressive detailing of life!

Dreaming

Elizabethan agriculture was undeniably organic. The 5 million people in England and Wales had enough food, cloth and fuel. Without modern storage and distribution methods, seasonal famines often affected large areas, but on the whole the land provided for everyone. Science, art and literature flourished; there was adventure and opportunity.

The winter, with its strange ice magic and long evenings by the fire, is the time for dreaming. The first Elizabethans dreamed of a mighty nation; perhaps we should dream of a resilient one.

The greatest journey begins with a single step – as long as you keep going, that is.

Onions

You'll notice that most of the savoury recipes in this book feature onions. They add bulk and flavour, providing a base for savoury sauces which helps prevent them going lumpy. If you don't like onions, substitute something with a similar light, crunchy texture and short cooking time, such as red pepper or celery.

Onions are part of the allium family, which includes garlic, leek, shallots and chives. They're the only food eaten all over the world. The oldest known cookery books – a set of three clay tablets from Babylon, four thousand years old – are filled with onion recipes!

Most resilience gardens can provide fresh food from this plant family all year. Grow leeks for harvesting from November to April. Spring onions take over then, until your traditional bulb varieties are ready to eat from June. Chives can stay green in mild winters, and the wild garlic leaves provide welcome vitamins in spring.

The alliums are rich in sulphur, vitamin C, copper and many other important nutrients. It's worth adding them to a meal as leaves if you can't stand your eyes watering when you chop onion bulbs. Cutting the root off last does help, as most of the irritant compound is found here. The best strategy, however, is to keep a tidy kitchen so you can get to the tap and a towel quickly, while having a safe place to put your glasses!

Something from the onion family should feature in your resilience garden. Other staple vegetables in your area will become apparent as you cultivate a garden, or even a few patio pots. Mine are broccoli, kale, spinach and rocket. All these self-seed and resist pests. Peas, courgettes, squash and potatoes thrive, although they need to be planted anew each year. Parsnip and carrots are starting to do well as I gradually convert the hard clay soil to a loosely packed loam. I still have no success with swedes or beans; the latter can't fend off the slugs.

It takes a few years of trial and error to find the crops you can rely on for resilience. They differ widely depending on the local microclimate, soil quality and access to sunlight. Use your books and the internet for research, and your garden diary to record results. Try growing your favourite vegetables; at the very least you will better appreciate the problems faced by organic farmers!

Recipes for December

Roast chicken

You can afford to buy an organic free-range bird, as you're going to be able to get up to twelve adult meals from it. Cheap factory farmed chickens tend to roast down to a withered brown caricature swimming in a pool of watery grease, and are not suitable for this series of recipes.

You'll find that using your own vegetables adds to the preparation time for a large meal. They need to be dug up, washed and trimmed before you launch into the actual process, as you don't want any mud involved. Economise on effort by cooking more than you need and adding the surplus to a stew the next day, then finishing off with a hearty soup. When most people had Sundays off, it was an opportunity to enlist the family in preparing the traditional roast, followed by a couple of easy meals on the workdays.

Plan a roast dinner carefully and allow a good couple of hours for the cooking. It's customary to have potatoes and at least two different vegetables with the centrepiece. If you only have two shelves in your oven, there's just room for meat and roast potatoes. You'd need to cook the rest on the hob. Choose your recipes accordingly; there's a selection following the main instructions.

A good-sized chicken for four people is around three to four pounds; one and a half kilos. Free range chickens from a butcher's shop tend to be larger than supermarket ones. Work with the size of your oven as getting those two extra shelves in use is important. You may get a bag of giblets; discard these in the outside bin if you don't know what to do with them.

Cooking times for all large pieces of meat depend on the weight, and are given for an oven preheated to the right temperature. The instructions here assume your hottest oven shelf is at the top; adapt them if it isn't. The element of some electric ovens may be in the base, making the lower shelves hotter.

Always prepare raw meat on a board, not your counter top, and carefully wash everything that it's been in contact with, including your hands. Don't cook frozen meat – allow it to defrost first.

Remove all the plastic wrapping, disentangle the rubber band and put the chicken in a lightly oiled, high sided roasting tin. Drizzle another few tablespoons of oil over it until all the meat is covered. Wash your hands. Did you make the stuffing? Packet varieties need some ten minutes to rehydrate, so do it quickly now!

Calculate your cooking times; it's helpful to write a list.

Preheat your oven to Gas Mark 8 (230C; 450F) for 10 minutes
Put the stuffed chicken in on the middle shelf and cook at this temperature for 15 minutes
Reduce the heat to Gas Mark 5 (190C; 375F) and cook for 20 minutes per pound weight (25 minutes per half kilogram). Include the whole weight, not just complete units.
Add another 15 minutes to the cooking time for the stuffing
Add a further 10 minutes for opening the oven door and letting all the heat out

A chicken weighing 1.65 kg takes 2 hours to be properly cooked. Medium rare is not an option with chicken. The juices must run clear, and the pink colour gone from the meat before it's safe to eat.

If you'd turned the oven on at 4.20pm, this chicken would be ready about 6.30pm. The roast potatoes would need be in the oven at 5.30pm, and the

other roast vegetables a little later depending on their exact cooking times. Carrots, swedes and other root vegetables are set on to boil around the same time; broccoli, sprouts and cauliflower a little later. Steamed leaves, such as kale, only need to cook for a few minutes right at the end.
Check the meat every 30 minutes and spoon hot oil over it. If it starts to brown on top long before it's cooked, drape a couple of slices of streaky bacon over it, or cover with silver foil.

As any roasted meat cooks, the top tends to dry out. Rather than being turned over, which can be tricky, it needs to be basted. Carefully spoon up hot oil from the roasting dish and tip it over the meat to keep the top moist.

After the meat has cooked for a while, the roast potatoes are next. Put them on the shelf above the meat until they are soft right through, when you can move them lower. Drained and covered, these are easy to keep warm once cooked, but can take longer than you'd reasonably expect. Allow a good 60 minutes on a high shelf for them.

Prepare all the other vegetables; once cut up, they should be kept in a pan of cold water. One of the prospective beneficiaries of the roast dinner could clean the kitchen and wash up, while making you a cup of tea. The busy stage is beginning; you'll need an empty sink and plenty of open surfaces ready.

You could move the meat down a shelf now, if it's looking nearly cooked. If it's slow – check the underneath too – try going up a heat setting, especially if you haven't used this oven before. It doesn't help to turn it up to high, as then you will only cook the outside. Wait until the chicken is very nearly done before starting the next stage.

Do use hand protection when moving hot oven shelves, always take the trays off and set them on a heat proof surface first. Be careful of hot oil; don't let your roasting tin get too full. Pour any extra into a bowl in the sink, then into the food recycling bin.

If the meat is on schedule, vegetables for roasting can go in the oven when the potatoes are getting soft nearly to the middle and there is about 40 minutes of cooking time left. Move the potatoes down a shelf so you can get these on top. Other roots are set to the boil at the same time and left to simmer.

Start cooking cauliflower and broccoli florets on the hob 20 minutes from the end; use hot water from the kettle to keep the timing right. Shredded green leaves can go in a steamer pan over these about 5 minutes before they are done.

When everything is cooked, preferably all at exactly the same time, have someone cut up the meat for serving while you make gravy – I use granules. Drain steamed or boiled vegetables, move the roasted ones out of their oil into a clean dish, and serve.

The idea is to smother everyone's plate with vegetables so that they do not notice there is only a small piece of meat each. Stuffing is for extra filler, and if you can make a proper thick gravy using the juices from the roasting dish, so much the better.

Hide the rest of the meat, or otherwise ensure no-one is going for seconds or midnight raids. Distract them with extra roast potatoes. There should be a mixture of the less popular vegetables left over. Keep these for the next day's cooking, when you will be making leftover stew. You can make a stock with the chicken carcass and use this as a base for the chicken and lentil soup on the third day.

Roast potatoes

It's worth devoting a large baking tray and a whole oven shelf to these, as they make a nice snack cold. Wash and peel a couple of medium-sized potatoes; chop them into your preferred size. Larger pieces will take a bit longer to cook. Arrange them on your tray so they are close but don't touch, and add more if there's room.

Then tip the chunks into a pan and cover with boiling water from a kettle. Bring back to the boil and simmer for no more than 8 minutes, then drain quickly and leave to stand a little while. Empty them back into the dry pan and toss them in plain flour with a scant teaspoon of salt added, and any finely chopped herbs you may fancy. The potatoes shouldn't be overcooked, or they will break up at this stage. Cut your losses if they do, and make a baked mash instead.

Have the baking tray heating up in the oven with a couple of tablespoons of oil, then carefully transfer the coated potato chunks into it, drizzle them with a little more oil, and return to a high shelf. Close the oven door while you're doing this; the meat is still trying to cook. Check them after 30 minutes and turn them over, or baste again.

Cooked alone, these take 40–60 minutes in a medium hot oven (Gas Mark 6; 200C; 425F). The oven is set slightly lower for the roast dinner, and cools a bit every time you open the door to fiddle with something, so allow the longer time then.

Experiment with different varieties of potato; some are much better roasted than others are.

Baked squash

Once you've hacked the hard skin off a squash and removed the seeds, cut it into chunks about an inch (2 centimetres) square. Lay these on a lightly oiled tray and bake for 20–30 minutes in a hot medium oven (Gas Mark 6; 200C; 400F) on a top middle shelf.

Alternately, you can cut the squash in half lengthways and, leaving the skin on, cut a crosswise pattern into the flesh and bake it like that. It takes a little longer and needs a lower shelf; it has to be soft enough to scoop out for serving. This is a good strategy if you haven't enough room for another tray.

Chunks of parsnip can be put in the oven while you prepare this; they take about 10 minutes more cooking. Leave half the tray clear, then add the squash. Always roast vegetables in a single layer, not a heap.

Glazed carrots

Clean and slice some carrots. Use at least one largish carrot (about 100 grams; 4 ounces) per person; they will be useful for the stew next day. Bring these to the boil in enough water to just cover them and simmer for 15 minutes. They should be starting to get soft but not cooked by then.

Add a stock cube and a pinch of salt. For every four large servings, stir in an ounce (25 grams) of butter and two teaspoons of sugar. Simmer uncovered for 10–15 minutes, until the water has reduced by half. Serve from the pan using a slotted spoon; if there's a lot of liquid left, you can thicken it with granules and use it as gravy. Garnish the dish with chopped parsley.

Brussel sprouts with onion and bacon

Using a pan, lightly fry chopped onions and bacon in a little butter. Remove the outer leaves of the sprouts, cut an X across the stem – to make sure it cooks right through – and add these once the onion is transparent. Pour in enough hot water to half cover the sprouts and simmer for 15 minutes or so until done to taste.

Make sure they don't burn by adding a little more water during cooking, but the idea is to be able to serve them straight from the pan complete with bacon and onion. You shouldn't need to strain this dish. Timing is quite important; if it's ready too soon, it's hard to keep warm without overcooking the sprouts.

Steamed cabbage, leeks and mustard

Trim a few of the large green leaves from your brassicas, pull a handful of leeks. Sauté the chopped leeks until just soft, while shredding the leaves. Stir these together in a steaming pan over some simmering root vegetables about 5 minutes before these are done. Cover and allow to cook. It won't take long for the leaves to wilt; take a little longer if you like them soft.

Mix a tablespoon of whole grain mustard (according to taste) into the cooked leek and cabbage before serving.

Leftover stew

Returning to the cooked chicken, which must have been stored overnight in a fridge. With scrupulously clean hands, strip the good meat from the carcass and set the rest aside. Cut into pieces and sauté using a little oil in a large thick bottomed pan, with a chopped onion. Add some water before it burns, then top up to about a third of the pan with hot stock. Use up any left over gravy, or just add cubes and water.

Add the cooked vegetables from yesterday's roast, bring to the boil and simmer for 30 minutes. Add extra vegetables if there isn't enough, but remember raw roots take a while to cook in a stew. Frozen peas are a good cheat. Thicken with granules and serve with boiled potatoes, mash or bread.

If you're using raw meat, sauté the pieces for longer until the meat is nearly cooked through. Cooking a full roast dinner in a makeshift oven would be very challenging, and spit roasting is harder than it looks in the movies. If you don't have an oven available, a stew might be your best option to feed a large number.

If you have a lot of chutney, adding a tablespoon or two to a stew is a good strategy for using it up. I prefer to make my chutney without adding raisins for this reason.

Chicken and lentil soup with stock

You can make this stock before cooking the stew above and use some of it there.

Break up the stripped chicken carcass and cover it with water in a large pan. Add garden herbs. I like thyme, bay leaf and chives; work out your favourite combination. Bring it to the boil and let it simmer for an hour, topping up with water if necessary. Don't let it boil dry.

When it's done, strain the liquid into another pan; this is your stock. Throw the bones and bits of herb away in an outside bin; it's less messy if you wrap these in newspaper first.

Sauté an onion in a large pan, add any small bits of meat you kept back, then top up with the stock and bring to the boil. How much you make depends on how many people you are feeding. For two, add around 700 millilitres of stock (a pint and a quarter); the lentils will absorb a lot of it. Turn the soup down to simmer and add 25 grams (1 ounce), or a small handful of red lentils for each person. A grated raw carrot is nice too.

Simmer for another 30 minutes, stirring from time to time to stop the lentils sticking to the bottom. Add some shredded fresh greens just before it's done. The soup is ready when the lentils are soft.

Baked apple

Take one large cooking apple in good condition per person. Don't peel it. Cut out the core without breaking the apple. If you can avoid cutting through the bottom, that's excellent; otherwise wrap the whole thing in foil to cook. Fill the space with a mixture of sultanas, brown sugar and a teaspoon of butter each. A dash of cinnamon is nice.

Here's a typical mix, per apple : -
1 flat teaspoon of butter
2 round teaspoons of soft dark brown sugar
1 tablespoon of sultanas
half a teaspoon of cinnamon

Place the apples on a baking tray and cook in a preheated low medium oven (Gas Mark 4; 180C; 350F) on the middle shelf for 30 minutes

Serve with cream or custard; use up a tin from your stores.

After cooking a roast dinner, the oven will be nicely hot. Take advantage of this by having a baked dessert ready to pop in after serving!

Carrot cake

100 grams (4 ounces) of self-raising flour, preferably wholemeal
Half a teaspoon of baking powder
2 medium carrots peeled and grated, about 150 grams (6 ounces) when whole
50 grams (2 ounces) sultanas
2 eggs, beaten
2 tablespoons (30 ml; one fluid ounce) of fresh orange juice
75 grams (2 ½ ounces) butter, just melted
Optional – 75 grams (2 ½ ounces) soft light brown sugar; the fruit provides enough sweetness in this recipe

Preheat the oven to medium (Gas Mark 5; 190C; 375F) and prepare a baking tin by greasing it, then scattering a little dry flour over the grease. Tap any excess into the cake mix. Many online recipes suggest a round tin, but I've always preferred using a one-pound loaf tin for this.

Mix together all the dry ingredients until the grated carrot is well coated. Add the eggs, butter and fruit juice. Stir together and tip into the tin.

Cook on the middle shelf for 40 minutes, turning down a little after half an hour. Check the cake at this point. If the top looks soft, shut the oven door quickly and gently. If it's hardening up, the cake can be taken out the oven briefly without collapsing. As the rising agent works, the gases have to be trapped in the setting mix; a delicate process.

A cake has to be firm all the way through; test this by poking a fork into it. It should come out clean, with no trace of cake mix sticking to it. If you're not sure, dig a little spoonful out of the middle and assess that.

Where the top is starting to burn, but the inside still seems runny, there are several things you can do. Move the cake to a lower shelf, cover the top with foil, or turn the oven down a setting.

Leave to cool in the tin for a few minutes after cooking, then turn out onto a wire rack to finish off cooling. If your cake sticks, try lining the tin with greaseproof paper next time.

Chapter Seven

January

After the winter solstice, on the 21st December, the days stop getting shorter. There's a bit more light, but it's often colder. For a smallholder, forage is thin on the ground, so your remaining stores are important. Learning how to harvest and store cereal crops was crucial to survival in the Northern temperate zone with its harsh winters.

Farm animals need food and shelter now. In the Viking long houses of old, there'd be a couple of stalls for prize cows at the end by the midden. Horses and sheep stayed out in the fields longer, but even they needed extra food. It wasn't unusual to send domestic animals out to forage in the woods. The much-reduced pig family and the small flock of chickens subsisted on household scraps, as did the dogs.

Wild forage

Wild animals are easier to spot in bare woodlands, can be tracked in mud or snow. Harvesting gave way to hunting. Small game was a tasty addition to stews made from withered roots and dried peas!

You're unlikely to be allowed to hunt squirrels in Britain today, but you can still walk the landscape. Without a covering of leaves, its contours are revealed. Take a good map and follow a footpath trail. Explore a forest. Learn how to identify trees and recognise animal signs.

Many plants are in a dormant phase. Exposed leaves are damaged by frost, so they are allowed to die off in autumn, sending the nutrients used in their structure to another part of the plant. Some will have seeded; others form large roots as a food store.

The seeds scatter and the roots are buried. You'll see a few berries, the discarded shells of nuts, some tattered nettles. Edible roots are there somewhere, but it's illegal to dig them up from the few remaining wild areas. Without their leaves, it's difficult to tell them apart from poisonous plants.

Ramsons often grow with bluebells and cuckoo pint; burdock can be similar to foxglove. The best way to find out about wild edibles is to go on a foraging walk with an expert. Learn about the conditions each plant likes

– damp or well-drained, sunny or shaded – and try to cultivate them at home. Watching them in your resilience garden, you'll become familiar with their various stages. If you manage to grow enough, and are confident of your identification skills, you could try cooking them.

Exercise caution when trying a new wild edible for first time. Make sure of the identification and only eat a little at first. Remember the foragers' warning "Everything is edible, but some things only once"

There's not much wild food around for humans in a British January, especially on high ground. Our nomadic ancestors probably headed towards the coast in winter. Rivers spread out into swamps; there were fish, waterfowl and frogs. Edible roots weren't locked in frozen ground. The sea, with its shellfish, birds and seaweed was within easy reach.

Famine foods

Although farming was a good strategy for surviving winter, it meant you were committed to staying in one place. In a bad year, you could be turning to famine foods as your stores dwindled. People who didn't have access to forests had to make do.

Snails hibernate in clusters and are easy to catch. Feed them on clean greens for a couple of days, in case they've been snacking on poisonous plants, then gut and cook them. Treated in a similar way, some large slugs are also edible; there's an inner shell to remove as well. Slugs and snails carry lungworm (Angiostrongylus vasorum); this can be transmitted to domestic animals who eat them raw. It's not usually known to infect humans, but always eat molluscs well cooked.

Most earthworms are edible; purged as above after capture and well cooked, whole. Although certain species are prized among the Maori of New Zealand, earthworm is far too bitter for most tastes. In a survival situation, you could try grinding dry ones into a powder and swallowing this mixed with something else, as they are rich in protein.

Many cultures celebrate their particular famine food as a delicacy. The French excel in recipes for frogs and snails; in Portugal, a dish of slugs may be proudly served. Lava bread, made from seaweed, is still popular in Welsh coastal towns.

Some famine foods are so complex that one wonders how they were discovered. In Iceland, during the Little Ice Age famine, the huge

Greenland shark was hunted for its oil rich liver. Fish oil was burned in lamps before the discovery of kerosene.

Unfortunately, its flesh contains urea and trimethylamine N-oxide, as an adaptation for swimming at depth. Eaten raw, or without careful prepaation, the latter produces symptoms similar to extreme drunkenness in both dogs and humans. This great mass of valuable protein had to be safely disposed of, generally by burying. As the ground was part frozen, the carcass would need to be covered with boulders.

The famished dogs would continue to try and get at it, and it was surely by watching them that humans worked out how to eat the shark meat. After a few weeks of cold and pressure, the toxic chemical is pressed out. Although the meat has started to ferment by then, it can be dried and eaten. It still tastes of cleaning fluid though; you'd have to be hungry.

Famine foods are not usually the dish of choice. Instead of rowing out in the icy treacherous Atlantic to wrestle a four metre angry shark with poisonous flesh, most people would prefer to eat bread and cheese, but the Little Ice Age ended grain cultivation in Iceland for many centuries.

Conditions improved, famine retreated into history. A prudent smallholder could easily amass ample stores again. Winters were spent conserving energy. People sat by the fireside spinning, carving, telling each other stories. They kept an eye on the bread rising in the warmth, stirred the pot of stew

There's still not a lot to be done in the garden at this time of year. Attend to regular chores when you're at home during daylight hours. Finish building your raised bed frames and fill them with soil, let it settle. Plan what you're going to grow, browse seed catalogues, order your own gardening book.

Some seasonal foods available in January

Dried pulses – peas, lentils, beans.
Stored grains, nuts, beans, dried fruit, dried mushrooms.
Your remaining stores of potatoes and other root vegetables.
Leeks, brassica leaves, winter kale from the garden.
Your butter stocks may be getting low, but there's still lard, suet and edible oils.
Eggs and fresh milk are in short supply.
Oranges and lemons are in season; they travel well from their countries of origin.
Apples stored in a cool shed.

Jams, syrups, chutneys and pickles from the autumn harvest.
Bacon, ham and sausages; salt beef, jerky and smoked meats.
Fresh meat isn't on the menu, apart from the occasional tough old boiler chicken, wild game or fish
Survival foods such as dock and nettle leaves, edible roots, bittercress, plantain and groundsel.

If you've managed to store enough of your own root vegetables to last this long, you'll notice they've begun to wither. The skins are tougher, the flesh harder. They need to be cooked slowly, in plenty of liquid. Stews and soups are the order of the day. There's often a few garden leaves to add to these recipes; a bit of fatty bacon, the last of the potatoes. These will begin to sprout soon, responding to the longer days, so use them up.

The importance of grain

Life in the cold North was pretty marginal for hunter-gatherers. The development of food stores and of keeping domestic animals were crucial for survival. Long before that, nearly two million years ago, we unlocked one of our most important discoveries. Cooking some foods releases its carbohydrates, makes proteins accessible. Humans can't digest raw grains. Cooked, they become the staff of life.

We soon discovered that dry grains store well; a buffer against seasonal famines. Wheat and barley were the first to be cultivated, followed by rice, millet, rye and other cereal crops. Some ancient granaries, the silo pits of Malta, could contain over fifty tons of grain each. With the right conditions, this could keep for over four years.

Grain must be kept dry, not even a bit damp as this encourages dangerous moulds. Freshly harvested seeds give off water, so they must be spread out to dry first. In wetter climates, granaries tended to be in raised buildings which allowed air to circulate, rather than pits.

Staddle stones, short pillars which curved outwards at the top, were used in Britain. The granary stood on top of these, protected from rats who couldn't climb around the curve. It was a challenge, storing the precious grain in the damp North. People often pre-empted the inevitable fermentation and brewed beer from their barley instead!

Whole grains are ideal in hearty stews, replacing the root vegetables as they run out. They also need long slow cooking, adding carbohydrates and bulk. It's a good time of year for making bread from freshly ground flour as well. It can rise by the fireside, bake in the inglenook oven, or cook on a griddle suspended over the embers. Dipped in a soup, even the hardest stale bread is edible.

Supplies needed to be conserved. Your stores were your lifeline through the winter. You were never sure how long it might last, nor what problems could arise. A cold wet spring would delay the planting of your summer food; mice may spoil a grain bin and leave you short of flour. January was a frugal month, even when there was plenty put by.

Recipes for January

Rabbit stew

1 rabbit, skinned and gutted. Any small game will do, such as squirrel, pheasant or pigeon
4 tablespoons of cooking oil, or 50 grams (2 ounces) of lard
A handful of fresh herbs according to taste to simmer with the stock
A couple of cloves of garlic, finely chopped
An onion, or some garden leeks, chopped
A few carrots, a parsnip, half a swede, a slice of squash, some bits of potato, whatever needs using up.
A tablespoon of plain flour
2–4 teaspoons of gravy granules. These should provide enough salt for the recipe. You can add more to your own bowl later.

Lightly roast the rabbit in half the fat for about 45 minutes in a low medium oven (Gas Mark 4; 180C; 350F) basting occasionally, until the meat is just cooked. It's easier to handle than raw meat. Strip off the meat – there won't be much – setting it aside. Make a stock with the bones, then discard them.

Consider how many people you are feeding, and how much they're likely to eat. If it's just for you, a stew will last a couple of days if kept cool. Adjust the amount of root vegetables to make a larger pot; the recipe will serve for a couple of people with good appetites.

Choose a thick bottomed pan of the right size. In the rest of the fat, fry the onions and garlic until they're transparent but not crispy. Take the pan away from the heat and stir in the plain flour, coating the onions. Add warm stock, a little at a time, stirring to break up any lumps of flour. When the mixture is smooth, top the pan up to half way with more stock liquid and set it to simmer gently.

Add the chopped root vegetables, the meat and any extra flavourings, then leave the stew to simmer for at least 40 minutes. If it takes longer, try cutting the roots into smaller pieces next time. Stir from time to time to make sure it's not sticking to the bottom.

Thickening a stew used to be quite an art, similar to making a sauce. Gravy powders also contained the brown colour we like to see – thickening with flour alone often gives a greyish cast to the stew. I stir in a few spoons of gravy granules towards the end. Add more hot water if you overdo these.

Test the roots. If they're cooked, it's time to put in the dumplings. The stew should be ready to eat 15 minutes later. Serve with bread and butter.

If you suspect a stew might have burned, don't stir it. You'll just mix the burnt taste right through. Pour most of it into another pan, then inspect the damage. How much you salvage mainly depends on how hungry you are, but remember to leave the burnt pot to soak or you'll never get it clean.

Invest in a good saucepan with thick walls and base. Investigate the use of heat spreaders if the cooker settings are a problem.

Dumplings

50 grams (2 ounces; two well rounded tablespoons) of shredded suet. There is an exactly equivalent vegetarian option available at most supermarkets
100 grams (4 ounces; four rounded tablespoons) of self-raising flour, with a bit more in reserve
a pinch of salt
some tepid water; about four tablespoons

These quantities will make six good-sized dumplings, which about fill up a large pan. As they have to be cooked on top of the stew itself, there's always a limited number!

It's a good idea to wear an apron. Stir everything together, adding warm water a spoonful at a time, until you have a sticky dough. You might not need all of the water. Have a small bowl of flour handy as you separate this dough into six equally sized balls. Sprinkle more flour in to make it workable. Try not to squish the mix too much as the rising process has already begun; you don't prepare them too far in advance for this reason.

Put the balls onto a floured plate and pop them carefully into the stew at the right time. I like to give the pan a last good stir first, then roll each dumpling over in the gravy before nudging them into their final position, well-spaced with plenty of room to expand. Once they're in, cover the pan and leave it for 15 minutes. It's very difficult to stir now, so it's important to get the heat right for this last stage; a gentle simmer.

The dumplings should double in size, being light and fluffy in the middle when cooked. Cut one in half to check; serve the meal quickly once you're sure they're done.

If you haven't got any self-raising flour or baking powder, use plain flour with one teaspoon of bicarbonate of soda (baking soda) and two teaspoons of lemon juice for every 4 ounces of flour. You'll need to make the mix faster and with a gentler touch, so it's good to get some practice using the ideal ingredients.

There's a definite lemony taste to these dumplings; they'd be nice with chicken or fish stews. Try adding some finely chopped parsley to the mix.

For a more savoury taste, substitute vinegar for lemon juice. Baking soda needs to be activated with an acidic ingredient; baking powder has one (tartaric acid) already mixed in.

Mince and barley broth

100 grams (4 ounces) of minced beef (or any other meat)
A dash of tamari (soy sauce) and a tablespoon of cooking oil
An onion, or some fresh leeks from the garden, chopped small
A couple of cloves of garlic, finely chopped
A few leaves of herb from your garden or pots
2 rounded teaspoons of plain flour
A stock cube
75 grams (3 ounces) of pearl barley; two small handfuls
A handful of shredded green leaves – brassica, spinach, nettle

Another dish which can be served with dumplings, though this is more of a soup. Whole grain has taken the place of root vegetables.

Use a large pan. Brown the mince in a little oil. A dash of tamari at this stage improves the colour. Add the onions, herbs and garlic. Stir till the onion is soft, then lightly sprinkle with plain flour and stir some more. Slowly add half a litre (a pint) of hot water as you stir, then crumble a stock cube into the broth.

Throw in the dried barley, bring it back to the boil, cover and simmer on a low heat for at least 50 minutes, stirring occasionally. Add the shredded leaves about halfway through, plus more water as the barley absorbs it. You'll need about half again as much, or you'll end up with a stew.

Serve with bread. This broth provides a nourishing meal for two people. Increase the quantities to feed more.

Adapt these basic recipes to your own taste. I like to add a teaspoon of made mustard, or a couple of tablespoons of chutney. You can substitute cooked dried beans from stores for the mince; boost the flavour with an extra stock cube. Combining pulses with grain gives a good all round protein.

Lentil soup

1 tablespoon of cooking oil or fat
A dash of tamari
About a litre (a pint and a half) of stock – this can be made from stock cubes and water
50 grams (2 ounces) of dried red lentils; a couple of handfuls
A quarter tube of tomato purée (the 130g tube size)
Garden herbs, especially oregano and chives
At least one onion or leek. Garlic, grated carrot and dried mushrooms also go well in this recipe
A rasher of bacon, chopped
You don't need to add salt

I use red lentils in my stores as they are quick to cook and don't require pre-soaking. This recipe is quite fast, so I don't use whole chunks of root vegetable in it, and use flavours which blend easily. If you're cooking from stores alone, you can use dried onions and a small tin of sweetcorn; leave out the first stage and just throw everything together.

Lightly fry the onions and bacon in the oil with the tamari; pour in the stock. Add the lentils, tomato purée, other vegetables, herbs and flavourings, bring back to the boil. Simmer for 30 minutes, stirring occasionally. Add more stock as the lentils absorb it; water will do. Try stirring in a tablespoon of green tomato chutney.

It's ready when the lentils are soft all through. This recipe will feed two, with a few slices of bread. With a longer cooking time, you can add small pieces of potato, thicken with gravy granules and turn it into a stew – again, suitable for dumplings.

Although making a stock originated as the best way to extract all the nutrition from a small carcass, it's a useful feature of many recipes. You can make a vegan equivalent.

Cut some sprigs of garden herbs, about a hand's length and a few of each type; choose about three. Chop a clove of garlic, maybe a small onion or leek, and put all these in a large pan. Cover with a little more water than the volume of stock you need; you can use the water from cooking other vegetables.

Heat to boil, then simmer gently for 30 minutes. Sieve out the plants, add two stock cubes per half litre (one pint) according to taste.

Leek and potato soup

A couple of large leeks from your resilience garden
A couple of medium potatoes from winter stores, chopped small
Stock – half a litre (one pint) for two people
Optional – some dried wild mushrooms. Practise with commercially available types

Acquiring the skills to collect and preserve wild mushrooms safely is quite a task. Try eating some already prepared first. You may not like the taste or texture! However, if you don't eat animal products, fungi can be an important source of protein.

Dried foods need a lot of cooking water, so it's best to add them to a stew or soup. Follow any instructions about pre-soaking on the packet, or online.

Slice up the leeks and sauté them in a little oil with a dash of tamari. Pour in the stock, add the potatoes and mushrooms. Simmer for about 20 minutes; it's ready when the potatoes are soft. If the mushrooms need longer – there are many different varieties – the rest of the soup is fine with that, as long as you keep the liquid topped up.

You can make this into a 'cream' soup. Allow it to cool so it won't scald you, then blend it. Warm it back up, stirring in 4 fluid ounces (100 ml) of single cream. Don't let it boil. Serve as soon as it's hot enough.

Although richer and more nutritious, this soup won't keep as long as the dairy-free version; it's best eaten up at one meal.

War soup – a modern famine recipe

4 tablespoons of dried milk
1 stock cube
2 tablespoons dried parsley or whatever green leafy stuff is around, shredded

Mix the dried milk with 2 tablespoons of water until it's creamy. Make up to half a litre (one pint). It should look roughly like milk. If it seems too thin, mix up another tablespoon of powder with a very little water in a cup and stir this in slowly to thicken it. Adding more dried powder straight to any mix often results in lumps.

Of course, if you have the packet, follow the instructions given to make up a pint.

Heat the milk gently, stirring in the crumbled stock cube and the leaves; serve at once.

Note the similarity to the 'cream of potato and leek soup' above. Both involve milk and stock cubes. Both can be expanded with garden forage or wild edibles. You would tend to use these recipes if protein from meat or pulses was in short supply. Milk supplies extra Vitamin D in the dark winter months.

Savoury crumble

75 grams (3 ounces) butter
200 grams (8 ounces) plain flour, preferably wholemeal
50 grams (2 ounces) grated cheese, plus a little more to sprinkle on top

For a savoury crumble, make up the mix as for an apple crumble, but leave out the sugar. Rub the butter into the flour until the whole mix is like largish breadcrumbs. Stir in the grated cheese.

You can make a vegan version: -

75 ml (3 fluid ounces) of hemp oil or other good quality edible oil.
200 grams (8 ounces) of plain flour, half of which should be wholemeal
75 grams (3 ounces) of ground up nuts

Mix these ingredients as for the cheesy crumble.

This is a splendid topping for a medley of vegetables in a thick sauce, a stew, or even a mixture of tinned foods from your stores. The filling should be already cooked, still hot, and not too wet. Strain off extra sauce or gravy and keep it for later.

Using an oven dish with heavy sides, like a casserole dish, pour in the filling and cover thickly with crumble mix. Pop it in the middle of a preheated medium oven (Gas Mark 5, 190C; 375F) for about half an hour. A bit of cheese grated on top gives you a good idea when it's ready, as this will start to brown.

Serve with potatoes, mashed swede, mixed greens, and gravy or sauce.

Marmalade

Assemble this equipment first:
A muslin bag or a square of clean muslin about large enough to contain a couple of whole oranges
A large stainless-steel pan, preferably with a thick base, able to hold up to 2.5 litres water (4.5 pints), two kilos (4.5 pounds) of sugar, a dozen oranges and the bag. If you haven't got a big enough pan, try halving the recipe, but you do need quite a lot of liquid due to the long cooking time
About 10 jars with lids, clean. Honey or jam jars are best; old pickle jars are best kept for savoury preserves
Four saucers and teaspoons being chilled in the icebox

1 kilo of Seville oranges (only available at this time of year)
1 lemon
2 kilos of sugar
Two and a half litres of water

Seville oranges have a stronger flavour than normal oranges; the bitterness contrasts nicely with the sugar. They are also very rich in pectin, the stuff that makes jam set, so this is a good preserve to try out first.

Wash the fruit, then cut in half and squeeze the juice out with a lemon squeezer. Save seeds and pith to put in the muslin bag; these are both rich in pectin so are cooked with the oranges. Finely slice the peel. Any bits of orange left on it fall away during cooking.

Tie up the muslin and put the bag in the water with the shredded peels and juice. The peel has to be cooked until it's very soft in the first stage; once you add the sugar, it won't soften any more. Simmer gently for two hours, uncovered, so that the liquid reduces by about half. Take the pan off the heat, remove the bag and let it cool – in a bowl! – before squeezing the last of the jelly-like pectin out to add to the marmalade.

Make sure the saucers are cooling in the freezer and turn your oven to a very low heat (under Gas Mark 1; 140C; 275F). Stand the clean jars upside down in the oven, along with any metal lids. This will both sterilise them and heat them; then the very hot marmalade isn't so much of a shock that the glass cracks. Pick the warmed jars up with a cloth. It's always best to have extra jars than not enough.

Add the sugar to the pan, heat gently and stir till it's dissolved. Use granulated sugar, as it's good to have slow dissolving. Preserving sugar has even bigger crystals, but often contains added pectin which isn't needed here.

When no grains are visible, increase the heat to a rolling boil, stirring occasionally. Be careful it doesn't burn; the mixture will be very hot after adding the sugar. Pay attention.

Skim off any scum as it rises, or add a dab of butter to disperse it. After 15 minutes of boiling, do the first test. Drop a teaspoon of the mix onto one of those cold saucers. Leave it a moment, then push the marmalade with your finger. If the surface wrinkles, then it's reached setting stage. If not, return the pan to a rolling boil, testing again every five minutes.

Marmalade can take up to 40 minutes to reach the crucial temperature of 104.5C. You can use a sugar thermometer to determine the setting point instead of the traditional method.

Leave it to cool for 15 minutes, then stir to mix the peel right through and ladle into jars. Leave a small gap at the top, and put on the lids while the marmalade is still hot. This is quite messy; do it on a tray. Wipe the jars down when cool, and label once dry.

Frothy jelly

One packet jelly (100–150 grams, as it comes)
One small can of evaporated milk (170 grams)

This is a good winter recipe, as it supplies vitamin D. It's useful if you need to use up the evaporated milk from your stores.

Make up the jelly with three-quarters of the total amount of water called for on the packet. Leave it till it's almost set, then whisk it until it's light and fluffy. Whisk the evaporated milk separately, then fold it into the jelly. Leave to set, preferably in the fridge.

The disadvantage of this recipe is the precise timing. The initial setting of the jelly takes longest, and all depends on how cool a place you can find to keep a large bowl of liquid for some hours. It has to be eaten freshly made; it gets soggy quickly. Use your practice attempts as snacks for the kids between meals.

Fifty years ago, this used to be a standard cheap and cheerful pudding. It's been replaced by instant packet versions. Far from being in the promised 'Age of Leisure', modern lifestyles often don't have enough spare time to let jelly set. Moving at such a frantic speed, the least upset – bad weather, a transport strike, a sudden illness – throws one totally off balance and sends elaborate timetables crashing to the ground.

To cultivate resilience, one should slow down the pace a little, especially in winter.

Interlude

Imbolc

Imbolc is a festival very closely tied to agriculture. As people moved away from the land, from being one of the key events of the year, it fell into obscurity. Six weeks after the Winter Solstice, in the first few days of February, Imbolc celebrates the beginning of Spring. From the perspective of a high-rise window, this may not be obvious. Down at ground level though, green shoots are appearing, buds are swelling. Even in the city, the days are clearly longer.

As lambs arrived in the pastures, so did a new supply of milk for hungry stone age farmers. After months of living on preserved food, with little access to sunlight, this source of vitamin D was essential for health. Imbolc customs often involved milk. The name itself may come from 'oimelc', an old word for 'ewe's milk'.

The winter was over in the minds of these early farmers. Whatever the weather, their thoughts had to turn to mending fences, digging the vegetable plots, putting plans into action. There was much activity around holy wells during Imbolc; weather oracles were anxiously consulted. The American tradition of Groundhog Day on February 2nd has its roots here; once it was a badger who popped out to test the air.

Bad weather on Imbolc – which is very likely – is seen as a good omen. The Callieach, a Celtic goddess in the shape of an old woman, was said to gather firewood on that day. If the cold weather was to last, she would cause it to be sunny so that she could gather a big pile. A wet day meant winter would soon be over, so she didn't need so much. This could be some consolation if your first day out for six weeks was spoiled by heavy rain!

> 'If Candlemas be fair and bright,
> Winter has another flight.
> If Candlemas brings clouds and rain,
> Winter will not come again'
> *Traditional English rhyme*

In the evening there would be a modest fire ritual. Great bonfires and loud parties weren't appropriate. Survival was still not certain, but depended on the coming season's crops. Candles were lit; it was a festival of hearth and home. Women encouraged the goddess of growing things to visit, sometimes by making a special bed for her.

In the Christian era, Imbolc became St Brigid's Day and was celebrated in much the same way. Straw dolls representing the saint were paraded from house to house, and special crosses woven. Once these were also of straw, probably linked to the previous harvest. Before the custom died out however, they began to be made of fresh-pulled rushes.

The official church feast is known as Candlemas; it has a similar theme. In olden times, it was customary for a new mother to undergo forty days of seclusion before a purification ceremony. Having been born on December 25th, the baby Jesus would have been presented to his community for the first time around this date. Birth and growth are honoured.

The element of ritual cleansing also goes back a long way. It survives in the tradition of 'spring cleaning', but may once have been far more important. Some stone circles are directed at the Imbolc sunrise, notably at Newgrange in Eire. The inner chamber of the Mound of the Hostages there shows such an alignment.

Although we don't know how these Neolithic people celebrated, we can imagine how they must have looked forward to the coming of Spring!

Chapter Eight

February

It's definitely getting lighter now, though the weather may not seem much better. It's time to put aside the gardening books and get to work! Fill up those raised beds, dig that new patch, sweep out the greenhouse. It all has to be ready to start sowing in March.

It's a time to tidy up. Warm yourself up with a fire of twigs from last year's prunings – not of laurel or other poisonous trees – while you clean flower pots, pull up the last carrots, take the dead leaves off the brassicas. Dig the ash in as fertiliser. Take frequent tea breaks to allow the birds to come in and pick over freshly dug ground; they hunt down harmful insects for you.

A smallholder would be busy mucking out the animal pens and preparing for the breeding season. The resilience gardener has an easier time of it. Pottering around doing chores in a leisurely fashion, you have plenty of time to observe the way light falls on your growing space, how the wind might affect your planned crops, whether some areas are particularly damp.

Greenhouses and cold frames

These are great if you're impatient to get started. If you're lucky enough to have one already, a few vegetables can be sown now. They'll be protected from adverse weather, able to take full advantage of the extra sunlight. It's best to study your growing area for a full year before investing in one, though.

Will your chosen spot be too sunny in August? Mature plants in a greenhouse need a lot of watering; is there a tap nearby? Will it be vulnerable to winter gales; site the door away from prevailing winds. Don't build it underneath an apple tree!

This is a good time of year to install a new one. It'll need level ground, hence many greenhouses are on concrete bases. This isn't essential for a modest walk-in one. In many places – such as allotments – it may not be possible to lay a permanent base. Level the ground in other ways, and lay some slabs inside the structure so the floor doesn't get muddy.

Even a flat pack greenhouse is quite difficult to put up, and you'll require assistance. Read the instructions very carefully; spread out a tarpaulin or dust sheet to unpack the boxes on, and have plenty of room to work. I recommend paying for this; it can usually be arranged with delivery. Could you make a better deal with an independent local garden centre than buying online? Investigate all large household purchases, as explained in the Resilience Handbook.

A full-sized greenhouse, big enough to move about in, is a major garden feature. It's nice to lay a path to the kitchen door, so you can water your plants whatever the weather. It can be pleasantly warm under glass; take a flask and watch the birds.

Where a traditional greenhouse wasn't feasible, cold frames and cloches were once widely used. These are large shallow boxes with glass lids. Sometimes they're filled with fine soil and you sow directly into them to transplant young plants later. Others are designed to hold seed trays or small pots. They work like a greenhouse, but you have to attend to ventilation or mould will form.

The chore of propping the lid open in mild calm weather and lowering it every night, or if the wind got up, reduced their popularity. Large sheets of glass close to ground level didn't mix well with free-range children, and they're now out of fashion in all but the most formal of gardens.

Lightweight plastic versions are available, which fit into small spaces. They're very vulnerable to wind; choose a sheltered spot. They still need to be opened for ventilation on warm days, and the plants watered regularly. These are more useful later in the year to get tomatoes, squashes and courgettes going.

There's always the windowsill, of course. Use round pots and stand them on plates to catch muddy drips. Once the seedlings are showing – but not before – they'll need watering. Excess water running out of the pots can spoil paintwork and stain wallpaper.

You could risk starting some peas in February. These are cold-tolerant, so they can go outside quite early. More delicate vegetables, such as tomatoes, should be sown a bit later. The weather needs to have settled into a steady warmth, with no danger of frost, before these can go out. Discover the date when the last frost is due for your area, and start these no more than six weeks before it.

Fresh greens

With a full-sized greenhouse, you can grow salad leaves, spring onions and radish now. It's not necessary to depend on these, however. Despite the continuing cold weather and the frequent heavy rains of 'February Fill-Dyke', new shoots are unfolding everywhere. The best sources of early spring greens are vigorous weeds.

You can look for wild garlic in woodland; if you have space under a tree in your garden, it will grow well there. Goosegrass, nettles, dock, plantain and bittercress are springing up and all edible. Lightly cooked and stirred into a dish of boiled grains, they provide a valuable tonic. Teas used to be made from the leaves, for the same vitamin boosting effect.

Keeping a controlled population of these wild plants in your resilience garden is useful. You can eat them knowing they haven't been sprayed with herbicide. They emerge just as your winter standbys – such as brassicas, spinach and leek – are moving their own energy from edible leaves to flowers and seed.

Farm animals used to be glad of the armfuls of goosegrass – also called cleavers due to its sticky seeds – you can haul out of your hedge, but generally there's far more than you can use and it goes to compost. These days, you can send your garden waste out into a council recycling scheme if you don't have room for your own heap.

Some seasonal foods available in February

A few fresh eggs and a bit of milk.
Fresh green leaves such as sorrel and wild garlic.
Fresh rocket and spinach for a scattering of salad, if it's not too cold.
Small game (rabbits and pigeons were a serious threat to spring crops) and fish.
Grains, flour and other dried stores – not much fresh carbohydrate-rich food is about.
Apples from the shed, a few potatoes and onions.
Leeks, brassicas, winter kale, rocket, spinach and chard.

The welcome arrival of milk and eggs provides relief from a diet of stew and dumplings. These are important ingredients in many common recipes as well as supplying valuable vitamins and minerals. The inactivity of winter was ending; people had to go out and get busy. They needed the boost from their domestic animals for the energy to look after their domestic animals.

Although this seems ironic, the hunter-gatherer would be struggling to find a few skinny rabbits in the same area. Early tribes had to be nomadic. Like the kingfisher, we would have headed to the coast for the fish and the milder temperatures. It was our alliance with animals which allowed us to colonise difficult environments.

A history of dairy products

Nomadic tribes began to keep prey animals with them, as a convenient source of meat. Since these were encouraged to breed, milk was a useful by-product. It was a valuable food for children.

However, the stomach enzymes which allow humans to digest fresh milk usually disappear after the age of eight. Milk sugar – lactose – has to be broken into two smaller sugars by this lactase enzyme before it can be absorbed. If it isn't properly digested, it passes into the intestines, where unfriendly bacteria use it as food. These produce gases and acids, which give rise to cramps, bloating and diarrhoea.

As milk goes off, turning into yogurt and soft cheese, its lactose content falls. Bacteria convert it to lactic acid, giving a sour taste. A controlled fermentation keeps harmful organisms out. Milk can also be soured by adding a weak acid, such as vinegar or lemon juice. This encourages it to solidify; useful in making cheeses.

Primitive farmers soon learned to process milk, initiating the dairy industry. Tribes with herds prospered; some could even settle on a good site all year without running out of food. Farming expanded to include growing fodder; people abandoned their light shelters and built in stone. The warmer Mediterranean areas gained a large settled population of these Neolithic farmers.

Then, around 7,500 years ago, there was a genetic mutation. Adults with this adaptation retained their lactase enzymes and could now digest fresh milk, which gave them another advantage. This may explain a sudden rapid movement north of farmers and herders, who displaced the original hunter gatherers and cultivated new lands.

In Britain and Northern Europe 90% of the population can drink milk, so could be descended from these mutant tribes. Where agriculture was already established, the original farmers stayed put and there is far more lactose intolerance.

Hard cheese

Hung in a muslin bag to let the whey liquids drain off, milk will turn into a sort of soft cheese as it goes off. This doesn't keep very well without refrigeration. Hostile moulds and other unwanted organisms can easily colonise this food source.

A hard cheese, on the other hand, will keep for years. Its use as a winter standby is enshrined in the term 'hard cheese' meaning 'tough luck' – eating hunger food. The rind of a good traditional cheese could be pretty chewy!

Cheese making goes back to prehistory. The earliest evidence, dated about 5500 BCE, indicates it was already an established practice back then. The oldest actual piece of cheese was found in China and dates to 1600 BCE. By Roman times, cheese making was a skilled art; later the craft was perpetuated and developed by monks.

Stone Age herders stored milk, like other liquids, in containers made from animal stomachs. Rennet, a collection of enzymes which curdle milk, is found in the stomachs of young animals. It was almost impossible not to invent cheese!

Techniques were refined to discourage harmful bacteria and improve shelf life. Medieval cheese making was a long and complicated process requiring continual attention. The milk must be kept at a constant warm temperature while curds form. These are separated from the whey in another series of stages, until a curd mass is ready to put in the cheese press. It sits there for twelve hours while the last of the whey drips out, after which it should be solid.

All the surfaces and utensils used have to be spotlessly clean – preferably sterilised. The dairy was kept as a dedicated room, away from other household activities. Dairymaids were always 'fresh and clean' in a culture where personal hygiene wasn't a priority.

Once out of the press, a cheese is dried for a few days then covered with cheese wax – using paraffin wax instead isn't recommended. Sealed by the wax, it needs to age for at least a month at a cool 10 degree Centigrade (50 degrees Fahrenheit) or slightly lower. A cave or cellar is ideal, as long as the humidity is right.

In warmer climates, cheese is often covered with a layer of olive oil and stored in jars instead. The cooler conditions in Northern Europe means cheese needs less added salt for preservation. A wider variety of friendly bacteria and moulds can be developed, giving a range of tastes.

Keeping a huge wheel of cheese is neither practical nor necessary for modern households. It's the sort of food store appropriate to more communal living. A farm used to feed a number of labourers as well as an extended family. If you look at the staggering quantities required in one of Mrs Beeton's famous Victorian recipes, it's clear she wasn't cooking for one.

A whole cheese used to be stored, carefully wrapped in waxed paper and butter muslin, in a cool dark place. A piece would be taken off, to last the week, then the cut surface wiped with vinegar and the cheese rewrapped. Ceramic cheese bells were a common feature of the walk-in pantry, even in early industrial times. Mass production meant this was still a staple food.

Today, there is a revival of artisan cheeses, made by traditional methods. If you're interested in making your own, the process does need a lot of space, and there's some heavy lifting. A gallon of milk makes about a pound of hard cheese.

Recipes for February

Pancakes

1 egg
300 ml (half a pint) of milk – can be made with dried or UHT milk from your emergency stores
120 grams (4 ounces) plain flour
About a tablespoon of oil for cooking

For the traditional filling –
A fresh lemon, or a bottle of lemon juice from stores
Sugar

Sieve the flour into a bowl. Mix the egg and milk together in a jug and add gradually, beating with a fork. Once it's all mixed in, you can use a blender to get rid of lumps. I like to leave the mix to stand for half an hour; this 'relaxes' the gluten in the flour and makes for a lighter batter.

Heat the oil in a thick bottomed frying pan. If your pan base is too thin, or rough, the pancakes will stick. It must be pretty hot, with only a thin film of oil coating the whole pan base. Tip any excess out into a china dish and add it back as required.

Test when it's hot enough by dropping a spoonful of the mix into the pan. It should hiss and bubble, then cook quickly without sticking. Flip it over to cook the other side, then take it out. A thin spatula, like a fish slice, is a good tool for this.

Check the oil still covers the pan, add a tiny bit more. If it begins to smoke, it's too hot; take the pan off the heat and let it cool down. Smoking oil can catch fire.

Add a ladleful of the pancake mix and swirl it around to cover the whole pan. Don't poke at it till it's nearly done on the side you can't see. You'll know because it'll be easier to lift away from the pan. Make sure it's unstuck all the way round, then flip it over to cook the other side.

Slide the cooked pancake onto a plate, add another small spoonful of oil to the pan and swirl. It's best to cook the whole mix in one session, serving as you go; they're best eaten freshly made. Extra batter will keep overnight in a fridge. If it separates, just stir it back together.

This recipe makes about four; you can't really make less. Double it for more than one egg.

Eggs are valuable as ingredients. This is a more economical way of using a limited supply than is eating them whole. If milk is also in short supply, a single glassful can make a family meal.

Traditionally pancakes are sprinkled with lemon juice and sugar, then rolled up and eaten in slices. A popular alternative is toffee sauce with thin slices of banana; you can experiment with all kinds of sweet fillings.

Savoury pancakes make a good meal. Lay a cooked pancake on a plate, spread it with a thin layer of warmed baked beans, or yesterday's cheese sauce, then roll it up. Sprinkle the top of the roll with grated cheese and carefully slide it all into a baking tray. Heat under the grill till the cheese melts; you can cook several at once. Serve with chutney and salad.

Yorkshire puddings

1 egg
300 ml (half a pint) of milk – can be made with dried or UHT milk from your emergency stores

120 grams (4 ounces) plain flour
About a tablespoon of oil for cooking

Yes, it's the same recipe as pancakes!

The high cooking temperature needed for these means that it's hardly worth making them unless they are part of a roast dinner. As they go in at the end, the oven will have been hot for some time. Prepare the mix as you are getting the root vegetables ready to go in, so that it has time to settle.

Use a tart or muffin tray; this mix will make four large puddings or six small ones. When you are nearly ready to start steaming vegetables, preheat the trays with a little oil in each – careful taking them back out of the oven! – before pouring the batter in. Fill them no more than half.

Cook on the top shelf of a hot oven; check after 15 minutes. They should have risen and browned, but make sure the bases are cooked as well, not stodgy. Give them another five minutes then, but these shouldn't be overcooked and need to be served at once rather than kept warm. This is the final bit of the intricate timing of a roast dinner!

Cheese sauce

1 medium onion or leek, chopped
1 clove of garlic, finely chopped
25 grams (1 ounce) butter
25 grams (1 ounce) plain flour
200 ml (half a pint) of milk
50–75 grams (2–3 ounces) of grated hard cheese, such as cheddar

Lightly fry the onion and garlic in the butter; don't let the butter go brown. You need to keep an eye on this recipe throughout. Take the pan off the heat and stir in the flour, coating the onions well. Add a little milk and mix to a paste; keep adding and stirring a bit at a time until all the flour is mixed in, then return the pan to a low heat. Keep stirring gently as it thickens; add any leftover milk.

This makes quite a thick sauce. If you're going to cover something with it and then bake it, you may want it a little thinner. Stir in small amounts of milk until it's reached the consistency you're after. Have patience; it's harder to remedy if it gets too thin. Don't add dry flour to a watery sauce to thicken it; mix it into a paste with water first.

Once you're satisfied it'll work, add the cheese and let it melt through. You have to cook this dish on a low heat and keep stirring; not every minute, but pretty often or it'll stick. Keep close to the cooker and have the meal ready to serve as soon as the sauce is done.

A cheese sauce is versatile. You can have it with cauliflower, broccoli, pasta, boiled potatoes and fish. Left over sauce can be used in savoury pancakes or baked pasta dishes; it's worth making enough for two meals. Store the extra in the fridge – it should last a couple of days – and add a little milk when reheating.

Using the onions to hold the flour is a good way to stop it going into lumps when you add the milk. If you want to try making more ambitious sauces, have the blender to hand! There are a lot of recipes online.

Nut roast

To serve four: -
1 chopped onion
A tablespoon of tamari
A tablespoon of cooking oil
170 grams (6 ounces) of ground or finely chopped mixed nuts
50 grams (2 ounces) of ground almonds
A couple of slices of bread, preferably wholemeal
150 ml (¼ pint) vegetable stock
A tablespoon of tomato purée

Fresh meat is limited to small game and fish. You're not going to eat your breeding stock now the spring fodder is arriving. What about grinding up stored nuts to make a roast dinner centrepiece? Many modern households have some nuts in shells left over from Xmas; this is a good chance to use them.

Put the bread in a low oven until it's dried out – this shouldn't take long, and will be quicker if you cut it up first – then crumble into coarse breadcrumbs and set these aside. You can buy ready chopped nuts, but if you'd rather choose your own mix, use a food processor. I like an ounce of walnuts, two ounces of hazelnuts and three ounces of cashews. I crush them with a mortar and pestle; cashews are quite soft! Brazil nuts, pine kernels and even cooked chickpeas can be used as well.

Meanwhile, sauté the onion in the oil and tamari, adding a bit of garlic and some chopped garden herbs such as chives and oregano. When these are soft, stir everything together and empty the bowl into an oiled oven dish. A bread tin gives a nice loaf shape. I use the larger two-pound tin, to make a thinner, flatter loaf which cooks right through.

Cook for 40–45 minutes at a medium heat (Gas Mark 4; 180C; 350F) on a low middle shelf, check that it's solid in the middle, run a knife around the edges to loosen it, and turn the loaf out onto a plate.

This mix is quite sticky. If the finished loaf is too crumbly, try adding an egg or some liquid from a chickpea tin, to bind it next time. Compensate for the extra liquid with more breadcrumbs, oats or a small amount of flour. Line the tin with greaseproof paper.

Mashed swede and carrot

Or just buy a packet of nut roast mix – they're useful in your emergency stores – and surround it with seasonal vegetables. Dig up those last root vegetables before they start to bolt. Chop these finely and simmer for about 20 minutes from the boil, until they're soft. Drain and mash; serve with butter and black pepper.

The traditional Scottish winter dish of haggis and neeps – mashed turnip – harks back to pre-Columbus root vegetables. These had less than half the calories of potatoes, so it was harder to fill the hunger gap.

Simmered nettles

2 cloves of garlic, crushed
250ml (a half pint) vegetable stock
2 rashers of bacon, chopped
Wear gloves, gather a bunch of nettle tops, rinse and coarsely chop them

Lightly fry the bacon pieces and garlic, add the stock and simmer the leaves for about fifteen minutes, till they are soft. Drain, reserving the liquid for a gravy, and serve.

Cooking the nettles gets rid of their sting, but they'll fight back till you get them in the pan!

Cakes

There are many cake recipes online and in books. These follow two basic patterns. Some call for equal amounts of sugar, butter and flour, adding rather a lot of eggs. I prefer this version, which uses more flour – the cheapest ingredient. This amount should fill two 'sandwich tins' or shallow baking tins of between 7–9 inches (18–22 centimetres) in diameter.

100 grams (4 ounces) sugar
100 grams (4 ounces) butter
200 grams (8 ounces) self-raising flour (or plain flour with a couple of teaspoons of baking powder)
At least one egg, preferably two. If you don't have an egg, you'll have to make something else
Flavouring – a teaspoon of vanilla essence is the default

It's important that a cake goes into a pre-heated oven, so turn it on before you start. Use a medium heat (Gas Mark 5; 190C; 375F) with one shelf just above the middle and one just below. Leave enough space for both halves to rise.

Put the butter and sugar into a bowl and cream them together using a fork, until there are no lumps of butter visible. Break the eggs into a cup to check they're okay before adding them. Beat them into the mix. If you're using vanilla essence for flavouring, add a few drops now. A tablespoon of cocoa for a chocolate cake is also better added at this stage, so it mixes through.

Now put the fork in the wash, and add the flour, stirring it in gently with a spoon a bit at a time. The idea here is to trap air in the mix and make it light, so don't bash away at it. A wooden spoon is ideal. The mix should be like a paste rather than a dough; add a little milk to moisten it.

Rub butter all over the inside of the tins, then sieve a little flour over this so that a thin layer sticks to the grease. Tap the tin on the side of your mixing bowl to dislodge the extra flour, which can be stirred into the cake.

Spoon the mix into the tins. Don't drag it as you level it out, or you'll disturb the thin layer which stops it sticking as it cooks. Cake mix is messy; you should be wearing an apron, especially if you like to sieve all the flour.

Now, the cake is going to rise as it cooks. This is a delicate process; the gas from the baking powder has to be caught by the setting cake before it escapes. Do not open the oven door for at least 15 minutes, and then do so carefully. If the cake is rising well, but still looks very soft, close the oven door gently and go away for another 10 minutes before checking it again. If you upset it at this stage, the rising dome will collapse and your cake will end up rather heavy.

The cake is ready when the end of a metal knife poked into it comes out clean; that is, without raw cake mix stuck to it. You may have to move the lower half up to the top shelf to finish it. Pay attention as the cooking ends; cakes can burn easily. This recipe needs about 25–30 minutes of cooking. If you're nervous, turn the oven down a little once the rising business is done.

Once you're happy that the cake is solid all the way through, loosen it by running a knife around inside the tin and carefully tip it out onto a wire rack to cool. Your grill pan will do, as long as you wash it first. If you let a cake cool inside the tin, it will go soggy.

Allow the cake halves to cool properly, then stick them together with jam or icing.

Jam alone is best if you plan to eat it as a pudding with custard. For a snack food use icing as well, and dust the top with a little sieved icing sugar. You can get a nice effect here with small cardboard stencils.

This basic cake mix can also be dolloped onto very well drained stewed fruit in your crumble dish, carefully spread to close the layer and baked. This will take longer, maybe 40 minutes, and it is tricky to tell when it is ready due to the liquid in the fruit.

As with all these recipes, you can adjust the quantities as long as the ratios remain the same. If you're short of flour, add some oats instead, but no more than a third of the total weight called for. You can try plain flour and make a flat, heavy cake; it depends how hungry you are. Your minimum is the one egg, so the smallest useful recipe would be

2 oz sugar
2 oz butter
4 oz self-raising flour
1 egg

You're unlikely to get a sandwich cake from that; you'd need very small cake tins. Make fairy cakes; the paper cases are not crucial. Just grease and flour a tart tin and they're unlikely to stick. Smaller cakes need less cooking time; a batch could be ready in 15 minutes. Cool on a wire rack as before. It's fun to decorate these.

Cake flavourings, icings and fillings

You only need a scant teaspoonful of any essence to add a lot of taste, so it's worth investing in quality. There are a number of interesting flavours available; investigate some specialist shops.
You can improvise. Any powdered drinking chocolate substitutes for cocoa powder. For a coffee cake, dissolve a teaspoon of instant coffee in a little hot water; allow to cool and add to the cake mix. A sharp citrus flavour comes from a tablespoon of grated lemon or orange zest; use the juice to mix an icing.

Stir in chocolate chips, add dried fruit or a few berries, but remember fresh fruit adds water and too much will make the cake soggy. Finely chop some of those walnuts that need using up and use a couple of ounces; this is nice combined with a coffee flavour.

For the really adventurous, I recommend 'The Flavour Thesaurus' by Niki Segnet...

A cake can be eaten on its own, or with custard, ice cream or jelly, but it's traditional to ice them. A butter cream icing will do to stick cake halves together as well as cover the top.

Beat together 75 gram (3 ounces) of butter and 150 grams (6 ounces) of sieved icing sugar to fill and cover an eight inch (20 cm) sandwich cake. It's easier if the butter is soft. Remember you have to add flavouring essence or juice, which should be done once half of the sugar is mixed in.

For a frosted icing, melt 25 grams (1 ounce) of butter with a tablespoon of full fat milk. Remove from the heat, add flavourings, and stir in 200 grams (8 ounces) of sieved icing sugar, until it's a smooth, thick paste. Pour the icing over the cake rather than spread it, and leave it to set. This is good as a topping for a single layer cake.

Or melt 50 grams (2 ounces) of plain cooking chocolate and add 50 grams of softened butter. Beat until smooth and shiny; pour over the cake. This will set quite hard in a few hours, depending on the sort of chocolate you use. Have the cake on a large plate, or in a tin, before you cover it with icing, and mark out slices before it sets.

The most basic icing just involves adding a little water to icing sugar; about 100 grams (4 ounces) should cover your sandwich cake. This isn't much use as a centre filling as it's too fluid; use jam instead.

Beware of icing sugar! Not only is the apron important again, but the least miscalculation in the amount of water you add will need half the packet to undo. It's safer to mash it into butter for a creamy filling, but if all you have is water, add this a teaspoon at a time and mix it in well before adding another.
It helps to have a mug of hot water to hand as you spread icing on top of a cake; dip the knife in this from time to time.

Extra icing will store well in the fridge; you'll have a few days to use it up. Spread it on plain biscuits; kids love decorating these!

Chapter Nine

March

The previous season's vegetables are nearly all gone now. The broccoli should be producing its lush purple sprouts; the leeks are developing hard stems ready to launch into flower. Mark your seed plants now by tying them to canes. Many will like to grow as tall as possible, then fall over to spread their seeds further, but you have other plans.

The weather is warming up; the daylight increases to a useful length. By Spring Equinox, around March 21st, the sun won't set until 6pm and the long twilight of Northern lands allows plenty of time for seasonal garden chores after a day's work. Gardening isn't hard graft at this time of year. A delicate touch and careful attention are required to start your baby plants off.

Preparing to grow

All your digging should have been completed in February and the soil allowed to settle down. If you have a ground level garden, it's important not to walk on the soil now. Lay out defined paths through your vegetable bed. I used to mark these with stone slabs or wooden planks. Slugs lived underneath them. Ants took advantage of the shelter and built cities, whose aphid farms infested the broad beans and courgettes to the point of destruction. Now, I use short pieces of stout metal grid to walk on.

The soil quality of the undisturbed area is better; it's far lighter, like a risen cake. A healthy soil with good drainage, texture and minerals is the key to growing healthy plants. Study the area around a well-used country gate. Different plants grow in the compacted soil. Just by creating a productive patch, the resilience gardener enhances community assets.

Using a long-handled hoe – space your paths so you can reach every part of the growing areas – scrape off any new weeds. Rake over the patch where you intend to plant. Leave it bare for the hungry nesting birds to pick over during the day, but you may need to cover it at night and once you have sown there. Local cats view your seed bed as an ideal toilet, ruthlessly scratching it up and scattering your efforts.

Cat guards need to be of solid wire. They have to allow light and warmth through on to the seedlings, but not entangle birds as a softer net might.

You should move them before the plants grow through the mesh, or it will be impossible to weed underneath the guard. I use a variety of small frames of chicken wire, upturned old hanging baskets and dismantled fireguards. You can find stuff like this at boot sales.

Once the plants have grown up a hand's length, the space is less attractive to cats. They're not such a problem in allotments; here, rabbits are the menace. You'd need to make taller, more permanent, cages to keep these out.

It's said that rabbits don't like reaching up to feed. A resident buzzard watches over our allotment, alert for any such carelessness. Growing in a stack of three tyres should discourage the rabbits if they decide to pick on you.

Hang an old CD disc on a nearby post, such that it spins in the breeze. The constant movement and flashes of light unsettle feeding deer, who will move on to less threatening ground. Raised beds protect against badgers, who can go through your plot like a small bulldozer. A light sprinkling of paraffin is said to deter mice from digging up pea seeds.

However, the animal life that will really give you problems is much smaller. Welcome to the complex world of the invertebrates; the insects, molluscs and mites!

Slugs and other pests

Although a continual aggravation, slugs are at their most destructive during the planting season. A whole row of your precious seedlings can be devoured overnight, your runner beans reduced to skeletons in a few days. How do you deal with this as a resilience gardener, avoiding the use of chemical controls?

You grow something else. Remember the low-maintenance principle? The quality of your soil, the prevailing weather, overshadowing by buildings – all are factors which combine to create a local micro-environment. Some plants will thrive in it, grow strong and fend off predators. Others will always need added support, extra work or expense from you. Discard these plants from your repertoire unless you're keen to make a project of raising them.

In a challenging environment like mine – a heavy clay soil on the edge of centuries old marsh land – only the hardiest vegetables survive. Leeks, broccoli, rocket, kale and potatoes succeed reliably. Peas and courgettes need protection until they get going.

There are a number of techniques for keeping slugs at bay. Some people swear by the 'slug pub', a jar of beer buried up to its neck, in which they drown. Others lay down copper strips, purchase predator nematodes or strew crushed eggshells. I find regular 'capture and kill' sweeps to be the most effective control in the long term, combined with reducing possible habitat areas within the vegetable patch.

With new seedlings, I surround them with a thick circle of bran, about two inches wide. This seems to offer some protection; you'll need a lot, so buy it from an animal feed shop, not a supermarket. It's a good soil conditioner too.

As the slugs and snails emerge from hibernation to start on your vegetables, so do the ants turn to nest building. Keep moving things around. If I leave so much as a bucket in one place for a week, I can find Ant City developing underneath it. Keep them out of the vegetable patch, but you can probably tolerate them elsewhere. They do prey on harmful insects for you; it's mainly their aphid farms which are the nuisance.

If you wish to develop the craft of gardening, there are a myriad of other pests and diseases which plants are subject to. If yours look unwell, explore the resources of the Internet, talk to fellow gardeners, decide on a strategy.

Your core resilience crops, however, should be those which like the local conditions, ones that any beginner can succeed with. Remember one of the aims of a Resilience Garden is to produce a good stock of seed so your community can get growing!

Deciding when to sow

Without the luxury of a greenhouse, seeds have to go straight into ground still wet and cold from winter. You must decide when it's safe to risk them. Too early and they may choke in waterlogged soil or succumb to frost. Leave it too late and you may have a poor crop. Some plants need to develop a good root system before the summer heat arrives.

Personal judgement based on experience tells you when to sow. Your garden diary records will help. You can try using a moon calendar; there are several variations. Sowing almanacs were best-sellers at the dawn of printing! However, the feel of the soil is the most important indicator. Is it soggy, sticky, cold to the touch? Then wait.

If impatience gets the better of you, try laying down a layer of potting compost about an inch thick and sowing into that. The dark colour will absorb heat; the dry mixture soaks up excess water. For larger seeds, such as peas, fill a small hole with this fine compost to plant in. You can always start raising these indoors, laying them on trays of wet kitchen paper until roots begins to appear.

There's only so much space on windowsills. In a cold wet spring, a greenhouse is a valuable asset. You can pot up your sprouting peas, set other seeds going. As soon as the weather improves, you have strong plants ready to go out and face the ravenous molluscs.

Once you've identified your core vegetables, they don't often let you down. Label the seed beds as you sow; it may be awhile before they show. Start another crop in pots if you're really worried they won't make it; you can always give these away.

It's the right time of year to get spuds in the ground. In Somerset we have a regular series of 'potato days' in March, where one can choose from many varieties on display in the village hall; a sort of travelling show of tubers! If it's really too wet use a tyre stack, or even plant in a large bucket with drainage holes poked in the base.

Early potatoes provide the first new carbohydrates of the year. Growing several different types ensures a constant supply over the summer, and enough for a few sacks to tide over the early winter months. After you've been gardening for a few years, see if you can work out how many plants it would take to keep you in potatoes from June to February.

Some seasonal foods available in March

A limited amount of fresh eggs and milk.
Hard cheeses and lard.
Fresh wild leaves; wild garlic, sorrel, nettles, dandelion, docks, goosegrass, plantain, chives, mint.
Purple sprouting broccoli, spinach, some leeks.
Stored grains, flours, imported pasta and rice.
Dried beans and peas; nuts.
Small game and fish.
Dried fruits.
Birch sap sugar.

Stored produce

Stores are your main source of fats, sugars and carbohydrates now. The coming of spring has brought on a spurt of growth. Seeds and roots are using up their own stores; animals are at the end of their fat cycle and pretty skinny. Hunter-gatherer tribes can suffer from 'rabbit starvation' caused by eating lean meat without carbohydrates, even when fresh leaves are available. This fatal condition can be swiftly reversed by eating fats and starches.

The warmer weather is causing the apples to rot in your shed. The root vegetables are intent on sprouting; potatoes have to be planted or thrown away. The green flesh they develop now is poisonous. Spring leaves grow in profusion however, and there are plenty of vitamins to be had.

Although less risky than harvesting fungi, it's necessary to take care when picking wild herbs. It's good to grow them in your garden so you can really get to know them – it's illegal to pick some in the wild anyway. Young plants may not display the characteristic traits which distinguish edible from poisonous varieties. Cuckoo pint often grows near wild garlic; hemlock can look very like chervil. As these plants mature, they become clearly recognisable. Until then, even an expert can make mistakes.

The better weather and longer daylight encouraged hunting forays for rabbits, pigeons and squirrels. People went out fishing again. The grass was growing up well in the pastures; the young animals were getting bigger.

Animal welfare and Lent

Sheep and cows aren't machines. They're producing milk because they've just created another animal and given birth to it. This is an arduous process. The mother needs to recover her strength, not provide milk for a human family as well. Since these families would be craving the nourishment after months living on stored food, powerful customs were needed to protect the welfare of the stock.

In the Christian era, an initial binge on milk and eggs would end with Pancake Day, usually some time in February. The following day, Ash Wednesday, marked a six week period of fasting. This lasted most, if not all, of March ending on Easter Sunday. These foods and others, including fresh meat, were forbidden. The farm animals were allowed to concentrate on raising their next generation.

Fishing

Fish emerge from their winter lethargy in spring, and are easier to find. Freshwater varieties such as roach, perch, pike and eels were once common fare in Britain. Fishing with a hook and line is a very ancient practice; the use of rods and reels came later. The first book written in English on the subject – a 'Treatysse of Fysshynge' – was written in 1496 by Dame Juliana Berners.

The strong hemp or nettle fibre twine used for lines was also good for net making. These were often used in community fish hunts. A long net would be held across a stretch of water by several strong men, and fish driven towards it. Larger nets were used for sea fishing.

Trapping was another popular method. River fish traps were often made of willow, woven into a funnel to force fish into the narrow end, where they became stuck. More elaborate cages were used by the coast to catch crabs and lobsters. Fish traps must always be checked at dawn. As soon as the sun begins to warm the water, the trapped fish may die, and the meat quickly spoil.

Using wicker fences and nets, some early English monasteries created fish traps on an industrial scale. Up to half a million fish a year could be caught; these were salted, dried and sold further inland. There is mention of these 'fish factories' in the Domesday Book.

As pollution from industrialisation and the growth of cities increased, rivers became less of a food source. Fishing in general moved out to sea. Tastes changed; small freshwater fish are very bony. Although there is now progress on cleaning up the rivers, angling has become a leisure activity rather than a necessity.

Recipes for March

Wild garlic pesto

2 rounded tablespoons of crushed nuts (50 grams; 2 ounces)
2 handfuls of wild garlic leaves (100 grams; 4 ounces)
1 tablespoon of Parmesan cheese – vegans can substitute yeast flakes
4–6 tablespoons of olive oil (100–150 ml; 4–6 fluid ounces)
a dash of lemon juice and a pinch of salt to taste

Wash the leaves and shake them dry. Blend everything together; a hand blender will do, but using a mortar and pestle can be tedious here. Make sure the oil covers the ingredients when you transfer the mix to a jar, or it won't keep so well.

Store it in a fridge and use part jars within a week; unopened jars will last longer. You can also freeze it for up to three months, but use it up at once when defrosted. These quantities will make a couple of jam jars full.

Pesto can be made from almost any edible spring leaves – spinach, rocket, watercress – as long as they are tender enough for a salad. Stir a tablespoon per person into cooked pasta and serve, or use as pesto in other recipes.

Wild garlic is also known as ramsons (allium ursinum). Like cultivated garlic (allium sativum), it's believed by many to have medicinal properties. Folk remedies employed it to reduce blood pressure and fight colds. The antioxidants in garlic may help protect cells against dangerous free radicals, but as yet there is no scientific evidence.

The active ingredient being studied, allicin, is only produced when the garlic is damaged by cutting or crushing. It's part of the plant's defence mechanism. Argentinian investigators found it releases more allicin-type compounds when you bake the cloves, while scientists at South Carolina Medical University believe peeling garlic and letting it sit uncovered for 15 minutes produces the highest levels of compounds to fight infection.

Garlic supplements may interfere with other medicines, but the amounts normally eaten in a meal are usually fine. Rather than wait until you are ill, then take industrial doses of chemicals which can be found in food, design yourself a healthy diet. Do your own research – who do you believe? Do you think their suggestions might work?

Pasta bolognaise

1 medium onion
2 cloves of garlic
250 grams (half a pound) of mince
a little cooking oil with a dash of tamari
A packet of tomato passata and half a 130 gram tube of tomato paste from your stores
A vegetable stock cube
A scant level tablespoon of plain flour
Pasta – these quantities are for two people

Extend this recipe with more vegetables rather than meat. Add a small red pepper, some celery or mushrooms. Replace the mince with cooked tinned beans (not baked beans) for a vegan option. If you'd pasteurised your own tomato passata in the autumn, the last of it would need using up about now.

Sauté the chopped vegetables in the oil, add the mince and keep stirring till it's browned. Stir in a little flour for thickening; no more than you need to coat the stuff in the pan. Use less flour than you would in a cheese sauce, as you thicken this one by reducing it.

Stir in the passata and tomato paste, crumble the stock cube in and mix well. Simmer uncovered for about twenty minutes, to thicken the sauce by evaporation. About halfway through, add vegetables such as peas, tinned sweetcorn, shredded leaves and cooked broccoli or cauliflower; these don't need so much cooking. What you use depends on what you have, though root vegetables aren't good in this recipe, except for a little grated carrot.

Cook the pasta as per the instructions on the packet; about 10 minutes in boiling water. Take a piece out and test it. Drain once it's ready and serve the bolognaise with grated cheese and salad leaves. It's useful to have Parmesan cheese in your stores; it keeps well and replaces fresh cheese as a garnish for tomato dishes.

Sorrel sauce

A small handful of fresh sorrel leaves (25–50 grams; 1–2 ounces)
A small onion or leek, finely chopped
A medium tomato, diced
25 grams (1 ounce) of butter
150 ml (5 fluid ounces) of double cream

You're unlikely to be able to buy fresh sorrel leaves, but they're easy to cultivate in a large pot and best from December to June. The sharp, lemony taste goes nicely with fish, especially baked trout or salmon.

Wash the leaves well and remove any hard stalks. Shred them finely. Sauté the onion in the butter, add the diced tomato and the sorrel. Stir for a few minutes till the leaves have wilted, then remove from the heat and add the cream. Reheat with care – don't let it boil – and serve at once.

An average sized fish fillet – about 15 centimetres long, 4 inches across and less than an inch thick – from a packet is roughly equivalent to a whole fish about a foot long from nose to tail. Unwrap the meat and read the instructions on the packet. You often cook them from frozen; raw fish goes off very quickly. The use-by dates are to be taken seriously.

Wrap your piece of fish, or your cleaned catch, in foil rubbed with a little butter or oil on the inside. Cook on a baking tray on the middle shelf of a preheated low medium oven (Gas Mark 4; 180C; 350F) for 25 minutes.

Unwrap one of the foil parcels and check if the fish is cooked right through. Raw fish looks a little transparent; the cooked flesh is cloudier. Give it another few minutes if it's not ready. Recognising when fish is cooked is a useful skill when using the uncertain heat of a fire!

Pilau rice

100 grams (4 ounces) of white long grain rice. The long cooking time of brown rice makes it difficult to use here, and it will need up to three times the amount of liquid.
25 grams (1 ounce) butter.
350 ml (12 fluid ounces) of stock – hot water with two stock cubes is fine.
Salt, pepper and herbs to season

Using a thick bottomed pan, cook the rice in butter until it is just going transparent. Stir in the hot stock and seasonings, bring back to the boil, and cover. Simmer for about 15 minutes without stirring – the bottom layer may burn if the pan metal is too thin. Once the water is absorbed, remove from the heat, take off the lid and cover the rice directly with a clean cloth. A folded tea towel is ideal.

Leave it to stand for 15 minutes, then serve.

Pilau rice can accompany a curry, or you can add small odds and ends to it for a complete meal. Use up tiny amounts of leftovers. Fry finely chopped red peppers or onions in the butter before adding the rice, stir in some frozen peas or shredded leaves just before you put the cloth over the rice. Parsley is a good addition, as is wild garlic.

Sweet and sour sauce

1 tablespoon oil
Half a tablespoon of soy sauce (tamari)
A small leek from the garden, chopped; an onion will do instead
1 rounded teaspoon of plain flour
1 tablespoon of vinegar, preferably a good quality one
1 tablespoon honey or sugar

120 ml (4 fluid ounces) of warmed vegetable stock

Fry the leeks in the oil and tamari, remove from the heat and stir in the flour. Mix the vinegar, honey and stock together and add this slowly. Gradually heat the sauce and simmer gently for a few minutes.

You can use this as a dip, or cook a variety of other ingredients and add these to the sauce a few minutes before serving. It's good with a Chinese style stir fry and rice.

If you want to experiment with a new dish, try sampling it first in a good restaurant or get it as a takeaway. With sweet and sour dishes, the vegetables should be crunchy and retain their identity as individual flavours, rather than merge with the sauce as in many curries.

Chinese recipes use their native water chestnut, bamboo shoots and bean sprouts to achieve this effect; you can buy these in tins, but then there's probably going to be a lot left over. Try using celery, peppers and onion to duplicate these textures with more readily available vegetables. White meat, such as chicken or pork, is best used here. Cut it into very thin strips and cook it a little, before adding the vegetables.

Pakoras

100 grams (4 ounces) of gram (chickpea) flour
About 4 tablespoons water
Half a teaspoon of turmeric powder
A selection of small pieces of lightly cooked vegetables such as cauliflower, onion and red pepper; peas are a nice colourful addition too
Oil for deep frying

Using a large bowl, mix the flour and water into a thick batter. Gently stir in the well-drained vegetables till they are thoroughly coated in this.

Scoop up a tablespoon of the mix and carefully slide it into the heated oil. It should sizzle if the oil is hot enough. Add a few more spoonfuls, leaving enough room so they don't stick together.

The pakoras will brown as they cook. It's important that their centres are cooked through, or they're a bit heavy. Lift them out with a slotted spoon and lay on kitchen paper to drain; cut one in half to see if it's ready. If not, you can put them back in.

Including more of the vegetables in your spoonfuls makes for a lighter result. Gram flour binds well – it's often used as a substitute for egg in vegan recipes – but it can be rather dense. For spicier pakoras, try adding a half teaspoon each of coriander and cumin powder, or even a little chilli.

Eat these with dips and salads.

Heat up left over curry for a quick sauce. Kormas aren't great the next day, but most of the other types are more robust. Don't reheat cooked rice.

Beer battered fish

150 grams (6 ounces) of raw unfrozen fish or chicken, cut into thin finger sized strips
100 grams (4 ounces) self-raising flour, with a large pinch of salt added
half a teaspoon of baking powder (not crucial)
200 ml (8 fluid ounces) of lager, preferably flat

A little dry plain flour in a separate bowl
A pan and oil for deep frying

Mix the self-raising flour and lager into a batter. Lightly coat the meat strips in plain flour, then dip into the batter and slide them into the hot oil.

Cook for five to six minutes, till the batter has bubbled up and the meat is cooked through. Extract with a slotted spoon and put on some kitchen paper to drain. Check the largest one to ensure the meat is cooked right through before serving.

This mix is more than enough; you could get away with half the amount. Try using the extra to coat thin wedges of raw apple, or chunks of banana, and fry as above. Experiment with other fruits, or drop spoonfuls of batter into the oil to make basic batter bits. Pat these dry with kitchen paper and serve dredged with sugar. This is a good high calorie snack if food is short.

If you want to reuse the oil, it will need sieved first, as this recipe leaves it full of bits. Never sieve hot oil through a plastic sieve.

Chicken nuggets

One free-range chicken breast – this will serve two people
A heaped tablespoon of plain flour, with a little salt sprinkled in
Up to three tablespoons of golden breadcrumbs
One egg and a little milk, beaten together

Cut the raw chicken into chunks, about an inch (2 cm) square or a bit larger if you prefer. It's best to work on a tray for the next stage, with your ingredients in separate bowls, and have a shallow oiled oven tin close by. Preheat the oven to medium (Gas Mark 5; 190C; 375F).

Dip each piece of meat into the flour to coat it lightly. Dip into the egg mix next, and then the breadcrumbs. For an extra crunchy coating, dip the piece into the egg and crumbs again. This will start to make the breadcrumbs wet, so don't put them all in the bowl at once. Keep adding them as you work.

Lay the finished nuggets on the oven tin. Cook on a middle shelf for 25 minutes.

This method can be used on whole fillets of fish as well; for two medium fillets, the quantities and cooking time are the same. Baking is a healthier way of cooking than deep frying, and much safer. Check the oven from time to time, and set an alarm in case you get distracted.

Rice pudding

50 grams (2 ounces) of pudding rice – this has smaller, rounded grains than ordinary 'long-grain' rice
25 grams (1 ounce) caster sugar
500 ml or a pint carton of milk

Combine all the ingredients in a thick casserole dish with a lid and bake in a low oven (Gas Mark 2;150C; 300F) for an hour and a half. Stir after half an hour; check again each half hour but don't stir it again.

The finished pudding will still look quite runny, but the rice should be soft. As it cools, it'll absorb more of the milk; if you cook it until it's solid, it'll end up quite dry. Serve it with fresh milk if that happens.

This recipe uses up a lot of spare milk with almost no effort and a very small amount of rice. It's good when you need to rotate dried or UHT milk from your stores. Adding a spoonful of jam to each serving is nice, and helps use up slow-moving jars.

This low oven setting will keep your kitchen warm. It's handy for autumn or spring days when it's a little chilly in the afternoons, but not enough to turn on the heating. Use the oven warmth to raise dough for bread, or turn it up and pop a pie in when the rice pudding is done.

Upside down cake

A tin of pineapple and its juice
100 grams (4 ounces) butter
100 grams (4 ounces) brown sugar (preferably light soft brown)
150 grams (6 ounces) plain flour with 2 teaspoons of baking powder, or self-raising flour
1 teaspoon of ground cinnamon; an optional half teaspoon of nutmeg
2 eggs
120 ml milk (5 fluid ounces)
50 grams (2 ounces) of caster sugar

A round cake tin about 20 centimetre (8 inches) in diameter with quite deep sides

Preheat the oven to a low medium (Gas Mark 4; 180C; 350F). Melt 25 grams (1 ounce) of the butter in the cake tin. Add 50 grams (2 ounces) of the brown sugar and stir till this is dissolved, then add a tablespoon of the juice from the pineapple can. Remove from the heat and lay the pineapple rings or chunks to form a pattern in the mix.

Sieve the flour, add the spices. Beat the eggs and milk with the remaining brown sugar and the caster sugar. Melt the rest of the butter, allow to cool a little, then mix it in. Stir this into the flour, adding a little more milk if the mix is too dry. It should be like a thick paste. Pour it into the tin, without disturbing the pattern of the fruit, and bake on the middle shelf for 50 minutes.

Allow the cake to cool in the tin for five minutes, then run a knife around the edge to loosen it and turn out onto a large plate.

Chapter Ten

April

The weather is very variable this month, and across the British Isles, but at some point in late April or early May, the land will explode into life. The tree leaves which have been the merest brush of green unfold into a canopy; the plants of the hedges climb up to meet it. Bare lanes become dark, mysterious tunnels where hidden birds sing.

Feeding the birds from your city balcony is good, but where can they nest? Even in rural areas there are not that many bushy trees out of reach of domestic cats. Learn about nesting boxes online. They're easy to make; an excellent first woodworking project. Some animal charities sell them to raise funds. Don't just go to a chain store and get an imported one. Read the Resilience Handbook to find out why this is so wrong!

Sowing

By now you should have a plan, some seeds and prepared seed beds. It's important to get everything started off now so it can endure the summer heat, which can begin as early as May. This is an exciting time, the moment you've been building up to!

Choose a calm day with a bit of sun, when the soil is still quite moist. If you're some distance from an outside tap, bring a couple of bottles of water and a bucket. You'll need to rinse the mud off your hands before opening packets or handling seeds. Wrap the bottles in a small towel to stop them rolling about. Another bucket is handy to carry the trowel, dibber, stakes to mark out the seed rows and a small bag of potting compost. Not forgetting the seeds, and a flask of tea is nice if you're out on an allotment. Gardening gloves keep your nails clean, but you'll have to handle seeds with bare hands.

Some are small and very round, apt to roll off into the ground. Others, like carrot, are tiny and you just have to scatter them as thinly as possible. Have the bed ready before you open the packet. Read the instructions, or refer to your favourite gardening book. Does the plant require a long shallow trench? How much soil do you cover them with? Don't overdo it; tiny seeds haven't much stored energy to get them to the light.

Larger seeds can be carefully spaced. Most packets will tell you the sowing distance. Gardeners generally over sow and thin out plants later. Sow some of your core plants in large pots as an additional back-up. If the first sowing fails, you can put these reserves out. This is useful when you're experimenting with planting times.

Some vegetables, like leeks, are started off in pots and transplanted later; by the time your early peas are finished, they'll be ready to fill the newly empty bed. Others, particularly root vegetables, prefer to stay put once they're sown.

Gardening can get quite complicated; keeping that diary really is useful. Once you've sown the seeds, it may be awhile before anything shows. Label the rows with wooden stakes, write with a permanent marker pen. Anything less won't stand up to the weather for long.

As an amateur gardener, April is your busiest month. Those seeds need a bit of looking after. If the weather is dry and warm, they'll grow quickly but risk drying out. If it's cold and wet, they'll need protection from the slugs. Check on them frequently; learn to identify the seedlings as they emerge. Be careful with weeding around them in case you disturb their fragile roots.

Plant identification

The resilience gardener understands the value of edible wild plants. Many, once common, are rare and protected now. Learn to recognise the weeds you can allow to grow as ground cover. Banish the valuable but invasive nettles to the wild patch; bittercress and groundsel can stay. Remove any inedible plants such as milkweed; compost them well so the seeds don't survive. Bindweed is so persistent that it's best put in the landfill bin, or burned.

Studying your own planned seedlings as they emerge helps you to recognise self-sown individuals much later. These may be particularly well adapted to the micro-climate; it might be interesting to let them seed. A resilience garden doesn't have to be about regimented rows. It's also a place where you can explore your relationship with food plants, a miniature edible landscape.

A low maintenance approach shouldn't be confused with neglect. Keep hostile weeds, especially bramble, at bay. Water your plants, take rubbish away, store tools safely. It's a fine line between valid urban permaculture and an eyesore, especially in a culture obsessed by tidiness. Explain to the neighbours what you're trying to achieve, allow them to take an interest. Your resilience garden could develop into an independent community project.

Cultivating mushrooms

This isn't the time of year when you'd expect edible fungi, but St George's mushroom pops up around 23rd April. If you mow too close to the edge of the lawn, you'll soon discourage it, which is a pity. Failing to attract or maintain this wild mushroom, you could always try growing your own. Remember they're a valuable source of protein if you don't eat meat or dairy products.

It's a complicated process, inoculating logs with mushroom spawn. If you develop the skill though, you can end up with a good supply of fresh shitake, oyster and other exotic fungi. There are ways of getting them to fruit in any season. This fascinating and productive hobby can be pursued even in a cold damp garden with hardly any room.

Our gardening group got funding for an expert to run free courses in the techniques. We've now progressed to exploring techniques of mycoremediation on a former industrial site nearby. Certain fungi are able to absorb a lot of poisons from contaminated soil; these are then taken away and incinerated in controlled conditions. By repeating this process, toxic wastes can be removed, and the soil made fit for growing food again.

Some seasonal foods available in April

Easter marks the end of the fasting season; plenty of eggs and milk are to be had.
Cream, butter, soft cheese, yogurt – last year's hard cheese tends to stay on the shelf now!
Fresh meat is still rare; there's less time to go hunting.
Stores of preserved meat – bacon, hams, sausages – could be getting low.
Fish and shellfish.
Some harder green leaves are ready, such as kale, nettle and borage.
There are plenty of tender salad leaves around too.
Edible stems, such as rhubarb and willowherb.
The usual dried stores – pulses, fruits, nuts, grains.
The last of the purple sprouting broccoli.
Fruit is in short supply until the strawberries are ready.

The root vegetables are all gone; now grains have to provide your carbohydrates until late summer and you can't replenish them until autumn. In a hard year, you'd need to make the most of them.

Grinding grains

Grinding the grains made them even more digestible. Weight for weight, bread has more nutrients than meat or vegetables, stores well and can be easily carried. The ancient Egyptians are credited with first using yeast to make dough rise into the leavened bread we know today.

Although bread can be made from a variety of grains, wheat is the most popular. One of the earliest known cereals, original varieties like emmer and spelt were selectively bred for heavier yields. Today, there is a resurgence of interest in these prehistoric wheats due to their resilience and suitability for organic growing.

If you try to grind wheat between two flat stones, you will lose a lot of grain as it rolls off the sides. A specially shaped tool had to be made, consisting of a containing dish and a smooth round lump of stone. There are pictures of these saddlestones being used in Egyptian tomb paintings.

When a simple rotary hand mill called a quern was invented it quickly became an essential item in the Neolithic household. Strictly speaking, only the lower, stationary stone of the pair is called a quernstone; the upper stone is a handstone. Querns were developed in many different styles; some with an added lever for faster grinding, others with hoppers on top for feeding in the grain. They are still used in some remote areas, and have even come back into fashion recently.

As settled life progressed, domestic animals began to make a bigger contribution to the energy available for a community. Simple mills, often powered by donkeys, were developed to grind flour for more than one household.

With a number of people working together, a much larger mill could be built, using huge stones moved by gears linked to a great wheel which was turned by the considerable energy of wind or running water. There would be a limited number of possible locations in any area for such a mill – close to a fairly large stream, or perched on a hill to catch the wind – so it would need to serve a reasonably sized community.

Most of the flour produced was consumed locally until industrialisation revolutionised transport. As towns began to grow into cities and create a demand for food, so mills became mechanised and more efficient. Combine harvesters and other machinery meanwhile reduced the time needed for growing wheat from over eighty hours per acre to two hours, thus providing a huge increase in the available grain.

In the 19th century, metal rollers and automated milling began to replace traditional mills. White flour could be produced for the first time, since the process was finely controlled. The bran and wheat germ were totally removed, along with most of the nutrients. The industry had to start adding vitamins to this depleted flour to make it worth eating. Some bran is returned to 'whole wheat' flour, but most is sold as animal feed or dietary supplements.

Bread and the Industrial Revolution

Once flour became a commercial product, storage was more of an issue. Unmilled grains can keep for many years, but destroying the protective husk allows heat, light and damp to begin spoiling the flour. The oils in the wheatgerm are especially prone to going rancid, which is why the germ is removed in commercial mills.

Unless used within two days, freshly milled flour needs to be stored for a fortnight or so before being suitable for baking. Without this ageing, it makes a dough which lacks the strength to trap gas and rise. Bleaches and other chemicals were found to duplicate these effects of storage in only a few days and are commonly used in America, although banned in Europe.

The trade-off between healthy food and large-scale production is clear when considering bread. Stone ground flour can be obtained again, now that the issues of food quality with mass produced bread are understood. With stone grinding, the oils were distributed evenly throughout the flour which allowed it to keep longer. All the nutrients are left intact and the food value is maximised.

You can get small hand operated or electric grinders for your own kitchen. Freshly milled flour can be frozen to extend its shelf life, but remember to bring it back up to room temperature before starting to make bread. Otherwise, don't put it in tightly sealed plastic jars; flour needs to 'breathe'.

As a general rule, store it in its original paper packets in a large crock or a clean metal dustbin. The cooler it is, the longer it will take for the oils to oxidise into that rancid taste. Protect it from mould, rodents and insects; wholemeal flour should keep for six months and white flour for a year.

Exploring the processing of grain is a valuable exercise in resilience.

Recipes for April

Scones

Scones are a good way of using up sour milk. The baking soda (sodium bicarbonate) used to raise flour in the olden days needed an acid ingredient before it would release bubbles into the mix. Sour milk is acidic, so it was essential for the scones to rise. Today we use self-raising flour, or baking powder which has tartaric acid added already, so the milk doesn't have to be sour.

If you want to try out the original method, use plain flour with a teaspoon of bicarbonate of soda, and properly sour milk.

200 grams (8 ounces) of self-raising flour
150 ml (6 fluid ounces) milk
A small handful of raisins (about 50 grams; 2 ounces)
50 grams (2 ounces) of butter

Wear an apron, turn the oven on to moderately high (Gas Mark 7; 220C; 425F).

Rub the butter into the flour to make a breadcrumb mix, stir in the milk, roll out on a well-floured surface to about an inch thick and cut with a 3 inch round cutter. Brush with fresh milk. It's better to transfer them to a clean plate for this so the milk doesn't get mixed up with the dry flour. Stand the raw scones on a shallow greased tray, leaving space between them for rising.

Cook on a high middle shelf for 10 minutes and cool on a wire rack.

For cheese scones, add 50 grams (2 ounces) of cheese instead of raisins, and reduce the butter slightly. After cutting into shapes and brushing with milk, scatter extra grated cheese over the scones and bake as before.

Apple scone

200 grams (8 ounces) self-raising flour
50 grams (2 ounces) of butter
50 grams (2 ounces) caster sugar
A quarter pint of milk, which can be sour (120 ml; 5 fluid ounces)
1 medium apple, peeled and grated
1 level teaspoon cinnamon powder
a teaspoon of sugar to scatter on top, preferably demerara

Preheat the oven on medium (Gas Mark 5; 190C; 375F) and grease a shallow baking tray.

Rub the flour and butter into a breadcrumb mix, stir in the caster sugar and grated apple, mix into a dough with the milk and put on the tray as a single cake. Brush it with fresh milk and sprinkle with sugar. Cook for 25–30 minutes. Mark into slices as it cools on the tray.

A nice way to use up the very last of your apple store, and it avoids the messy rolling out stage!

Drop scones

100 grams (4 ounces) self-raising flour
A pinch of salt
1 egg
90 ml (6 fluid ounces) of milk
A small handful of raisins or sultanas (optional)
Sugar for dusting

Mix the ingredients into a batter, which many say is best left to rest for half an hour. It should be thicker than a pancake batter. Heat some oil in a frying pan, then drop large blobs of the mix in with care. You need more oil than for pancakes; the deeper the oil, the thicker the scones will be as the hot oil stops them spreading out.

Fry two or three at a time. Cook until the top sets, then turn them over and do the other side. Mind the oil doesn't overheat; remove the pan from the heat if it starts to smoke.

Lift onto absorbent paper to cool when cooked, sprinkle with sugar. They're best eaten fresh. These quantities make about eight.

You could leave out the raisins and sugar to serve these with a savoury dish. Drop scones are good with a fried breakfast!

Soda bread

200 grams (6 ounces) of plain wholemeal flour
200 grams (6 ounces) plain white flour
2 teaspoons of bicarbonate of soda
1 teaspoon of salt
300 ml (half a pint) of sour milk. You can use ordinary milk with 2 teaspoons of vinegar, or plain natural yogurt, as a substitute for this

Pre heat the oven to medium hot (Gas Mark 6; 200C; 400F).

Combine the dry ingredients in a bowl, form a well in the centre and pour in the milk. Mix this in, turn the dough out onto a floured board and knead lightly for a few minutes. Pat it into a round loaf and transfer to a greased, floured baking tray.

Cut a deep cross in the top of the bread, and bake on a middle shelf for 40 minutes or so, until the loaf is a golden brown colour and sounds hollow when tapped. Cool on a wire rack.

Soda bread is best eaten freshly made, but is good for toast the next day.

Kedgeree

100 grams (4 ounces) white rice – brown rice takes longer to cook and needs more water added
25 grams (1 ounce) of butter
1 onion, chopped finely
Half a teaspoon of turmeric
500 ml (1 pint) of stock – use water with only one stock cube, as the fish is salty
2 hard-boiled eggs, cut into quarters
200 grams (8 ounces) of smoked haddock, defrosted
A tablespoon of fresh parsley, chopped – optional

Set the eggs on to boil in a small pan. Using a deep frying pan, sauté the onion in the butter until it's soft. Add the turmeric when they're nearly done. Stir in the raw rice, coating it well in butter, then pour in the stock. Cover and simmer for 12 minutes.

Meanwhile, put the fish in a pan of boiling water and simmer for 4 minutes. Allow it to drain and cool a little on a plate before breaking it up into flakes, discarding the skin and bones.

Check the rice. It should be quite soft for this dish. If there's still too much water in the pan, uncover it and let some evaporate. When all is well there, stir in the fish, eggs and anything else you might add. I like to use tinned sweetcorn to keep up the yellow theme, but garden peas and chopped raw tomatoes are also nice.

Simmer gently for another 3 minutes, taking care not to let it stick as the water should be nearly used up now. Stir in the parsley just before serving.

Garnish with sprigs of parsley and lemon slices to squeeze over the dish.

To boil eggs, put them in a pan and cover with cold water. Bring this to the boil then, when it is bubbling properly, cover the pan – this is essential – and turn off the heat. Leave the eggs in the hot water for 4 minutes if you want them soft boiled, 6 minutes if you hate runny eggs, or 10 minutes for hard boiled. Take one egg out and check it before throwing the hot water away!

Pasta bake

Cooked pasta to fill the size of oven dish used – about 100 grams (4 ounces) dry weight will do for two people
2 eggs
60 ml (2 fluid ounces) of milk
An onion or two, chopped and lightly fried
120 grams (5 ounces) of grated cheese
Other odds and ends to taste, such as lightly fried mushrooms, red pepper or bacon, steamed purple sprouting broccoli, garlic and a few oregano leaves
A sliced tomato and a sprig of parsley to garnish

Pre heat the oven to medium (Gas Mark 5; 190C; 375F). Grease the inside of the oven dish. Mix the cooked pasta with half the cheese and the other dry ingredients: tip into the dish.

If you can break an eggshell clean in half, one half shell full is the traditional measure of milk used here and in many old recipes. Stir up the eggs and milk, pour them evenly over the pasta. Scatter the rest of the grated cheese on top and bake on a middle shelf for 30 minutes. The egg mix should be set and the cheese on top starting to brown.

Serve with salad, chutney and baked beans.

Pasta bake is a great way to use up leftovers; a couple of mushrooms, a single rasher of bacon, the last of a packet of something. Add some odds and ends from the vegetable garden too.

Cooked pasta from the fridge should be put in a pan of hot water briefly, then well drained, before mixing the ingredients, or the cooking times may be out.

Purple sprouting broccoli

The resilience gardener can eat purple sprouting broccoli all spring, harvesting a small handful every day. It goes in most stews, risottos, soups and pie fillings. Only use the budding tops and the tender part of the stem. If you allow the yellow flowers to develop, that plant will stop producing these edible shoots.

If you have enough to serve as a vegetable on the side, lightly boil until the stems are soft, drain and serve with a knob of butter melting into them.

Burdock root

After spending a couple of years making very sure you can distinguish burdock from foxglove at all stages of development, and having the landowner's permission, dig up some burdock root.

If you have room, grow some in your resilience garden. Burdock matures into a large plant, with sticky burrs for seeds – if you have a long haired pet, this plant may not be for you! It likes damp edges, not full sun, but not too shady either. The roots are thick and long, providing quite a lot of food value; burdock is cultivated in Japan, where it is known as gobo.

You can make a sort of kinpara – a Japanese cooking method where roots are sautéed then braised (simmered in liquid till done). There are more elaborate recipes for burdock online.

Burdock roots will be muddy. Scrub them clean, scrape lightly. Don't peel if possible; the peel has a lot of the flavour. Try and leave some of the thin brown skin on.

The white flesh begins to brown as soon as it's cut, so put your prepared roots in a bowl of water, with a little vinegar added. Acidulated water is a good way to stop this oxidation process, which is also seen in cut apples. Use lemon juice to halt the browning when making sweet dishes.

Some cooks recommend soaking the burdock roots in water for 15 minutes, until the water starts going brown. This reduces the flavour, which is strong and earthy like beetroot or mushrooms.

Cut the roots into pieces about 6 centimetres (2 inches) long, halved lengthways. Stir fry these in a tablespoon of oil, with a teaspoon of tamari added, for 4–6 minutes, until lightly browned. Add hot vegetable stock to cover the roots and simmer for 10 minutes, until the roots are cooked through but still crispy.

If you prefer them softer, add them to a stew of other root vegetables and cook this slowly for an hour or so. It's fine to include meat or beans in this recipe.

Burdock root has a high energy yield. While carrots and swede give less than 60 calories per 100 grams, burdock supplies 72 calories. They are nearly as nutritious as boiled grains (around 85 calories) or potatoes (100 calories).

Urban survival oyster mushroom broth

If you master the art of cultivating exotic mushrooms, you can grow them in a city environment. They'll add important nutrients to stored food. Both shitake and oyster mushrooms are tougher than normal supermarket mushrooms, so they need to be sweated or lightly boiled before adding to a recipe as an equivalent.

To make a small bowl each for two people: -

Oyster mushrooms – up to 100 grams (4 ounces)
about half a pint (300 ml) of vegetable stock – water and one stock cube will do
1 teaspoon of miso paste
2 teaspoons of tamari (soy sauce)

Slice and cook the mushrooms in a little hot oil for about 2 minutes, until they are browned and softened. Take them out of the oil and set them aside to drain on kitchen paper.

Bring the vegetable stock to a boil in a saucepan. Add the mushrooms, reduce the heat to low, and simmer for 4 minutes. Stir the miso paste and soy sauce together in a small bowl; add this to the broth and continue cooking for another minute. Pour the soup into bowls and garnish with some finely chopped fresh leaves.

Miso is a fermented soy bean paste used in many Japanese recipes. Its many health benefits are being explored since it was credited with the survival of patients in a hospital very close to the Nagasaki atom bomb in 1945. Miso may lower blood pressure, despite having a high salt content; work continues on its role in protection against radiation.

Noodles with shitake mushrooms

100 grams (4 ounces) dry weight of medium egg noodles, cooked
A couple of ounces of shredded cooked meat
A few lightly boiled and chopped shitake mushrooms
Some finely chopped vegetables such as spring onions or garden greens
A little oil for frying, with a dash of tamari

Sauté the meat and vegetables; you can use a wok to imitate the Japanese style. Stir in the noodles, heat through and add extra sauce to taste. You can use Worcester sauce instead of soy, though it's not vegan.

This dish is nice with a chutney, or a spicy pickle, on the side.

Mock knotweed crumble

As roots wither, shoots fatten. Edible stems were important in spring. Young knotweed shoots are a delicacy in Japan, and can be eaten just like rhubarb, or steamed like asparagus. It's illegal to cultivate it in Britain, and wild plants may be contaminated with spray.

Burn any scraps from preparing it – don't compost them or even send them to landfill.

Although knotweed doesn't set viable seed in this country, it can regenerate from the tiniest of pieces. It's likely to be around long after weed killers are. This recipe is a good basis for edible stems in general.

20 pieces of thin rhubarb stems, each about 8 centimetres (3 inches) long
1 banana, or well-drained tinned fruit
4 tablespoons of apple juice
1 teaspoon of powdered ginger

Make your crumble mix – one part butter (or another fat), one part sugar and two parts plain flour; rub the butter into the flour and stir in the sugar – put the oven on medium (Gas Mark 5; 190C; 375F) and grease your crumble dish.

Lay the rhubarb in the dish. Cut the other fruit into the gaps, sprinkle with the ginger and pour the apple juice over it all. Cover with crumble mix and bake for about 30 minutes on a middle shelf.

You can adapt this recipe to try out other edible stems if you're keen to explore foraging. For example, young stems of rosebay willow herb are edible, though many find them somewhat bitter.

Remember that young plants may not show the characteristics which identify them as poisonous; I recommend that you go out foraging with an expert until you feel confident.

Impossible pie

2 eggs
100 grams (4 ounces) caster sugar
50 grams (2 ounces) plain flour
50 grams (2 ounces) desiccated coconut
1 teaspoon vanilla essence
200 ml (half a pint) of milk

Just mix everything together and pour it into a deep oven dish, about 8 inches in diameter. Bake for 45 minutes at a low medium heat (Gas Mark 4; 180C; 350F). The flour sinks to the bottom to form a pastry-like base while the coconut rises and browns like a cake topping. The centre is like a set custard.

Nettle beer

Nettles (a kilo; a couple of pounds)
Water
450 grams (a pound) of sugar
A large tablespoon of cream of tartar (40 grams)
The juice of one lemon, or a tablespoon of bottled lemon juice
Some brewing yeast

Wearing gloves, pick a full carrier bag of young nettle tops. Older plants have more oxalic acid in them, so they're not so edible; spring is the time to eat nettles. Cut them up and stuff them into a large stainless-steel pan; mine holds a gallon and a half. Cover with a gallon of cold water and bring to the boil. Simmer for 15 minutes, pushing the leaves back under the water as they rise.

Strain into a sterilised food grade plastic bin with a lid and add the sugar, lemon juice and cream of tartar. When the mix has cooled to blood heat, add the yeast. If the liquid is too hot, you'll just kill it; if it's too cold it will take a while to get going.

You leave this in the bin, in a warm place, for three days. Then you're supposed to bottle it. I don't recommend this, unless you already have experience with beer making, as it's very fizzy. Use extra strong glass bottles with swing top lids to withstand the pressure; ordinary glass bottles may even explode. I found half the beer shot out of the top as soon as I opened it for the daily check! So I don't bottle this anymore.

Instead, I rack it off the sediment into another plastic bin and leave it covered for a few days, then either draw the beer from that for drinking or transport it in plastic bottles to the nearest Beltane party!

Technical terms used in brewing

Sterilising

Use a food grade sterilising powder, designed for home brewing or baby utensils. Follow the instructions on the packet and rinse the container in clean water after sterilising. If you can't get these, pour about a gallon of boiling water into the bin, put the lid on tightly and let it cool.

Brewing yeast

You ought to use a beer yeast, but a wine variety works. Sterilise a bottle, cool about half a pint of boiled water to blood heat – that is, when it feels comfortable on your finger – stir in a teaspoon of dried yeast and a teaspoon of sugar and pour it into the bottle. A small funnel is useful here. Leave the yeast mix in a warm place until it froths; this can take a couple of hours. Read the label on the yeast carefully. Some are yeast compounds; those that aren't will need a little yeast nutrient, bought separately, to bring out the best in them.

Racking

The beer or wine needs to be siphoned out of the original container without disturbing the layer of sediment which has fallen to the bottom. This layer is full of dead yeast and other impurities, so you need to get rid of it.

Interlude

Beltane

You can relax for a moment now. The seeds have been sown, the new plants are growing, there's plenty of good food around. The sun has already risen when you get up, the air is warm, the lawn is dry.

Halfway between spring equinox and summer solstice, Beltane marked the beginning of summer as Samhain (Hallowe'en), opposite it in the calendar, marks that of winter. It was one of the most important pagan festivals and never managed to take on many Christian elements, remaining a folk event to this day.

Thanks to the better weather and longer daylight, people could travel safely across the wild landscape between settlements and visit their neighbours. The feast also celebrated the cattle moving to the summer pastures. The grass was well grown, the new young animals strong enough to make the journey. Many villagers would go with them to enjoy life in their summer huts on the hillsides. A few would remain to tend the growing crops; it was a festival of meeting and parting ways.

Unlike the quiet holiness of Imbolc, wild enthusiasm is the theme of Beltane. It's a fire festival; not candles but 'balefire'. Huge bonfires were lit, the fresh nettle beer passed around, feasting tables laden with meat. Teenagers met again after a long winter cooped up with their families, and disappeared into the woods. Men, excited by drink, engaged in trials of strength; old women gathered in gossiping groups to exchange news and mull over the events of the winter.

Even the ceremonial aspect was energetic. Decorating everything with yellow flowers, dancing around the maypole, the Obby Oss chase; these made sure the children were ready for a good night's sleep during the party! The festivities could be dangerous. Cattle were driven between twin fires for luck. Feats of leaping over the flames were encouraged, and most of the community were drunk.

No wonder the spirits were said to be particularly active around May Day!

As with Hallowe'en, abundant folklore and customs have survived around May Day. The maypole was nearly consigned to history during the fossil fuel diaspora of the Fifties, but is now enjoying a revival as people return to the countryside. Thousands flock to Padstow in Cornwall to see the Obby Oss. Elsewhere, the sound of the accordion fills market squares as the Morris is danced with clashing staffs, chiming bells and waving handkerchiefs.

Walking in procession around boundaries – 'beating the bounds' – is still carried out in some shires but the custom of washing one's face in May dew to magically enhance the complexion is no longer very practical. However, Beltane still celebrates youth and beauty with the crowning of a May Queen, garlanded with summer flowers. The landscape is exploding into colour and the air is warm!

May Day has a long history across Europe. The Romans celebrated Flora, goddess of flowers. Catholic Christians hold it to be a festival of the Mother Mary. The Germanic people, in a strange reflection of Hallowe'en, called the night before May Day 'Witches Night'.

The witches were said to meet on a high mountain, and spirits were abroad. People would wander the streets in a carnival atmosphere; teenagers would play pranks. The night of 30th April is called Walpurgisnacht now. May 1st is the feast of St Walpurga, credited with bringing Christianity to Germany. It's also a feast day for St Joseph the Worker, but this is quite recent. The Pope established it in 1955 as a response to the communists naming May Day as International Workers' Day.

The echoes of Beltane have come down the centuries. Even today, there is a Bank Holiday in Britain. Weather permitting, the bonfire feast can be recreated in the first barbecue of summer!

Chapter Eleven

May

Long sunny days are here at last! Although the weather can still be wet, even chilly, the danger of frost has passed for all but the most northern areas. The growing season in Britain is defined as starting when the temperature on five consecutive days is over five degrees Centigrade, and ends after five days when it is below five degrees. On average, it's just over eight months.

Growers pay keen attention to the 'last expected frost' date. Fruit trees are blossoming. Each flower is a potential fruit; an icy wind can strip their petals, costing you an entire harvest. There's little to be done about that, but you can protect more accessible crops.

Planting Out

It's time for putting those seedlings in the ground. Many of your delicate young plants, raised in the shelter of a windowsill or greenhouse, can be killed off by a night's frost. Your first strategy is to work with the weather. Move your seedlings outside during the day to 'harden off', returning them to shelter in the evening. Pay attention to the forecast in case of any freak conditions threatening, and put the hardened plants into well-prepared ground after a few days.

Handle the plants carefully with fairly clean hands. Don't break the stems. Transfer as much soil as possible with the roots. Fragile root hairs do most of the work when it comes to taking up water, so you need to keep these intact where you can. Make the hole deep enough so the roots don't get squashed; fill it with water and let it drain. You can add some liquid plant feed here. Hold the plant upright while you fill in around it with fine soil or potting compost. Pat this down gently.

I prefer to plant out in the morning, on a day when I'll be at home to do several light waterings, the last being well before sunset. The main hazard young plants face in my garden is molluscs. Slugs and snails come out at night and travel easily across wet soil. In a hotter, drier garden, there would be less of these. Tender seedlings may wilt in the afternoon sun here and be better off planted in the evening.

The novice gardener would do well to keep some seedlings in reserve until observation and experience leads to the right judgements for their particular locale. Pay attention to the instructions on the seed packet, they'll be appropriate for the variety. Write your sowing and planting out dates in your diary!

Use the new space on the windowsill for sprouting courgettes and squash.

The Dangers of Stakes

Some plants may need to be tied to a support. Using bamboo sticks is a popular solution. Lengths of two to three feet are good to support most vegetables. They are also invisible from above. You are constantly bending over in a garden. As you dive down on that stray dandelion, you may not notice the stake in front of you. If you're lucky, it'll miss your eye.

Use thicker stakes. Cutting up a length of timber, about 2" by 1" in cross-section, is safer though a bit cumbersome. Taller pieces of bamboo – about head height – will do the job. Both these solutions are more expensive. Instead, you could cover the end of the stake so it's visible and not so pointy. An upended plastic drinks bottle is ideal; the two litre ones are less likely to blow off in a stiff wind.

This can look a bit untidy. For a neater job, find some old socks, preferably of a light colour. Stuff one with rags, and tie it in place with gardening string. Hemp twine is, of course, ideal; plastic cord can be harmful to birds. Or cut a slit in an old tennis ball and pop that on to the stake end.

Take the trouble to cover them, it's worth the bother!

Protecting your plants

As you get used to your growing space, you'll be able to identify the main dangers to your crops and work out low cost, non-chemical strategies. I don't mulch around growing plants, and keep the soil of the vegetable plot quite bare. This reduces slug habitat. In a drier garden, on a sandy soil, a mulch suppresses weeds and holds valuable water where it's needed. You can use the cut grass from mowing the lawn.

Drying out can be a major problem in early summer. Water down at root level. If you sprinkle the leaves during a sunny day, the droplets can act as tiny magnifying glasses, focussing the light and scorching them. Your newly planted seedlings may struggle; the warmth is causing them to give off moisture from their leaves, but their roots haven't recovered enough to replace this. Wilting reduces the surface area of a leaf, so it loses less water. Pay special attention to plants which are starting to droop.

A well-established potted herb which suddenly starts to wilt may be harbouring an ants' nest. In the confines of the pot, their secretions damage the roots. You'll need to evict them. Move the pot over to your wild area and – wearing wellies – tip the whole thing out. Shake the plant gently; submerge the root system in a bucket of water. Go and have a cuppa while the birds pick over the debris. Next day, wipe out the pot, fill with fresh soil, and replant the herb. Standing pots on old plates rather than bare ground helps prevent this invasion.

Aphids – blackfly, greenfly and whitefly – can be a nasty problem. Try spraying them with dilute washing up liquid. Predatory insects keep these in check; your task is to attract these. Grow companion plants, such as calendula marigold, on which the adults feed. They then seek out an aphid infestation to lay their eggs in and their larvae eat all the aphids.

Trouble is, when they've all gone, the hoverfly or ladybird will have to go elsewhere to lay. Unless you have nettles in your wild patch. These harbour the nettle aphid, harmless to other plants. Your predators will quite happily snack on these while keeping an eye on your vegetables growing next to those tasty flowers.

If I can't control an aphid infestation – and I find whitefly particularly resistant – I cut off the affected part, even pull up the whole plant, and bin it. They often attack my seed broccoli; I keep some two-year-old seed in reserve as I don't want to breed from a plant which turns out to be bad at fending off these insects. Broad beans struggle with blackfly in my garden; I grow peas instead. Remember the Resilience Garden rule: "if at first you don't succeed, try growing something else!"

You're unlikely to see common plant diseases this early in the season, though this is when the experienced gardener protects against such attacks. Poor growth or ill health may be due to a mineral deficiency in the soil. There are useful charts online and in gardening books to match symptoms, such as yellowing leaves, with possible problems.

Liquid plant feeds

Liquid feeds contain useful nutrients. Add some to your watering can as a matter of routine. Buy these, or make your own. An aerobic compost tea provides a quick fix when you've identified a particular deficiency.

Comfrey contains potassium, also known in gardening as potash. Wood ash from a fire suitable for cooking is also a good source of this mineral, hence the name. Plants which are producing fruit need potash rather than nitrogen, which may make them too leafy.

For a nitrogen boost, chop up dock leaves, borage and nettles. Throw these into your lidded bucket, fill up with water and keep covered for a couple of days. Stir to a froth regularly to keep the process aerobic. Sieve off the liquid and water your ailing plants with it.

Seaweed is worth adding to any mix, as it contains the whole spectrum of micronutrients. Unless you live within easy reach of the seaside though, it may be tricky to source. Gather a bucket full on an expedition and use it to make the anaerobic compost tea described in December, which is about when you'd have to start making it to be ready now.

Store the completed product in labelled plastic containers and add a very little to your remedial mixes.

Don't give extra nitrogen to peas or beans. It'll just irritate them. Legumes have a deal with friendly bacteria who are provided with housing in special root nodules. In return, they supply the plant with easily digestible nitrogen, extracted from the air, which helps form the protein-rich crop. When you dig up old pea plants, rinse the roots clean and take a look. You can see these nodules as small lumps on the root hairs

If you want to develop gardening as a craft rather than just see what you can do, there's plenty of equipment you can invest in. You can buy a fleece roll to spread out over new plants to protect from frost, make miniature poly tunnels against heavy rain or hail, set up elaborate trellis work for peas to climb. However, it's always good to try things out without spending money in your first season. You're better able to make informed retail decisions after that.

Some seasonal foods available in May

Fresh green shoots are being replaced by mature leaves.
Winter standbys like kale and rocket are going to seed.
There's a selection of salad ingredients already; lettuce, radishes, cress.
Abundant milk, cream, cheeses, butter and other dairy products.
Eggs.
Stored grains are still your main carbohydrate.
The only 'fruit' around is rhubarb, but there are some large edible flowers such as elder.

It's getting too warm for fish and shellfish – there isn't an 'R' in the month. Small game is harder to catch in the thick undergrowth but there's occasional fresh meat from farm animals.

Sugar and honey would have to come from stores at this time of year; it could be in short supply, carefully hoarded for the summer fruit jams. People satisfied their craving for sweet tastes by eating nectar rich edible flowers and looking forward to strawberries. There was plenty of cream to go with rhubarb pie and elderflower fritters though, so it wasn't all bad.

Checking your stores

Outside the busy dairy, there's not much to do in May except watch things grow. Having gathered the news about harvest prospects from the local area at the Beltane feast, the prudent housekeeper does an edit of the stores. The warm weather will make some items, such as bacon, spoil faster. These need using up. It looks like a good bean harvest, so finish off the old stores. People said the bees weren't happy; put some honey aside in case there's a shortage in autumn.

We don't seem to have paid much attention to the resilience stores yet. However, every recipe in this book can either be made from stores and easily available foraged food, or can be quickly adapted. Where butter is called for, try using coconut oil. This, kept in a jar, can stand warmer temperatures than butter. It just melts and sets again, unlike butter which separates.

Onion in a recipe can be replaced by dried onion. You could explore the use of a dehydrator and make your own. The rabbit stew recipe will serve for any small game, even a tough old boiler chicken. Vegetarian mince can be used in the barley broth. The resilient household forages where it can and knows what to do with the results!

Most of the time your emergency stores won't be used for a really serious emergency which affects the whole country, disrupting mains services and distribution networks. They have to be capable of seeing you through one of these – a fortnight is a good target period – but you'll mainly be using them up due to the sell-by dates. You'll have access to the trappings of civilisation like cookers, water and shops; you can use ordinary recipes, even exotic ingredients!

Checking stores at regular, if infrequent, intervals is part of a resilient lifestyle. The month following each 'cross quarter day' is easy to remember. May follows Beltane, so you would do one of your four annual routine checks about now. Don't put things in your stores with short sell-by dates; you should only have foods that keep for at least six months.

Go through your stores. If you've got the space, such as a loft or large shed, you can have several large (50 litre) plastic stack boxes, and separate newly bought from older stock. Another strategy is to stick a bright label with the expiry date written large onto the product; this is useful in a dimly lit store. Take out anything with less than three months to run and put it in the kitchen to get used up.

Write a list of what you need to replace. Inspect the remaining items for damp, rodent attack and other dangers. Tough plastic boxes will protect food against most hazards, and are the safest, lightest storage containers.

You'll end up with an odd selection of ingredients which need to be used up quite soon – suet, salad cream, stock cubes. It's difficult to be enthusiastic about stew and dumplings on a hot summer's day, or a salad in December. The cross quarter days are when the seasons change. For a few weeks, you can have a variety of weather before it settles down into the next period. It's a good opportunity to get those random items used up!

Adapting recipes

Be inventive. Is it possible to make a summery suet pudding? It might involve the mysteries of steaming; you'll need to do some research. Nobody likes the nut burgers; could you use the mix as a topping for a vegetable casserole instead? Have a reserve meal planned in case of disasters. Although it's wrong to waste food, you are not a dustbin! Everyone makes mistakes when learning; the important part is not to repeat them.

Light a small fire in your garden if it's permitted and neighbourly; try cooking on it! Use special pans you picked up from the boot sale as they will probably have black soot on the bottoms afterwards. It gets everywhere; wrap them and keep them in the shed. What sort of pan handles really don't work with an outside fire?

Pay attention to kitchen hygiene and understand the principles behind it. It's not so easy if you're camping out in the mud, though probably more important. Think about how you could manage, try it out for a weekend; hopefully you'll need to imagine the mud part! Is it worth packing a small plastic tray in your grab bag to prepare food on? A sealed packet of disinfectant wipes?

Cook meat well, especially pork, chicken and game. Those TV foragers aren't just being picky when they cook their squirrel instead of eating it raw. Unlike farm animals, wild creatures aren't inspected for parasites. Some can lurk in the muscle tissue – the meat – and infect your gut. If you're thinking about doing survival skills as a hobby, you need to find out about these unpleasant creatures.

Learn to break a recipe down into elements and understand what each one does. Some, like eggs and flour, hold the food together. Sugar makes the difference between a sweet or savoury dish. Stock cubes and herbs provide flavour. Can you replace flour with oats? Butter with hemp oil? Does it affect the texture, the cooking time? Is it completely inedible or would you eat it if that's all there was? Remember, grains have to be cooked to access their carbohydrates.

Experiment!

Recipes for May

Pastry

One part fat
Two parts plain flour
A little tepid water
A pinch of salt (optional)

That's it. You'll need an apron. Turn the oven on to medium. Rub the fat into the flour to make a breadcrumb mix. Add the warm water a tablespoon at a time, stirring it in until the mix becomes a dough. It needs to be quite firm, and not sticky, as you have to handle it a lot. Spread a thin layer of dry flour on a clean surface to roll the pastry out on; sprinkle flour on the rolling pin too. If you don't have one of these, improvise.

Work confidently when rolling and cutting your pastry. The more you handle it, the heavier the finished product will be. Try lifting it with the help of a fish slice if it sticks to the surface, but you can squish it back into a ball and roll it out again if all else fails. Don't make it too thin, or the next stage won't go well.

Use a pastry cutter for small tarts, if you have one; you could cut around a saucer or jar lid if you don't. Transferring a larger sheet to a baking tray is trickier. Make sure the tray is well greased and floured. Using a shallow one is best, as then you can turn the pastry over the top edge, which stops it shrinking away from the sides as it cooks.

Folded pastry tends to stick to itself. Picking it up by the edges, the centre may stretch and tear. Make sure it's the right size for the tray, and isn't stuck to the surface, then dust the top of the sheet with flour. Lift it carefully into exactly the right place on the baking tray and pat into shape, pushing the corners in and trimming the edges.

If there is a tear, or a gap in the sides, your filling will leak out and burn. Fix these using the leftover pastry. Roll out a patch, brush the area with a very little water and gently press it down.

Now you need to bake the pastry 'blind', that is, without the filling. Spread a layer of silver foil or greaseproof paper over the whole base. Weigh this down with dried beans, even raw pasta will do. You can use the same lot many times; just keep them in a separate jar so they're not accidentally eaten. Pop the tray into a medium oven on a middle shelf for 15 minutes, then take it out. It still has to go through another round of cooking, so you don't want the edges to burn.

You can keep this pastry case for later, or carry on with a filling.

Using an eight inch sandwich tin, 4 ounces (100 grams) of butter and 8 rounded tablespoons of flour should make sufficient pastry for an open tart. Add half again if you want a covered pie. It's better to have made too much pastry than not enough.

Quiche

Early summer is another time of year when there's small amounts of a wide variety of vegetables, but not enough of any one to make a meal. There's some peas, a few tiny carrot thinnings, an assortment of leaves. You could make a stew, but it's not much use on a picnic. Added to an egg mix and held in a pastry case though, these scraps make a very portable meal.

First, choose your baking tin. How thick do you want the egg layer? I prefer mine quite thin, less than an inch deep. How many slices do you want to provide; how many people are you feeding? For this recipe, I'll use the eight inch (20 cm) sandwich tin from the pastry recipe.

Preheat the oven to medium (Gas Mark 5; 190C; 375F). Make a pastry case using: -

120 grams (4 ounces) of butter
240 grams (8 ounces) of plain flour

6 tablespoons of tepid water
A pinch of salt

Prepare a selection of lightly fried or steamed seasonal vegetables – spring onions, peas, mushrooms – cut small. Let them cool a bit. Mix in some shredded ham or sliced cooked sausage. Use enough to fill halfway up the side of the pastry case.

For the egg mix: -

Three or four eggs
Up to four half eggshells of milk (120 ml; 4 fluid ounces)
4 tablespoons of grated cheese
pinch of salt (optional, and not if you're using preserved meat)

Break three eggs into a bowl, measuring a half eggshell of milk for each one. The amount of milk is thus directly related to the size of the egg. Combine the eggs and milk, then stir in the other ingredients, reserving half the cheese.

Pour the mixture into the baked pastry case. Is it full enough? Save the other egg. If not, whisk it up with milk and add to the filling. Sprinkle the rest of the cheese on top and cook on a middle shelf until the egg is set and the cheese on top browned. Check it after 20 minutes; it should be done by 30 minutes.

This size of quiche will make six small slices for a buffet, or provide a meal for at least two adults if you add salad, chips and baked beans.

Vegetable pie with cheese pastry

For the pastry, use the same eight inch round tin, 6 ounces of butter (150 grams) and 12 ounces of plain flour (300 grams). Stir 2 ounces (50 grams) of grated cheese into the mix before adding the water. Set aside a third of the dough for the lid, and make a pastry case as before with the rest, baking it blind.

Again, prepare a selection of lightly fried or steamed seasonal vegetables. You can use a tin of chickpeas or similar to provide bulk. Heat everything together in a pan, add a little stock, a tablespoon of chutney, a bit of passata or ketchup. The filling has to be moist, but not too runny. Thicken the liquid with a teaspoon of gravy granules, or by reducing, if necessary.

Pour this into the pastry case – it should be filled to the top but no more. Brush the edges with water. Roll out the lid, making it just a little too big and drape it over the pie. Press it down around the edge; the water will help it stick. It's easier if the cooked pastry is still a bit soft.

Prick a few holes in the lid with a fork, brush it with milk, or an egg yolk, scatter grated cheese on top and return the pie to the oven for half an hour. Use the same shelf and setting as for cooking the pastry case.

It'll be ready when the pastry lid looks cooked, as long as the filling was hot when you put it in. If it needs more cooking, check it every five minutes. Serve from the baking tin; pies don't need to be taken out to cool like cakes do.

You might have seen a pie chimney. They were often made to look like a blackbird, after the nursery rhyme. It's a small ceramic tube, with a wavy base. The chimney was put in the pie and the lid cut out around, then sealed. It acted like a vent for the filling, to prevent the pie going soggy.

Pastry shapes, tarts and pasties

If you only have a small amount of pastry left over from making a pie, you can cut it into shapes to decorate the lid. Apply them after brushing the milk on.

With a bit more, you can make a small batch of jam tarts. Or cut the pastry into shapes, sprinkle with sugar and bake on the bottom shelf for 15 minutes while the oven is on for the pie. Make strips of cheese pastry, twist them and dust with some Parmesan.

You can roll a six inch pastry round, dollop a tablespoon of left over vegetable pie filling in the centre and fold it over to make a pasty. Brush the edges with water first so they stick together; it's a knack. Expect them to leak. Pinching or folding the edges over can prevent this; a milk glaze over it all acts as a light glue.

These need about twenty minutes baking, on a middle shelf in a medium hot oven; longer if the filling is cold or contains meat.

Instead of jam, try using soft cheese for bite-sized savoury tarts. Mix mashed potato, bacon, fried onion and grated cheese for a different pasty filling, or use well-drained stewed fruit for a sweet version.

Pastry is very versatile!

Read the labels on pasties in supermarkets to get a useful idea of cooking times for various sizes and types. Meat pasties generally need 30–45 minutes baking from cold. You don't put raw meat in a pasty; always cook it first.

Chilli con carne

250 grams (8 ounces) of minced beef
1 onion and a couple of cloves of garlic, chopped
1 medium-sized chilli, finely chopped – wash your hands afterwards before touching your eyes!
1 small tin of kidney beans, or fully cook 50 grams (2 ounces) beans by dry weight
1 small tin of tomatoes
Half a teaspoon each of ground cumin, paprika and coriander
A pinch each of fennel seed, cayenne pepper and dried oregano
1 red pepper and half a courgette, chopped – optional

Lightly fry the chopped vegetables, add the chilli and spices just as these become soft, then stir in the mince. Once this is cooked, after about 15 minutes, add the drained kidney beans and tomatoes. Adjust the taste at this stage; add more chilli with care, as you can't take it back out!

Simmer uncovered on a low heat for 40 minutes; add a little water if it starts to stick. Serve with rice, or in wraps topped with cheese melted under the grill.

Dried beans – bought for stores or harvested from your own garden – require quite a lot of preparation. First soak them in cold water for several hours, preferably overnight but not much longer or they may start to ferment. Throw this water away, rinse and drain the beans.

Put them in a large pan – they will double in size at this stage – and cover well with clean water. Bring this to a fast boil and turn it down to a steady simmer after 10 minutes. Continue this for a couple of hours, keeping the beans covered with water at all times. Don't add salt yet, as this will toughen the skins.

Some people recommend a second rinse after the boiling, using another lot of clean water for the simmering. The exact cooking time varies depending on the type of bean you are using; look it up.

Skim off the white scum which rises to the surface. Once the beans are tender, rinse them again, discarding the water. You now have a recipe ingredient.

Beans contain a toxin called lectin, which is destroyed by cooking and drained away with the water used. Kidney and soya beans have particularly large amounts of this. Symptoms of lectin poisoning are stomach ache, nausea, diarrhoea and vomiting. These usually pass a few hours after onset; it is rare to be hospitalised.

The smaller beans, such as mung or aduki, are more user friendly. They're a good source of protein for your stores, and can even be sprouted to provide fresh micro-vegetables.

Bean and pasta salad

As well as providing a healthy and colourful side dish, a salad can be a meal in itself.

Open a tin of mixed beans from your stores, drain and rinse. Or prepare some dried beans; if you don't cook these regularly, buy packets with instructions. Bad preparation can lead to stomach upsets.

Cook enough pasta quills for the number you're serving. Drain, mix in the cooked beans and allow to cool.

Using tins from stores, this quickly makes a large dish for several people. Add a small tin of sweetcorn, some olives, and seasonal salad vegetables from the garden. Stir together with a tablespoon of hemp, or olive, oil and serve.

Banana bread

250 grams (9 ounces) of self-raising flour, with half a teaspoon of baking powder added
85 grams (3 ounces) butter
150 grams (5 ounces) of light soft brown sugar
3 ripe bananas
100 ml (3 fluid ounces) of milk, which can be sour, or natural yogurt
2 eggs
85 grams (3 ounces) of chopped walnuts (optional)

Grease and flour a two-pound loaf tin, preheat the oven to a low medium (Gas Mark 4; 180C; 350F).

Mash the bananas up well. In a separate bowl, rub the flour and butter together until they look like breadcrumbs, and there are no lumps of butter. Stir in the sugar.

Add the mashed bananas, eggs, milk and nuts. Beat till well mixed, then transfer into the loaf tin and bake on a middle shelf for up to 90 minutes.

Check after 1 hour, then every 10 minutes. A skewer should come out clean when the cake is done. Leave it to cool in the tin for 5 minutes, then turn out onto a wire rack.

The finished cake is quite heavy, due to the bananas. This is why it's referred to as a bread, though the recipe is actually more like cake. Banana bread is often spread with jam, and can even be toasted.

Elderflower cordial

Put a kilo (2 pounds) of sugar into a stainless-steel pan. Add 500 millilitres (1 pint) boiling water and stir over a low heat till the sugar dissolves.

Remove from the heat and add 30 grams (one and a quarter ounces) of citric acid, the grated zest of a lemon and the sliced fruit. Add 12 washed, drained elderflower heads.

Cover and let it stand for 12 hours. Then strain and bottle. Drink diluted with water, or use as a syrup in recipes.

Elderflower cordial generally keeps for a few weeks in a sealed bottle, since it is little more than a flavoured sugar solution. Even so, you should always keep home-made syrups in bottles suitable for beer or other pressurised drinks. The absence of industrial preservatives may allow them to ferment through the action of wild yeasts, producing gases.

Keep opened bottles of cordial in the fridge, and use within a week.

Chapter Twelve

June

All your seeds should be planted by now. The weather can be mixed, but the days are longer and the soil is warm. Things grow at an alarming rate, including weeds. You've made sure your vegetables had a head start, and they are defending themselves by shading out the ground beneath. Unless you're experimenting with ground cover, pull up anything that gets too close to give your plants a clear run at the nutrients.

Selective weeding

As soon as you create even the tiniest patch of bare ground, plants will try and move in. Learn to identify these; some are useful. There's often a gap between clearing an early crop and planting for the winter. It's best to have friendly weeds colonise the space.

Encourage plants which are easily uprooted and useful. Edible weeds, correctly identified, can be fed to pets; guinea pigs are said to be very fond of groundsel. Flowering ones attract those aphid-eating insects. Some lure pests away from your crops. The dreaded Cabbage White butterfly prefers nasturtiums to brassicas for its caterpillars.

Nasturtiums as weeds? Only in the relatively tame confines of your garden can you create your own set of weeds. Any robust plant which reliably self-seeds will do. Just clear away all the rest; you'll soon be able to identify your favourites from very small seedlings.

My garden has calendula marigold, borage, nasturtiums, rocket and spinach as regular features. If I couldn't cultivate it for a while, these loyal and decorative edibles are capable of hanging on for several years before being overrun! The blue speedwell and scarlet pimpernel are always ready to oblige with low ground cover; I tolerate these for their lovely little flowers until I need the ground cleared.

Dock, nettles, thistles and dandelion are discouraged by the competition, and by digging them out or hoeing them off while they are small. They could have a place somewhere in your garden but, like bindweed, horsetail and couch grass, they can regrow from small pieces of root left in the ground so clear them all from the vegetable patch itself.

Bindweed has pretty flowers, but isn't otherwise useful. If you don't spot it in time, its tendrils, which grow at great speed, wrap around your plants. They can be knotted into a clump, unable to grow and subject to mildew if the weather is damp. It's quite difficult to disentangle, especially if you've been on holiday and it's had a free hand. Dig up the whole bindweed plant with all the fat white roots as soon as you spot it, and bin it. It might look quite decorative on landfill sites.

Water and the garden

On the whole, the surfeit of water which causes mildews and moulds isn't your normal summer problem. After spending half the year dealing with floods, frost and hail you can expect to spend the other half coping with a shortage of water. Plants which were growing well suddenly become high dependency.

It's a pleasant image, pottering around in the sunshine with a watering can. You can even create a productive resilience garden which needs no more maintenance than that. However, if you're going for traditional vegetables, there's a bit more work needed.

Current lore recommends a good soaking every few days, rather than regular sprinklings. Target the roots. Don't use the rose on the watering can – this is to break up the flow onto delicate seedlings – but pour water directly onto the soil. A hosepipe is an ideal delivery system; set it to a steady flow, not a jet. If it has a sprinkler nozzle, you can wash the dust from leaves with an evening watering.

There are many situations where this isn't an option. There's the cost of the water to think of as well. Collect rainwater where possible; if choosing a barrel, consider how you'll get the water out again. Is the tap high enough, the lid sufficiently wide? Can you install it at the top of a slope? Some people create entire irrigation systems, aided by solar powered pumps and even timers!

Grey water from the house can be used on the garden. Technically, this is all your waste water apart from toilet flush. In practice, only bath water is accessible without adapting your plumbing system and using eco-friendly cleaning products. Learn the trick of using a bath siphon. This water is best used for trees and perennial plants, not salad vegetables.

Water from washing machines, dishwashers and the kitchen sink could all be reused. A simple ultraviolet sterilising system and some basic filters would render it safe for piping to community gardens. Until housing and estate design catch up with resilience though, this resource continues to be wasted.

For many gardeners, and especially the beginner, summer watering can be quite a chore. You don't need to carry many heavy watering cans from the kitchen sink to the far end of the garden before your thoughts turn to easier ways of doing this. If you can't set up a better water delivery system, consider what you're growing. Some plants have deep roots and are better able to withstand drought.

Pots are especially vulnerable to drying out; move them to a shadier spot, stand them in a shallow tray of water. Balance the value of a mulch in retaining soil water with the slug habitat it provides. Keep empty buckets in the most difficult to reach areas, to gather rainwater. It's important to give your vegetables enough to drink during this intense growing phase; it'll affect your crop later.

Some seasonal foods available in June

Soft fruits; strawberries, currants, early raspberries, gooseberries.
Mint and other leafy herbs; salad leaves in abundance.
Milk, cream, butter and soft cheeses are in plentiful supply, as are eggs and young chickens.
Young carrots, kale, peas, asparagus.
Early potatoes can be harvested from June (if you're very good at growing).
Stored nuts, beans and mushrooms may be running out; vegans need to keep an eye on their remaining dried proteins if the weather gets damp. They still have to last until the autumn crop.

Strawberries, cream and haymaking

The season of abundance begins as the soft fruits ripen. The sweetness of fresh strawberries combined with the richness of cream was the defining taste of summer for centuries. A cool north facing pantry comes into its own for trifles, jellies and salads. There was some leisurely jam making, but on the whole, it was more pleasant to just binge on fruit.

Even at the height of summer though, there were some serious preparations for the winter. As soon as the weather allowed, a harvest of hay was gathered. In the old days, this would have been cut and turned by hand before building the dried grass into the traditional haystacks, which vanished from the countryside not that long ago. Generally, the whole community pitched in to support the scythers; it was hot and thirsty work.

Water supplies

People and animals need water. Rivers, streams and springs were attractive to Neolithic farmers, as their flocks could drink easily. In drier pastures, a dew pond could be constructed. A thick bed of trampled clay lined a large shallow pool. The animals coming down to drink kept the clay edges free of grass. Water condensed on this bare surface during the night and trickled down into the pond.

This isn't a garden feature. You're unlikely to have a well either, and you can't dig one just anywhere. Apart from the legal complications, not every hole in the ground fills up with water. It's quite an art, creating a well, and worth protecting those remaining.

You need to drink between two and three litres of water every day; about half a gallon. In hot weather, you'll need more, especially if you're working hard. It's difficult to store enough for a fortnight and you may not have a local off-grid source. If you're thrown on your own resources during an emergency, start planning to replenish your drinking water before it runs out. You won't last a week without it.

Not all water, even that from a well, is safe to drink. A clear liquid in an unlabelled, or previously opened, container may not be water at all. As well as the natural hazards of bacteria and parasites, we have to consider contamination by chemicals when purifying water for drinking. Some volatile compounds are even resistant to distillation.

Some indications of chemical pollution are:

A foam or scum on the surface
Dead or dying plants
Algal bloom and choking weeds

Boil off a small amount of suspect water – don't breathe in the steam – and study any residue.

Stagnant water is a breeding ground for parasites and germs. Avoid it where possible; filter and boil well if not.

Emergency drinking water

You can make some effort to shift chemicals by leaving your prospective drinking water in an uncovered container for a few days, as you would for topping up a fish pond with tap water. Chlorine and other light chemicals evaporate away, but your water has probably got bits in it now.

The rainwater barrel will be in a similar condition; you'll need to do some filtering. The stages are much the same whether you're supplying a village or processing a couple of litres in conveniently-sized plastic bottles as an experiment, so I'll describe the latter.

You can dispel gases by aerating the water. Shake the bottle hard for a minute, then pour the water back and forth between two containers. Let any bubbles escape. How clear is the water? If it's very muddy, leave it to stand and let the heavier particles settle out.

With a bit of research, identify the right sort of alum to use, and add a tablespoon to see how this brings the dirt into clumps, which fall into a sediment faster. This chemical is often used in water treatment plants. Otherwise, leave the bottle to settle for a few hours.

Now for your filter system. Take one of those two litre plastic bottles and cut the bottom off. Cover the top with a clean filter – old (washed) tights, a coffee filter – securing this tightly in place with a rubber band. Turn this upside down; it'll look like a funnel. Put into another bottle which you've cut the top third away from. You're about to make it top heavy, so prop it up with something; the next stage can be wet.

Fill your funnel with three layers. First add a layer of well washed pebbles, then coarse sand and top with fine sand, like a playsand. Run some clean water through the filter once it's in place. Pour carefully to avoid disturbing the top sand layer, and use this rinse water on the garden. Your filter is now ready for your settled water.

Carefully tilt and pour the cleaner water from the muddy sediment into a clean container and run it through this filter. Leave it to drip; you should be able to clean even quite dirty water with this method. It's still not fit to drink yet. As the final stage, you can add your purification tablets or boil the filtered water for at least a minute. Then leave it to cool and transfer to clean, labelled bottles. Keep these in a dark place and repurify after a couple of days.

In certain circumstances it may be easier to distil drinking water. Boil it, preferably in a kettle, and direct the steam onto a cool clean surface. Water vapour will condense and run off into a usefully placed clean container below. You could easily construct an apparatus to save having to stand too close to the fire or hold hot objects. This water is usually safe to drink straight away.

It's quite hard work to process dirty water; remember you'll need clean water for cooking too. Even if your storage space is limited, try and keep a few litres of bottled water. Fill up larger containers from the tap as soon as you find out that mains supplies might be interrupted.

Recipes for June

Barley water

2 tablespoons pearl barley (50 grams; 2 ounces)

Wash and blanch and strain the barley. Put it in a jug with sugar and pour a pint (half a litre) of boiling water over it. Leave the jug covered and strain the barley out when it's cool. Add the rind of a lemon, thinly pared and the juice of half a lemon to make lemon barley water.

Lemonade

Take 4 lemons and pare them thinly, place the rinds in a jug with 50 grams (2 ounces) sugar. Pour on a litre (2 pints) of boiling water. Strain when cool, add the lemon juice. Don't expect it to be fizzy.

These recipes are useful if you are having to boil drinking water anyway. They're refreshing, low sugar and boost your vitamin C.

Herb teas

This is another way to flavour boiled water. The simplest method is to wash a sprig of fresh herb and cover it with hot water, just as you would use a herbal teabag.

Try mint or lemon balm for a refreshing alternative to coffee. Sage or cleavers make a good tonic. You could use these light herb teas instead of commercial flavoured waters. Add a little honey to sweeten to taste.

This is an infusion. If you were making a stronger brew – for example sage tea is said to be good for sore throats – you'd crush the leaves and infuse them for up to twenty minutes before straining off the liquid and using it.

A decoction is an even stronger brew, usually used for medicinal roots and bark. The plant is simmered in water for a while – again, usually about twenty minutes – then left to steep and strained when cool.

Always research unfamiliar plants thoroughly before using them.

Iced tea

1 teabag per cup, preferably a blend of black and green teas

Steep the teabags in hot water for 5 to 10 minutes, then remove the bags. Cover, cool to room temperature and chill.

Serve this and other summer coolers with flavoured ice cubes. Make up a small jug of elderflower cordial and fill your ice cube tray with this. Add some borage or marigold petals to each cube and freeze.

Try different combinations of cordials and flowers. A strawberry syrup frozen with mint leaves can give you an improvised Pimms!

Raspberry syrup

1 cup of washed raspberries, loosely packed not squashed down
Half a cup of sugar
Half a cup of water

Use the same cup, mug or jug for all the measuring. As raspberries can be hard to come by, measure them first and adjust the other quantities accordingly.

Mix the sugar and water in a pan and simmer gently till you can't see the sugar any more. Be careful of hot sugar solution; it's hotter than boiling water.

Allow this to cool a bit, then tip in the raspberries and crush them with a potato masher or fork. Leave them to steep for 30 minutes or so, then strain the syrup into a bottle or jar.

Dilute to taste as a cordial – especially nice with sparkling water – or use as a syrup in cooking.

This doesn't keep as well as the elderflower cordial, maybe a week in the fridge, unless you pasteurise it. Raspberries themselves go mouldy quickly too; if you get a bargain box from the supermarket, this syrup is a good way to extend its usefulness.

You can use a variety of other flavourings in a basic sugar syrup. Instead of raspberries, infuse it with shredded fresh herbs such as basil, rosemary or lavender. Steep the herbs till the syrup cools to room temperature, then strain into a jar as above, and store in the fridge for up to a week.

Use these flavoured syrups to design your own cocktail recipes!

Seasonal salads

The summer salad is the equivalent of the winter stew in that you can use up small quantities of things before and after their main crop. Experiment with different combinations. Try grated carrot, or even whole baby carrots from your thinnings, mixed with chopped spring onions and radish. Sprouted seeds with fresh peas and parsley on a bed of salad leaves garnished with mint sounds good. Add nuts and fruit to the mixtures for extra variety.

Use a protein rich centrepiece for these salads, served cold. Pork pie, scotch egg, boiled egg, cold nut roast, quiche, ham slices, samosas. Pack up the meal and take it on a picnic!

Here's some salad recipes to celebrate the decadence of summer, using quite a few non-local and non-seasonal ingredients. You'd have to be an expert to raise cucumbers in June, and celery isn't usually ready till the autumn. Without the modern food distribution system, fresh oranges would be rare now.

Smoked trout and orange salad

300 grams (12 ounces) smoked trout, flaked
Half a thinly sliced cucumber
2 oranges chopped into bits
2 sticks of celery, sliced

A serving dish lined with lettuce, or other largish salad leaves. Mix the other ingredients and spoon in.

For a dressing: -
a tablespoon of grated apple
a tablespoon of lemon juice
2 tablespoons of mayonnaise

a tablespoon of creamed horseradish
Mix; dust with cayenne pepper

Red cabbage salad

100 grams (4 ounces) of red cabbage shredded finely
50 grams (2 ounces) grated carrot
50 grams (2 ounces) grated fresh beetroot, not pickled ones out of a jar
50 grams (2 ounces) raisins
50 grams (2 ounces) chopped walnuts

Mix in 3 tablespoons of French dressing, then toss in 3 tablespoons of salad cream or mayonnaise and sprinkle with fresh chopped parsley. Alternately, stir in 4 tablespoons of orange juice. This last version will keep in the fridge overnight.

This is a good way to get people to eat beetroot. You hardly know it's there.

Spinach, bacon and avocado salad

75 grams (3 ounces) of raw baby spinach leaves
6 rashers of crispy bacon, cut small
An avocado, peeled, sliced and dipped in lemon juice to stop it going brown
A few chopped walnuts

Mix everything together and serve.

For a dressing, combine : -
2 teaspoons lemon juice
2 tablespoons olive or walnut oil
Half a teaspoon of Dijon mustard
a pinch of black pepper.

Tuna pasta salad

1 can of tuna
1 can of sweetcorn
Cooked pasta to serve up to four, cooled to room temperature or below
2 tablespoons of mayonnaise

Drain the cans, mix everything together. This is a fast meal, and a good way of using up stores. Shred salad leaves into it or have a green salad on the side.

Falafels

1 tin of chickpeas from your stores – about 180 grams drained weight
1 clove of garlic, crushed
Half a teaspoon each of cumin, coriander, turmeric and cayenne pepper
1 teaspoon of lemon juice
2 tablespoons of gram flour
A little fresh parsley and chives, finely chopped
A pinch of salt and a touch of ground black pepper

Blend all the ingredients together, or mash the chickpeas up with a mortar and pestle first. You can pick out the skins then, which makes for a smoother finish.

Divide the mix up into balls, about the size of ping pong balls, and slightly flatten them. Pan fry in a little oil until golden brown. This recipe makes 6–8 falafels.

Serve with salad or a dipping sauce.

Braised broad beans

100 grams (4 ounces) of shelled broad beans; the pods are heavy, so this will be quite a lot
100 grams (4 ounces) of shelled peas
3–4 spring onions, chopped
1 small leafy lettuce, the sort that grows in your garden
50 grams (2 ounces) butter
1 rasher of smoked bacon, cut up small
300 ml (half a pint) of stock with a pinch each of sugar, salt and pepper added

Optional – 2 tablespoons of double cream and 2 tablespoons of very finely chopped chervil

Sweat the bacon in the melted butter, then add all the vegetables and cook for 5 minutes over a low heat, stirring. Add the stock, stir, bring to a gentle boil and cover. Simmer for 15 minutes, until most of the liquid has gone.

Remove from the heat, stir in the cream and chervil, serve at once.

Asparagus

This is an edible stem which has become a luxury food. It doesn't preserve well, so is relentlessly seasonal. You can grow it in an allotment or large garden; the plant requires a lot of space for a very short harvest. Its delicate fronds are rather decorative the rest of the summer though, and very colourful in autumn.

Cut the emerging stems at ground level before they are 20 centimetres (8 inches) long. Trim the thicker white end, which can be woody. Tie a bundle of about a dozen stems together with cotton string, not plastic, and put this into a large pan of boiling water.

Leave at a gentle but firm boil for 10 minutes, then take out your bundle and let it drain for a minute in a colander. Cut the string and serve with melted butter and salt, as a dish on its own.

Gooseberry and blackcurrant tart with sweet pastry

250 g (8 ounces) plain flour
125 g (4 ounces) butter chilled and chopped
70 g (3 ounces) caster sugar
1 egg yolk
1 tablespoon cold water
350 grams (12 ounces) fresh gooseberries
100 grams (4 ounces) fresh blackcurrants

Mix the flour and butter into breadcrumbs, stir in the sugar. Stir in the egg yolk and water and mix into a dough; use your hands if necessary. Turn this out onto a floured plate, knead very lightly, then wrap and chill for 30 minutes.

Prepare the gooseberries and blackcurrants by the tedious process of topping and tailing, cut the gooseberries in half and simmer the fruit gently in a pan with a little water for about 5 minutes. Turn off the heat and leave covered while you make the tart base.

Grease and flour a 20 centimetre (8 inches) tin. Roll the pastry out on a well-floured surface. Handle it carefully as it's stickier than savoury pastry and more inclined to split when you lift it, so roll it thicker than usual. Carefully lift into the tin, gently push down the base and trim the edges.

Cover the pastry with metal foil, held down with baking beans or raw pasta, and bake blind in a preheated low medium oven (Gas Mark 4; 180C;

350F) for 15 minutes. Strain the warm fruit, saving the juice, and stir in a little sugar to taste.

Fill the partly baked tart base, roll out some strips of left over pastry and lay these across the top. Fix them to the crust with a dab of water, brush them lightly with milk and sprinkle a little sugar over them.

Bake on the middle shelf of the low medium oven for about 20 minutes, until the sugar has started to brown. Serve with cream.

Whipped cream

It's nice to pour cream over puddings, but you can go one better and make it into a decorative topping by whipping. It's the butterfat content of the cream which determines how well it keeps its shape. Clotted cream is almost solid, with a 60% fat content; you'd use this as it comes. Double cream is about 48% butterfat and is the best for whipping. It's also called whipping cream, heavy cream or rich cream. Single cream won't work.

Chill everything before you start; the bowl, the whisk, the cream. If you're using an electric beater, start with a low speed and increase gradually to avoid splashes. Beat the cream until lifting the whisk out leaves soft peaks in the cream, which slowly fold over. If the cream starts to look buttery, you've overdone it.

Once these peaks form, it's ready to add to your dessert. For a more elaborate cream, you can add sugar – preferably sifted icing sugar – and flavourings. A dash of vanilla essence is nice, as is some liqueur, fruit syrup or cocoa powder. Stir it in carefully, so that the trapped air doesn't leave the mix.

The icing sugar will help the cream keep its shape. You can add gelatin (an animal product) for an even firmer finish. Dissolve a little in hot water and add it with the flavourings. Store whipped cream in a cold place, protected from flies, and eat it the same day.

Cheesecake

For a 20 centimetre (8 inches) round tin: -
200 grams (8 ounces) of digestive biscuits
100 grams (4 ounces) of butter, melted
125 grams (5 ounces) of cream cheese, such as Philadelphia
120 ml (4 fluid ounces) of double cream
90 grams (3 ounces) of caster sugar

Use a loose bottomed tin if you can

Crush the biscuits in a bag, using a rolling pin, stir into the melted butter and cover the base of the tin in a firm layer. Allow to cool.

Beat the cream cheese and sugar together until smooth. Whip the cream till it forms peaks, then fold this in carefully. Spoon the mix over the cooled base and leave in the fridge until ready to serve.

You can add various flavours to this basic mix, such as a capful of vanilla essence. For a firmer set, stir in some melted white chocolate, or find a recipe which uses gelatin.

Cream cheese is a soft cheese with a mild taste, made from milk and cream. It's not matured, so needs to be eaten fresh. Even so, it was first mass produced as early as 1872 by an American dairyman called William Lawrence. He called the brand 'Philadelphia' after the city, which had a reputation for quality foods.

Chapter Thirteen

July

One hopes for a hot and sunny July in Britain, but it can be wet and not very warm. In a dry summer, the large leaves of your maturing plants create shade to keep moisture in the soil; if it rains a lot, the dampness encourages mildews. Clear away some growth and try spraying affected leaves with a bicarbonate of soda solution. Tie plants up to let air circulate.

Main crop potatoes are in flower now; these are surprisingly pretty. The green seeds which follow, looking like tiny tomatoes, are poisonous, and divert energy from the roots, so pick them off. Borage flowers are very popular with bees, and a lovely shade of blue. Arum berries show as flame orange among hedges; birds can eat them but you can't.

A resilience garden is colourful as well as useful!

An allotment can be difficult to manage in June with the heavy watering. By July, the mature plants are better able to protect themselves from drying out with deep roots and broad shady leaves. Use their natural defences to save you work.

Permaculture

Wild plants have worked out their relationships with local climate over thousands of years. They're not very productive from a human viewpoint though. Remember those hunter gatherers needed hundreds of acres to forage from.

Gardening is the process of creating your own small ecosystem, populated only by the flowers and vegetables you want to grow there. In the developed world, the appearance of a garden often takes precedence over its usefulness. In the name of tidiness, the land is drenched in pesticides in concentrations that would make the most industrialised farmer wince. Soil micro-organisms and helpful animals are collateral damage in a culture which only values pretty flowers, well-shaped vegetables and lawns of grass so short it may as well be AstroTurf.

There's a new cultivation ethos emerging however. Permaculture and forest gardening work with natural systems to grow a selection of plants which work well together. Once established, these plots produce food in a pleasant, natural environment. There's very little effort or expense involved. The plants are expected to sort themselves out regarding pests and water, though you can help them to cope. It's only fair.

Your yields aren't as high, but the growing area as a whole is far more resilient. Vegetables aren't grown in neat rows, but scattered throughout the plot. The harvest is spread over a longer period, as plants get different amounts of sunshine and nutrients. You can pick enough for daily meals over several weeks rather than having to deal with a sudden glut. Use the selective weeding techniques to encourage self-seeding, and you can end up with an impressive array of food plants.

There's a lot of information online about permaculture; some good books as well. To become an expert, able to assess a new piece of ground and design a plan, you'd really need to take a course. Applying the knowledge to your own garden is much easier and the practical skills gained will help you understand more advanced techniques.

Annuals, perennials and self-seeding

Using your journal, observe and take notes. You're supposed to do this for a whole year before starting to plant, but until you start growing you won't really know what you're looking at. Try things out. Perpetual onions work more like giant chives than the familiar bulb onions, but they add the same flavour to a recipe. Fruit bushes provide shade; established around the edges they can shelter wildlife from cats. There's a project in Bristol to link a number of gardens using 'wildlife corridors' and encourage the return of hedgehogs, those useful slug-eaters.

Permaculture uses more perennials than annuals. Perennial plants continue growing year after year, even though the top part may vanish during the winter. You harvest leaves, fruit or seeds as you need them. Edible roots mainly come from bi-annual plants; you sow in spring, the plant gathers energy from the sun over the summer and builds up a carbohydrate store in its roots. As its foliage dies away ready for the winter, this store is at its maximum; that's when you dig it up.

Left alone, the plant will use this to grow again in spring, faster and taller than before. This is its flowering phase; this year it will seed and die. Annual plants – peas, for example – complete their cycle in a single year. They're often good at self-seeding. Observing vegetables through their whole life-cycle allows you to study the survival strategies left over from their wild ancestors.

Spinach will grow to a tremendous height, then fall over, crushing the surrounding plants in order to reduce competition for its seedlings. A rocket patch expands around the edges; they are brassicas, a hungry lot, and the old plants have used up all the nutrients.

Resilience gardening also calls for leaving plants to go to seed. Dry stems are left standing; solitary bees like to overwinter in them. Your garden doesn't look like a picture in a catalogue.

This may lead to complaints from your neighbours or landlord. If you know the purpose of each plant, each pile of debris and each patch of weeds, you can defend your practices. Permaculture is not the same as idle neglect but you may need to compromise, depending on your situation.

Other gardeners have cause to complain if you host a lot of dandelions or willowherb, whose windblown seeds will lodge in their patches. They should be grateful if you decide to cultivate nettles though. They provide that important food reserve for aphid predators. Urban ecology is quite a new concept. Consider putting up a small notice explaining what you're doing.

'No Dig' gardening and fungal networks

There's a lot of debate about no-dig gardening. Instead of digging in compost to nourish the soil, you simply spread it on top and let the worms mix it in. You clear weeds with a hoe – obviously you're allowed to dig up the roots of invasive ones – and leave them to rot on the soil, or compost them. No-dig methods work very well with raised beds, but you can also apply them at ground level.

Most people think of fungi only in terms of the visible mushrooms or toadstools, but these are merely the fruits springing from a huge underground system of roots, or mycelium. Recent studies have revealed some astonishing properties of these fungal networks. They can carry nutrients between plants, and generally attend to the health of an ecosystem in other surprising ways.

These mycelia grow slowly but persistently; some are thousands of years old. Digging the top layer of soil is going to break these up. Experimental growers, such as Charles Dowding, have found no-dig methods produce larger crops, even on a commercial basis. There's a lot to be explored in gardening!

Forest Gardening

A forest is clearly a no-dig situation. You can tell an ancient woodland by its smell of fungi in the autumn. Wild forests used to be extensive in Britain; they were an important source of animal fodder, firewood and forage. Many were cut down for fuel at the start of the Industrial Revolution; there are few left now.

However, there is a revival of interest in tree planting. With a careful mix of species, a whole variety of nuts, fruit and ground floor edibles can be established. A fully formed forest garden has up to seven layers of productivity.

You don't need acres of land to explore this technique. A single fruit tree – even hawthorn – can provide the nucleus. Plant wild garlic around the trunk. It comes up early and is finished before the new leaves shade it out. Put low fruit bushes, like blackcurrants, a bit further out so they can get more sunshine. That's a three-layer forest garden!

In my Resilience Garden, there's a conventional plot for annual vegetables close to the outside tap. Around the edges and out of the way I keep trees, bushes and other perennials. They need much less watering. I like to keep the remaining lawn quite long; even allowing the grasses to go to seed. Wild meadows are another shrinking habitat.

Some seasonal foods available in July

Blackcurrants, cherries, plums, raspberries and strawberries.
Herbs, edible flowers and salad leaves are flourishing.
Early potatoes.
Carrot thinnings, radish from regular new sowings, early runner bean pods.
Meat from chickens, lamb and small game.
Eggs and dairy produce.

Hydroponics

Permaculture and forest gardening follow the ways of nature to produce food. Other innovative cultivation methods rely on the appliance of science to increase crops while reducing labour costs.

Hydroponics is the technique of growing plants without soil. Photosynthesis uses sunlight, and the green chlorophyll in leaves, to combine carbon dioxide with water. This produces sugar, which the plant uses for energy and growth, and gives off oxygen. In a similar way to animals, plants also need various minerals and other nutrients, in a soluble form, to remain healthy.

These are found in a good soil, but the roots need to seek them out. A hydroponic system uses an inert growing medium, like clay pebbles, just to hold the plants upright. Water with nutrients in exactly the right mix is delivered direct to the roots. The leaves and fruits develop faster, get bigger.

There's less water wastage, and no need for crop rotation. With added light and heat, hydroponics can work in a totally artificial environment. Unusual growing spaces can be exploited, such as derelict urban infrastructure or deserts. Large scale hydroponic farms are encouraged by the high yields and production of seasonal vegetables on demand.

Intensive cultivation often suffers from outbreaks of pest or disease. These are often treated with chemicals, which means the product won't be organic. There's toxic waste to dispose of, and current systems often rely on fossil fuels.

Aquaponics

Aquaponics combines fish farming with hydroponics. The nutrients needed by the plants are provided by edible fish; the plants clean up the water in the fish pond. No pesticides or artificial fertilisers can be added, as they will kill the fish. Produce from an aquagarden is generally organic.

You can set up a small aquaponic system in your garden; it takes up no more room than a pond. There's no digging, and you can take it with you. Ornamental fish are just as effective at supplying nutrients as the edible tilapia, trout or perch are. Flowers absorb them as well as vegetables do. Use a small solar powered pump to circulate the water; you need to add more occasionally to compensate for evaporation.

Both hydroponics and aquaponics can produce large crops in small spaces. They're ideal for urban ecosystems. A future city could even support a low-meat or vegan diet using its own local produce combined with preserved foods bought in bulk. Keeping and feeding animals larger than fish would be more complicated.

Urban food production
Incredible Edible Todmorden, based near Manchester in Britain, are pioneers of edible urban landscapes created by and for the community.

Their iconic vegetable plots in the yard of the local police station have inspired countless other projects. Many cities now boast beds of cabbage, onions or tomatoes, tended by small bands of volunteers. Notices tell people when the vegetables are ready for picking; these are public Resilience Gardens!

Rooftop beekeeping and vertical gardening are other ways to provide food in a city as its hinterland contracts from global to local. Selective breeding can produce plants adapted to urban life. It's better to let them work it out for themselves than to interfere using genetic modification. They've been plants for a long time and know what they like.

Organic growing methods are important in a city ecosystem. Chemicals washed into waste water increase the cost of processing it. Pesticides can't be sprayed over a wide area. Urban permaculture requires new approaches to food as a whole.

Recipes for July

Chicken curry

One free range organic chicken breast, cut into small chunks
1 onion, chopped
4 cloves of garlic, sliced
1 red chilli, chopped (optional – add more for a hotter curry)
1 teaspoon of cumin seeds
1 teaspoon each of coriander and garam masala
A tablespoon of oil, preferably coconut
100 grams (4 ounces) of creamed coconut, or a tin of coconut milk
3 tablespoons of tomato puree
150 ml (5 fluid ounces) of stock – use hot water and one stock cube

Optional extras: -
A 2 centimetre (one inch) cube of ginger
1 teaspoon each of fenugreek seed and black onion seed
One small red pepper, chopped
Half a dozen mushrooms, quartered
A few young runner bean pods cut into inch lengths
A small handful of shredded leaves, such as kale or borage; these are added towards the end

Sauté the onions, garlic and ginger in half of the coconut oil. Dry fry the seeds in a separate pan until you can smell them, then crush and add to the onion. Add the chilli and the rest of the spices, remove from the heat and stir in the tomato puree and stock.

Lightly fry the chicken and other vegetables in the rest of the coconut oil. Add to the spice mix and simmer, uncovered, for 10 minutes.

Add the coconut milk, or creamed coconut, bring back to the boil and continue to simmer for another 30 minutes. Stir regularly and top up with more water if needed to stop it sticking – use a pan with a thick base.

Serve topped with sprigs of fresh coriander.

To use red meat, about 200 grams (8 ounces) will do for two people; less if you include more vegetables. Fry it for a little longer than you would do chicken; until it is brown all over.

Mushroom curry

250 grams (8 ounces) of mushrooms, sliced thin
1 onion, chopped
2 cloves of garlic, crushed
1 teaspoon each of garam masala and ground coriander
1 teaspoon of cumin seeds
Half a teaspoon of ground ginger
2 teaspoons of paprika
2 teaspoons of plain flour
2 tablespoons oil
1 can of chopped tomatoes
1 tablespoon of tomato paste

Optional seasonal garden produce, such as red peppers, courgettes or celery, cut small

Sauté the mushrooms, onion and garlic in the oil for 5 minutes, along with any other vegetable odds and ends you're including, except for shredded leaves which always go in towards the end of cooking. Add the spices, stir well and lightly fry for another 5 minutes. Sprinkle the flour over to coat everything and move the pan off the heat.

Sieve the tomatoes, stir in the juice and the tomato paste, crumble in the stock cube. Return to the boil and simmer gently, uncovered, for 15 minutes. Add more water if the sauce looks like sticking.

Transfer to a casserole dish, cover and bake in a low medium oven (Gas Mark 4; 180C; 350F) for 30 minutes.

Serve with rice and sauces.
If you don't use the whole can of tomatoes, store any left overs in a china dish with a lid. Tomato products react with the metal in tins once they are opened, and quickly acquire a nasty acidic taste.

Spiced potatoes

250 grams (half a pound) of cooked potatoes, preferably new ones, cut quite small
1 small onion, chopped
2 cloves of garlic, thinly sliced
1 small red chilli, finely chopped
1 teaspoon of cumin seeds
1 teaspoon of medium curry powder
1 tablespoon oil
a pinch of salt

Cut the potatoes into chunks about 2 centimetres (one inch) squarish.

Fry the onion and garlic in oil for 5 minutes, then add the seeds and fry gently for another 5 minutes, stirring often. Continue to stir as you add the curry powder and a tablespoon of water; cook for a further 2 minutes.

Tip in the cooked potatoes. Stir fry these until they are well coated in the mixture and warmed through; about 10 minutes. Add a little water from time to time to prevent sticking. Try mixing in a tablespoon of chutney at this stage.

Serve with curry and a cooling sauce.

Cucumber raita

125 grams (5 ounces) of natural yogurt
1 tablespoon of fresh mint leaves, chopped very fine
A chunk of fresh cucumber, about 3 centimetres (a generous inch) long
A pinch of salt and a touch of black pepper

Peel and coarsely grate the cucumber. Mix all the ingredients together and serve with curry.

Potato salad

150 grams (6 ounces) of new potatoes
3 tablespoons of mayonnaise
A handful of garden chives, chopped small
Boil some new potatoes, let them cool and cut into chunks. Mix the chives with the mayonnaise in a cool bowl and stir in the potatoes.

Store in the fridge and eat the same day.

Early potatoes were important to fill the hunger gap in July before the new grain harvest, which could be a very lean month for villagers depending on grain stores. They arrived from the newly discovered Americas in Elizabethan times, and were soon a staple crop.

Unfortunately, not being native plants, they can be vulnerable to disease. Digging up and using a few of your own potatoes before the main crop is ready will show you if there's a problem developing.

Coleslaw

A quarter of a white cabbage head
2 medium carrots
A medium onion
3 tablespoons of mayonnaise

Chop all the vegetables finely and mix together well, then stir in the mayonnaise and serve. It's best eaten freshly made.

This recipe makes quite a lot, and the size of the onion is the limiting factor. Use half the onion in another dish at the same time – burgers or quiche, for example – and you can make less. Carrots and cabbage keep better once cut than onions do.

A slaw is a mix of any finely chopped or grated raw vegetable, bound together with mayonnaise. Coleslaw is specifically cabbage, carrot and onion, but you can use the principle to invent your own combination.

Thousand Island dressing

3 tablespoons of mayonnaise
1 teaspoon of tomato paste
Half a teaspoon of paprika

Mix together. This is the sauce you find on prawn cocktails.

Pork steak with pepper

2 small pork steaks, not too thick
1 onion, chopped
1 teaspoon of crushed or milled black peppercorns
1 teaspoon of Worcester sauce
1 tablespoon lemon juice
4 tablespoons of double cream
1 rounded teaspoon of butter
1 tablespoon of brandy (optional)

Gently fry the onions and peppercorns in the butter for 5 minutes, stirring constantly. Add the steaks to the pan and cook to taste, turning often.

The juice from the thickest part of the meat should run clear, as with chicken. Unlike beef, undercooked pork can be dangerous. A loin steak will take around 15 minutes; a thicker chop more like 20 minutes.

Stir in the Worcester sauce, lemon juice, double cream and brandy. Heat gently without letting the sauce boil; serve straight away with mashed potatoes and greens.

Strawberry trifle

Some cake – this is a good way to use up stale cake; scrape off the icing first
Fresh strawberries, washed and drained
A packet of strawberry jelly
Custard – a tin from stores, or make your own
A small carton of double cream, whipped
A scattering of borage petals

Break the cake up into 2 inch (6 centimetre) chunks to loosely cover the bottom of your chosen bowl. You can buy packets of special trifle cake, which has a long shelf life, or forage a sell-by bargain.

Remove the hulls – the green bits – from the strawberries and cut them in half or quarters. Dot these around the cake and pour the made up jelly over it all. Use a little less water than the packet suggests; about three quarters. Leave this to set firm, covered, in a cool place; it will take a few hours.

Next, spoon a layer of custard on top. If you've made your own – it's easy, using custard powder, sugar and milk – let it cool first. Then add the final layer, the whipped cream, and serve.

The exact quantities are determined by the size of your bowl. To use all the jelly and a full tin of custard, make the trifle in the sort of large bowl you'd use for making bread, but this is a lot for one person as it should be eaten on the day it's made. Trifle is really a party food; serve it after the barbecue!

Creme fraiche tarts

Make some jam tart cases and bake them blind for 15 minutes in a preheated medium oven (Gas Mark 5; 190C; 375F); check them after 10 minutes. It's handy to do this while something else – such as a quiche – is in the oven already. Let them cool right down.

Spoon a dollop of crème fraiche into each and top with jam. If your summer fruit jam ended up a bit runny, this is ideal.

To make crème fraiche, special bacteria are added to pasteurised cream. It's matured for a day or so, kept in a fridge. The original French method used unpasteurised cream which naturally contained these bacteria.

You can make your own crème fraiche using double cream and buttermilk; there are recipes online. Take food hygiene seriously when dealing with dairy products.

Blackcurrant syrup

Fresh blackcurrants (300 grams; 10 ounces)
A litre of water (2 pints)
A kilo bag of plain white sugar (about two pounds)

Three clean swing top bottles, preferably sterilised

As the blackcurrant harvest reaches its peak, you may end up with quite a lot. This recipe dispenses with the tedious process of topping and tailing the fruit.

Just wash and crush the blackcurrants. Add them to the water in a large pan, bring to the boil and simmer for 20 minutes. Allow to cool down a bit then strain the juice in a sieve and measure it.
Discard the fruit pulp.

If you press the fruit in the sieve too enthusiastically, you may end up with a fruit jelly rather than syrup. Stand the bottles in warm water to turn it into a liquid again, so you can pour it out. Process it into something else, like jam.

Add a pound of sugar for every pint of juice; a kilo of sugar for every litre. You probably won't need the whole bag. Mix the sugar in well, then reheat the syrup to a gentle boil and simmer carefully for 20 minutes, stirring often. Take care with hot syrup, especially if there are small children around.

Cool, then pour into the bottles, using a funnel. Fill them to within an inch of the lid, no lower. Use partly filled ones within a week, storing them in the fridge. A full, unopened bottle should keep for at least a fortnight in a cool place.

After that, unless you've pasteurised it, it may ferment which causes a build up of gas. Ordinary screw top bottles might break under the pressure. Sometimes a mould may develop where the syrup meets the air; bottle necks are made narrow to reduce this point of contact. If you're in survival mode, strain this out and reboil the syrup.

This recipe can be used for other fruits, such as elderberries. Adjust the amounts depending on your taste preferences and availability of the fruit.

The ratio of sugar to liquid must stay the same, although it seems like a lot of sugar. The syrup will definitely go mouldy if you use less; besides it's diluted with water before being drunk.

On the positive side, you aren't using any artificial sweeteners or preservatives. At least you know where you are with sugar.

Raspberry jam

Half a kilo (one pound) of raspberries, washed and patted dry, with any stalks removed. Frozen fruit is fine, as long as most of the juice is drained off
Granulated sugar (half a kilo; one pound). You can use preserving sugar here, as this fruit needs the extra pectin
Juice of a lemon
A small knob of butter (optional; for settling the froth which rises to the surface. You can scoop this froth off instead)

Tip the fruit into a large pan, add the sugar and the lemon juice. Heat this gently, stirring, till the sugar has dissolved. Then bring it to a rolling boil, paying the usual careful attention to this hot sugar solution, for 15 minutes.

Pay careful attention if you are making these small quantities of jam. If your pan is too thin, it can easily start to burn. Take it off the heat if it does, and test for set. If you've used extra pectin, it may be ready after only 5 minutes.

If not, pour into a clean pan and reboil until done.

As with the marmalade, you need some china saucers cooling in the icebox to test the jam for setting. Take a teaspoonful of jam out and drop it on the cold saucer. Allow it to cool for a minute, then poke the surface. If it wrinkles, it's probably done. If not, keep the jam at the rolling boil and test again every five minutes until it's ready to set.

Let cool a little, then transfer to warmed, sterilised jars; have about half a dozen ready. Work on a tray, use a jug and funnel to fill the jars; this is messy. Leave a little space between the acidic jam and the metal lid, only about a centimetre (half an inch).

Wipe round the tops of the jars and put the lids on while the jam is hot, then leave them to cool down before you wash off their sides. Dry the jars and label them; store in a cool place, and in the fridge once opened.

Raspberries, like many summer fruits, are low in pectin. You may struggle to get your jam to set; it can still be used in puddings as a fruit syrup.

Add pectin by using preserving sugar, or make your own from lemon pips. Saving these in the freezer as you encounter them is easier than trying to find them at short notice. Put a tablespoon of these pips in a saucer of water overnight. Discard the pips and add the liquid to your jam recipe. Or tie the pips up in a muslin bag and put them in the pan while cooking.

Citrus fruits are very high in pectin, which is one of the reasons you often see lemon juice added to a jam recipe. In the days before easy access to fresh oranges and lemons, making summer fruit jam was quite a skill. Native fruits with a good pectin content include apples, crabapples, gooseberries, currants and quince.

Dehydrating fruit

Soft summer fruits don't keep well so they have to be eaten or preserved quickly. Freezing isn't always satisfactory. You might not have time to attend to jams or syrups, or you might not want to use so much sugar. Try dehydrating the fruit.

Oven drying is generally more expensive, and less effective, than using a dehydrator. These come in a variety of sizes and prices, and are quite a large piece of kitchen equipment. They run on electricity; each session takes an average of 24 hours, and costs around £1 depending on your provider. Look up product reviews online if you're considering a purchase.

Of course, if you had your own off grid system, it'd be free. You'd be running dehydrators in the summer to use up surplus solar power, as housewives of old used to cook things just because the fire was lit in the winter.

If you're interested in advanced learning, you can even make your own dehydrated survival meals to take on your foraging weekends. Beware, because you will have left the realm of safe sell-by dates; do your research, and avoid experimenting with rice.

Interlude

Lammas

It's difficult to see the 1st of August as the start of autumn, but it's soon going to be six weeks since the sun turned back south at the summer solstice. The evenings aren't quite so long and, by the end of the month, there's the hint of chill in the dawn air.

Summer weather lingers on into autumn, but the long hot days are coming to an end. By Autumn Equinox, around the 21st of September, the sun is only in the sky for twelve hours. Britain's northern latitude means that it stays light for a bit longer than it does at the equator. We have dawn and dusk due to the angle of the sun's rays.

With cooler weather and shorter days comes a flurry of activity across Nature. Once this would have been your busiest time of year as you gathered, stored and preserved. Plants and animals prepared their food stores for winter, and so did you. Unlike the gentler pace of Spring, with its emphasis on delicate young things, the work of autumn was intense.

Well fed and rested, you harvested to the limit of your resources. The months of leisure ushered in by Beltane ended with Lammas. Today, it's as obscure as Imbolc; the importance of these festivals in the farming calendar is lost on city dwellers.

Before potatoes were introduced to Northern Europe, the grain harvest was crucial to communities living from the land. Stored grain was their only source of carbohydrate in summer; it might be running low by July. As people eked out the last of their flour, they would anxiously watch their new crop maturing. Threatened by storms, diseases, wild animals – their hopes for the coming year could be destroyed overnight.

As soon as the wheat or barley was ready and the weather favourable, it was scythed down and hauled off to dry. The grains were beaten out by threshing, separated from the husks by winnowing, then ground up by milling. It was a very physical activity – the folk song 'John Barleycorn' describes how it felt like a battle!

Some early Lammas customs actually involved a ritual fight between Lugh, the harvest god, and the demons of blight. Lammas celebrations were as excitable as Beltane, but with a strange edginess. The hopes and fears of Imbolc have crystallised into practical reality; the wheel has spun and the winnings collected. Winter is coming to test your resilience.

As well as the bonfires, feasting, storytelling, trading and gossip of a large festival, Lammas often featured athletic contests, horse racing and other extreme sports. Of all the cross-quarter days, it was the hardest to schedule. The name probably derives from 'Loaf-mass' and featured the first loaf made from the new grain. It'd make sense to celebrate after the harvest was secured, but organised religion requires a set calendar regardless of nature. As Lammas was tied to August 1st, the custom compromised with a gift of wheat ears – these didn't have to be actually ripe!

In a more fluid society, Lammas was often held around the first full moon of August. The lunar cycle was in tune with crop growth; the extra light helped the weary but excited harvesters travel to the feast. It could be as late as mid-August, but no later. The grains and the hay may be gathered in, but there was plenty other harvesting to be done back at the farm.

The long summer holidays of British schools reflect these old connections with agriculture. Even after the Industrial Revolution, many families left town and spent August camping out to help with the harvest. We should retain this possibility as part of a national resilience strategy, rather than impose an artificial timetable on the school year.

Chapter Fourteen

August

British people are notorious for talking about the weather. This is because it's so changeable. The country is on the edge of the Atlantic Ocean, so winds from the west bring rain and storms. The great land mass of Eurasia to the east sends cold dry winds from the Siberian north; hot dry winds come from the desert south. These weather fronts often collide over the British Isles, producing an interesting and unpredictable mix.

The gardener has the challenge of this lucky dip weather to deal with every year. August may be hot and dry; it may be cool with long spells of torrential rain. You can rely on at least one period of sunny weather during summer, and there is usually some rain. You just don't know when. The ideal mix is sunshine with a gentle rain just before dawn every few days; these clement conditions occur more than the non-gardener might realise.

Preparing to harvest

August is the beginning of the harvest season. The asparagus, soft fruits, salads and early potatoes – they were just to keep you going. The next round of produce is for preserving as well.

If it's been wet, dig up your potatoes before the slugs get the tubers. As the spuds develop, the leaves wither and die, so you can tell if they're ready. Sort out your compost heap ready to add more vegetation; have some manure or soil conditioner to hand for feeding bare ground before the autumn sowings of rocket and winter kale.

Use some of the cleared space to plant out the leeks you sowed in March. They should be about as thick as pencils now. Broccoli and cabbage seedlings can be transplanted too; they'll need a lot of room for their next stage.

Pick baby runner beans and courgettes as they form; these delicious micro-vegetables are a luxury only available to gardeners. Thin out the tomato crop and pick any which are ripe. If you have pumpkin or squash, make sure they have plenty of room. Their long tendrils can expand into cleared areas, but keep them from smothering your winter vegetables.

Collect the jars and bottles you may need for jams, syrups, wines and chutneys. You'll find a large stainless-steel pan, a wooden spoon and a metal sieve useful too. Tidy up your freezer to make more room; if it needs defrosting do it now before the final round of fruit comes in.

Pests

While you were on holiday, those pretty white butterflies have used your brassicas as a nursery. Even if their yellow and black caterpillars have eaten the leaves down to the bone, the plants may still recover. You don't harvest them until after winter, when these pests are long gone.

Give your plants a helping hand by donning rubber gloves and picking off the caterpillars. You'll have to kill them; squish them with a pinch and drop them into a bucket of water. If you release them they will return, or perish miserably from starvation. Most caterpillars can only eat a few types of leaves.

Ones that they do like are nasturtium. These sprawling stems with edible flowers and large tender leaves flourish in August. Grow them close to your brassicas, which encourages the butterflies to lay there instead. Some years, this works really well. However, the price of purple sprouting broccoli in February is vigilance in August.

What strategies can you use to protect and nurture your vegetable crops? Should you mulch against a shortage of water, or keep the ground bare to discourage slugs? You can always deploy the bran again, which is a somewhat expensive way of doing both. To encourage your vegetables towards a successful harvest, you need to respond to prevailing conditions. As you walk on the paths among the plants, applying water to their roots, watch out for signs of pest attack.

Take notes, print some photos for your journal, search out organic solutions on the internet. If a plant looks like it's losing, it may be best to dig it up and bin it. Don't add sick plants to your compost heap. Where slugs are the problem, leave the chewed remains in place as a distraction while you prepare counter measures.

Wild birds are a big help in controlling your insect pests all year, but they can ravage your fruit crops. Protect these with wire netting. Birds become entangled in soft nets draped over bushes. Watch out for signs of rabbit and deer if you live in a rural area. You may need to enclose your garden if your wild areas attract these larger animals.

Pleasure

Gardening isn't all hard work; far from it. It's mainly watching things grow. A resilience garden is particularly designed for the leisurely cultivation of friendly and co-operative plants. Vegetables aren't just a uniform dull green either. The white flowers of rocket and peas brighten up the spring, followed by the lovely pink of radish. Blue flowering borage contrasts with the vivid summer oranges of marigolds and nasturtiums. The large yellow courgette flowers mark the transition into autumn.

Stroll down garden paths scented with lavender, lemon balm and mint, picking leaves for your herb tea. Watch the butterflies on your nettle patch. Gather watercress from your solar powered water feature, nibble on nasturtium flowers. Relax in the sunshine listening to the humming bees. A low maintenance resilience garden is more interesting than a lawn, and far more useful.

Some seasonal foods available in August

New potatoes and small tender root vegetables.
Courgettes and runner beans.
Borage and wild herbs.
Cherries, blackcurrants, plums.
Early tomatoes, cucumbers, salad leaves and onions.
Fresh lamb, beef, chicken and pork – but it's not the season for bacon, ham and sausages.
A variety of wild meat.
Eggs, cheeses and dairy products.
Grains and flour – the new harvest is coming in!

Foraging

August is a popular month for holidays. It's a good time to test your resilience by camping out. Once you've mastered living in a tent on a site with facilities, you're ready to try out a survival weekend. Not all of these involve yomping up Snowdonia. Many teach you simple woodland living and ancient crafts. You can spend time with expert foragers, make your own string from nettles, chip out a stone knife, cook on an open fire. Study the equipment brought by experienced participants; there's quite a range available.

There's a lot you can learn from camping, but for now we'll look at developing food-related skills. Hunting and foraging are complex and difficult crafts. It's not enough just to read about them. You need to do field work. If a long stay in the woods isn't possible, try a day course. Take the bus out to a nature reserve, or follow a footpath walk across country.

Edible wild plants are a key feature of the Resilience Garden. It's important to observe them in their natural environment. August is a good time for the beginner to test their knowledge. All the leaves, many flowers, even some seeds, are on display. Plant identification is easy.

Sometimes, however, the plant is most useful for food during a season when its obvious features aren't present. Wild garlic leaves are only above ground in spring, but the edible bulbs are present underground all year. So are the poisonous bulbs of bluebell and cuckoo pint, which grow in the same places. How can you learn to tell them apart?

It's illegal to dig up wild plants without the permission of the landowner, as well as threatening an important food reserve. Here's where your miniature forest garden comes in handy. Plant all three, in the ground if you want to live dangerously, or in pots to prevent them spreading and getting mixed up. Bury the lower two thirds of the pots to better reproduce their natural environment; the cool, moist shade of a tree.

Once you've got your specimens going well, you can dig up and compare the bulbs at your leisure. They really are quite different, except in the first year of growth. Once the roots are about pea-sized, their identifying features are clear, as you need to see for yourself. Much the same can be done for any wild edible. Recreate its natural conditions, get the plant established and then harvest some of it to experiment with recipes.

Try cultivating burdock for its starchy roots – a lifesaver in winter. The early leaves are quite similar to foxglove. Once you're familiar with both, you'd no more mistake them than you would confuse Nokia with Nike. Country folk of old could read the landscape better than you can navigate a supermarket.

Don't underestimate your experience with common garden weeds. Edibles such as dock, dandelion, nettles, groundsel, plantain, willowherb, yarrow and bittercress all feature in the wild, especially on the edges of cultivation. Learn the meaning of the landscape as you go for a walk. Use plants as clues to history. If you want to play detective, get yourself a copy of the fascinating book 'How to Read the Landscape' by Patrick Whitefield.

There are probably animals around too, though you're unlikely to see any but birds. If there's mud, look for paw prints. Thorny bushes can snag a few strands of hair. Small paths may wind across a field, vanishing into a hedgerow. How easy is it to get close to a wild animal?

Survival skills

Mastering the art of twisting cord from natural materials is up there with fire and stone tools. String made from nettle stems is strong enough for a bow. You can also equip yourself with nets, fishing lines and snares. These ancient crafts are part of your heritage and ought to be learned even if you never expect to use them in a survival situation.

Finding food isn't much good if you don't know how to eat it. Treat foraged roots much like parsnip. Tender leaves go in a salad or garnish; tougher ones are steamed like cabbage. Seeds are generally ground or crushed. Fruit is eaten raw or lightly stewed. Always cook wild meats thoroughly.

Once you get the hang of campfire cooking, it's possible to devise an oven for baking. Meanwhile, cooking on a barbecue is a good start, and will get you through a few days of mains outage if you have a safe place to use it.

Fire safety

I was brought up in houses with open fires. Few people are, these days. There's quite a bit to learn about lighting them and keeping them going. Meanwhile, here's some tips to stay alive.

Fire can burn you. Don't lean over it in wafty clothes. Tie your hair back. Be careful picking up metal objects, like pans, which are close to the fire as they can be very hot.

Fire can spread. Don't light fires unless you know what you're doing and have a current permission from the landowner. The surrounding area may be too dry to risk it. Flying sparks can set fire to tents pitched too close. There should be room for a ring of chairs around the fire, and for people to pass behind these, before the nearest tent.

Some fuels give off poisonous fumes. Don't burn laurel or rhododendron, plastics or artificial wood. Fresh wood torn from living trees won't burn. You need to look on the ground for dry fallen branches.

Ideally, a fire should be lit on bare ground or short grass. If this can't be done, either avoid concrete and tarmac surfaces, or keep your fire on a sheet of metal, held up with bricks. Avoid using galvanised metal.

Recipes for August

Beans and sardines

A tin of baked beans
A tin of sardines in tomato sauce. Drain them if they're in brine or oil
Some bread

Going camping? Travelling light? This meal is tasty, nutritious and only needs a single pan. Break up the sardines into the beans and heat through. Serve in bowls with bread, or have some baked potatoes ready.

Gipsy toast

For each person: -

Two large slices of bread
An egg
A half eggshell of milk

Another quick and easy camping recipe. Heat a little oil in a frying pan. Mix the egg and milk in a shallow bowl. One at a time, lay the bread slices flat in this mixture, turn over to soak the other side and flip into the hot oil. Let it sizzle for a minute, turn to seal the other side and cook for a few minutes on each side, turning often.

Serve at once, with tomato ketchup and a pinch of salt.

Gammon and pineapple

2 gammon steaks
1 tablespoon of made English mustard
1 tablespoon of soft, light brown sugar
1 small can of pineapple rings, preferably in juice not syrup

Find an oven tin which fits under your grill, or line the clean grill pan with silver foil. Lay the gammon steaks on this, and pour the mixed mustard, sugar and juice from the can over them.

Grill for 10 minutes, then turn the steaks over and spoon the liquid over the other half. Cook for another 10 minutes, then put a pineapple ring on top of each steak and grill until these are browning; serve.

Hash brown potatoes

250 grams (half a pound) of peeled, cooked potatoes
15 grams (half an ounce) of butter
1 tablespoon of vegetable oil
A pinch of salt

The potatoes should be quite firm, not fluffy, as you have to grate them. If they're not, make potato scones or something instead.

Heat the butter and oil in a large, thick bottomed frying pan, stir in the coarsely grated potatoes, add salt. Use a fish slice, press the potatoes into a round cake and fry gently for 15 minutes. Turn over and cook the other side until brown.

Traditional bubble and squeak is a similar dish. Mix mashed potatoes and a bit of fried onion with a medley of cooked vegetables left over from the night before, especially cabbage. Tip the mix into a frying pan with a little warm oil and press it into a large burger shape. Turn up the heat and fry on both sides until it's heated right through and the outside is browning.

This makes rather a loose cake, difficult to flip over, so it tends to come out very greasy since the oil gets well mixed in. It's good for fuelling a long day's hiking!

Burgers

The weather's warm; you don't want to be stuck in the kitchen making elaborate meals over a hot cooker. It's the season for barbecues and picnic foods. Burgers are quick and easy; serve in a bun with salad.

250 grams (half a pound) of beef mince
Optional tablespoon of fried onions, done a little brown
Optional egg for binding

If I'm working with raw meat, I use a china plate rather than the wooden chopping board, as it's easier to clean. Wash your hands and all utensils as soon as the meat is ready for cooking, and before you go touching the pan handle.

Squish the mince into two burger shapes. They'll hold together if you handle them carefully, but you can bind the mix with a beaten egg for greater firmness. This is recommended if you're adding the onions. Heat a little oil in a frying pan and slide the burgers in with a spatula.

Cook gently for 10 minutes each side, flipping them over from time to time. The oil should be quite shallow so it doesn't splash you. Don't wander off when you're frying food; it might burn or even catch fire.

Grilling is safer and healthier, but needs a bit more managing. The grill tray may be too far from the heat and cook really slowly; if you put the burgers on a baking tray, they may be too close and get scorched. Every grill is different, but you soon get the hang of your own one.

Everything you expect in a salad is available now, even tomatoes and cucumber. Regular small sowings provide you with spring onions and fresh leaves. Only radish is out of season; this is its flowering time, and you'll have trouble persuading it otherwise.

Add a selection of salad vegetables and sauces to burger buns or wraps for quick summer meals.

Tomato ketchup

Commonly known as tomato sauce.

500 grams (half a pound) of tomatoes
1 medium onion, chopped
A couple of cloves of garlic, finely chopped
50 ml of good white vinegar (2 fluid ounces)
50 grams (2 ounces) of golden caster sugar
1 tablespoon of tomato puree
A pinch each of spices to taste – coriander, allspice and black pepper are good ones

Fry the onion in a little oil till transparent. Add the chopped tomatoes, all the other ingredients and simmer for about 40 minutes, until the tomatoes are squashy and the liquid in the pan has reduced by about a third. Cool and blend, or press through a sieve. If the ketchup is still too runny, return it to the heat and simmer gently, uncovered, until the liquid is further reduced.

Freeze it for later, or store in the fridge, in airtight jars for several weeks.

Mustard sauce

3 tablespoons of mayonnaise
1 teaspoon of made English mustard
1 teaspoon of lemon juice
1 teaspoon of tomato ketchup
1 teaspoon of Worcester sauce, or tamari

Mix these ingredients into a smooth paste, serve with sausages.

Guacamole

1 avocado
1 teaspoon of lemon juice
Half a teaspoon of tabasco sauce
1 clove of garlic, crushed
A salad onion, finely chopped

Peel and mash the avocado well, then stir in the other ingredients.

Cut avocado goes brown quickly. Cover a cut surface in lemon juice and store it in on a small plate in the fridge; even so, it will keep for less than 24 hours.

Most of these fresh dressings and sauces need to be eaten straight away; keep this in mind when deciding quantities.

Ratatouille

1 red onion
4 cloves of garlic
1 red pepper
1 small aubergine
1 courgette
Other odds and ends of summer vegetables
6 tomatoes and a few tablespoons of water, or a tin of tomatoes
A few leaves of basil, a bit of vegetable stock, and a splash of red wine (optional)

This recipe is a summer vegetable bake. Roughly slice all the vegetables – use all the aubergine, as it doesn't keep well once cut. Put them in a casserole dish with a lid. Add a pinch of salt and a little ground black pepper, the basil and wine.

Cover and bake for 35–40 minutes in a pre-heated low medium oven (Gas Mark 4;180C; 350F). Check every 10 minutes. Add a little more stock if it looks dry. Serve with baked goats' milk cheese and crusty bread, or use as a pasta sauce.

Beef Bourguignon

250 grams (8 ounces) of stewing beef
A glass of red wine
2 rashers of bacon
1 medium onion
1 clove of garlic
300 ml (half a pint) of stock
Fresh herbs, such as oregano, finely chopped
2 tablespoons of plain flour with pinch of little salt added
1 tablespoon of oil

Cut the meat into chunks, coat it in the flour and lightly fry until browned. Meanwhile chop up the onion, garlic and bacon. Sauté these in a little oil, in a pan with good thick walls, then tip in the meat pieces and herbs.

Add the wine and simmer gently for 15 minutes, stirring often, then add the hot stock. Simmer for an hour, until the meat is tender, stirring regularly. The sauce should be quite thick; if it starts to stick, add more stock, a little at a time.

Serve with potatoes and assorted garden vegetables.

Pigeon casserole

2 pigeon breasts per person
125 grams (5 ounces) of chuck steak or other cheap beef
2 cloves of garlic
A medium sized carrot, sliced
A courgette, sliced
A small handful of French beans, chopped
A few leaves each of thyme and oregano
300 ml (half a pint) of stock

Pigeons were a menace at this time of year as the grain ripened; they were often killed for the pot. Their meat is very dense, almost like liver, and strongly flavoured. They are undeniably free range; watch out for stray shotgun pellets!

If you have the carcasses, boil them for stock and use it in this recipe. Most of the meat on a pigeon is breast though, so you may as well buy these ready prepared from your local butcher and save trouble. Use odds and ends from your garden too; carrot thinnings, baby courgettes, young runner bean pods.

Heat a little oil in a casserole dish, cut the beef into chunks and lightly fry till it's browned, then stir in the vegetables, lay the pigeon breasts on top and add the stock. Cover and bake in a low oven (Gas Mark 3; 170C; 325F) for an hour.

Left over casserole can easily be turned into a pie filling by reducing the liquid and thickening with gravy granules (or cornflour).

Cobblers

These are similar to dumplings, but lighter; the recipe is the same as for cheese scones. As with dumplings, you can only cook as many as will fit side by side in the casserole dish, so just bake any leftover mix as scones.

To make about 6 cobblers, you'll need: -
75 ml (3 fluid ounces) of milk, which can be sour
100 grams (4 ounces) of self-raising flour
25 grams (1 ounce) of butter
50 grams (2 ounces) of grated cheese
A pinch of salt

Rub the flour, salt and fat into a breadcrumb mix, stir in the cheese. Add the milk to make into a dough; add extra flour if it's too sticky. Roll out on a well-floured board to about an inch thick and cut into rounds with a two inch cutter. Place these gently on top of the pigeon casserole after it's been in the oven for twenty minutes.

Bake uncovered for a further forty minutes. The top of the cobblers should be brown when they're done.

Dauphinoise potatoes

3 medium sized potatoes
1 clove of garlic, sliced
25 grams (1 ounce) of butter
1 teaspoon of dried mixed herbs
50 ml (2 fluid ounces) of single cream
50 ml (2 fluid ounces) milk
Parmesan cheese to taste

Thinly slice the potatoes, melt the butter in a casserole dish and soften the garlic and herbs in it for a few minutes. Add the potatoes, milk and cream.

Cover and bake in a pre-heated low medium oven (Gas Mark 4; 180C; 350F) for 40 minutes, until the potatoes are getting soft. Top with Parmesan cheese and bake uncovered for a further 15 minutes, until the cheese browns.

You can adapt this recipe for use with celeriac, sweet potatoes, parsnips or butternut squash, or add grated cheese to the mix for a gratin.

Green tomato chutney

Not all the tomatoes on your plants will turn red. Thin the fruit out and use the pickings to make chutney.

2 medium sized cooking apples, grated – you could use the truly seasonal options of courgettes or young marrows instead – about 250 grams (half a pound) of these
A few small onions, also grated. Use thinnings from your onion patch
About 500 grams (a pound) of green tomatoes, chopped fine
A level teaspoon of salt
200 ml (7 fluid ounces) of malt vinegar
100 grams (4 ounces) of demerara sugar
A small chunk of root ginger
A teaspoon of dry mustard
One quarter teaspoon each of cayenne pepper and turmeric

You could add a couple of sticks of celery and a handful of raisins. I leave the fruit out these days, so that I can use the chutney in stews. Some people are allergic to celery.

Prepare 8–10 jars, by sterilising them and warming in a very low oven, as for jam. Handle them carefully in case they've got too hot.

Mix everything together in a large pan, bring to the boil stirring frequently and simmer for about an hour. The mixture should be soft and quite thick. Allow to cool a little, then remove the ginger and spoon the chutney into jars.

Fill these nearly to the top, but not touching the lid, as for the jams. Wipe them down and label with the date. It'll be ready to eat in a month, and keeps well unopened.

Lemon ginger crunch pie

100 grams (4 ounces) butter, preferably unsalted, melted
200 grams (7 ounces) of ginger nut biscuits
300 grams (10 fluid ounces) condensed milk – tins are around 397 grams
Finely grated zest and squeezed juice of 3 lemons, or 3 tablespoons of lemon juice
150 ml (5 fluid ounces) double cream

Crush the biscuits and mix with the melted butter, as for a cheesecake. Tip into a 20 centimetre (8 inch) round sandwich cake tin and press down firmly with the back of a spoon. Leave to set for half an hour.

Beat the condensed milk, lemon zest and juice together until thickened. Lightly whip the cream and fold into the mix. Pour it all onto the biscuit base and chill for several hours before serving.

Damson jelly

The autumn fruits are starting to arrive, beginning with garden plums and wild damsons. You can stew these for crumbles, pies and cakes; they don't make great syrups or wines. It's easy to pick lots though, and they do make a nice jam. It can be difficult to get rid of all the large seeds, however careful you are. These can ambush you in a sandwich. Make a jelly instead.

You'll need a kilo (two pounds) of fresh damsons, washed and patted dry, with the stalks and seeds removed
Granulated sugar (one kilo; two pounds)
Juice of 2 lemons

You should also have a jelly bag, a large bowl or deep pan, and a way of holding the full bag over this. Try fitting a sieve over the bowl, with a wooden spoon laid crossways to support the handle.

Simmer the damsons in a couple of tablespoons of water, with the lemon juice added, until the fruit is soft; about 30 minutes. Pour the fruit carefully into the jelly bag and keep this over the bowl for several hours, or overnight. The longer you leave it, the more juice you get. Squeezing the bag helps extract the pectin which makes your jelly set.

Measure the juice back into the pan. Add a kilo of sugar to every litre of juice (or a pound to a pint). Have the china saucers and teaspoons cooling in the icebox, ready to test for set. Stir over a low heat until the sugar has all dissolved, then bring it to a rolling boil, paying the usual careful attention due to a hot sugar solution.

After 15 minutes, take a teaspoonful of jelly out and drop it on one of the cold saucers. Allow it to cool for a minute, then poke the surface. If it wrinkles, it's done. If not, keep the jelly at the rolling boil and test again every five minutes until it's ready to set.

As damsons have a high pectin content, it is possible to overdo this stage, which will make your jelly too thick and sticky, rather like toffee. If it hasn't set after three trials, you could settle for a syrup instead, which will come in handy to flavour apple puddings next month!

Let cool a little, then transfer to warmed, sterilised jars, as for the marmalade.

Chapter Fifteen

September

September is a time of change. It can be warm and dry, but summer is over and the nights are drawing in. Youngsters are rounded up and sent back to education. Tourist resort owners contemplate their own holidays. Among the fading green leaves, red and purple berries decorate the hedges.

Plants are preparing for winter. Seeds and fruits are developing, roots swelling, leaves withering. The pace of harvesting picks up, there's not much time left to gather stores. September is a busy month in farm and kitchen.

The grain harvest is complete; cattle and sheep were once allowed to graze on the stubble, fertilising it for the next crop. Pigs were driven into the woods to feast on fallen acorns and beech nuts. These 'pannage' rights were jealously guarded. In northern countries, it's difficult to grow enough protein for livestock. Today we import a huge amount of animal feed, which reduces our resilience.

There's a lot of knowledge required to store your own produce through the winter. This developed over thousands of generations, and has been nearly forgotten within a single century. Fortunately, the same century brought us the internet, where much of this information can be found.

Harvesting root vegetables

It begins with harvesting. The way you dig up your vegetables influences their storage capabilities. Roots accidentally cut with a spade won't keep; set them aside for eating now. Once you've dug up potatoes, it's important to keep them in the dark, or they develop poisonous green flesh. Clean wet soil off harvested roots, and store them in a cool, dry, dark place.

Carrots are good for experiments in storage techniques. They can be eaten raw, boiled or roasted. Finely grated into a meat stew, you'd hardly notice them. They need a loose soil to expand into; if yours is hard clay, grow them in pots with a mix of sand and peat. Carrot seed is tiny, so it's hard to sow them well spaced. Pull most of them up over the summer and use them in salads, leaving plants at least a hand's length apart for the final harvest.

Dig up half of these mature carrots. If the roots are thin or divided, the soil mix may have been too hard. Note this in your gardening journal. Assuming you have a few good ones, cut off the stalks. Green material will rot in storage and encourage moulds. Wash away the soil and leave the carrots to dry on newspaper.

Find a large shallow box. Cardboard will do, but not plastic; roots give off moisture as they're stored. Buy a bag of play sand. Lay the dry carrots on a layer of sand, not touching each other, and cover them completely with more sand. Store the box in the cool, dry place.

Revisit this store at intervals over the winter, eat a few of the carrots. Are they keeping well? If they're going soft or brown, your storage area may be too warm. A garden shed is ideal, as long as it's not damp, but then the mice may discover your stores. Once, the old chap next door could tell you what to do; now you have to learn for yourself.

The carrots you left in the ground are observed in a similar way. Do they get any bigger over the winter? Are they attacked by pests, eaten by rabbits, frozen into the ground? Let the strongest ones grow into tall, handsome plants to flower in the spring and provide you with seed.

Collecting seeds

The established resilience gardener will be harvesting these as well in autumn. Some seeds – mainly peas, flowers and brassicas – will have been gathered already as they turned brown. This is the last chance to collect the rest before they fall. You need dry weather, preferably for a few days in a row. Pods should be dry, brittle and easily broken up. Discard as many bits as possible, as they can rot in storage and spoil the seeds.

Seeds are heavy, while husks are light. Practise the ancient technique of winnowing. Tip your seeds onto a sheet of newspaper and gently blow away the dry plant material, without sending the seeds all over the floor. Or put them in a large envelope and shake well, picking out the husks as they rise to the top.

Large seed heads, with their resident insects evicted first, can be brought indoors to ripen if the weather starts to get damp. Hang them upside down inside a paper bag, collecting the seeds as they fall. Store all seeds in paper bags, clearly labelled with the type and year, in a dry place.

Gathering fruit

Seeds and roots keep well because they're still alive. Fruits are designed to be eaten, to tempt animals into spreading the seeds they contain. If left on the ground, they soon rot away to let these seeds reach the soil.

Soft fruits – plums, blackberries, tomatoes, courgettes – need to be preserved within a few days. If they're picked on a wet day, they go mouldy faster. It's much better to gather fruit on a sunny afternoon. Take a picnic, explore some footpaths! Don't be too greedy with hedgerow produce though. Wild animals depend on it for their winter supplies.

Fruits like squashes, pumpkins and apples have harder skins and firmer flesh. They ripen a bit later, and can be kept whole in a cool, dry, dark place for some time. Apples for storage should be picked straight from the tree and handled gently. If they have fallen to the ground, they'll be bruised, even if it doesn't show.

Some seasonal foods available in September

Tree fruits; early apples, late plums, damsons, nuts, sloes.
Jams and syrups made in summer.
Fresh eggs and milk are still available, but fodder will become scarce soon.
Butter, cheese and edible oils are in good supply.
Fennel and other seeds, nuts and fungi.
Potatoes, tomatoes, courgettes, onions, garlic, carrots, parsnips, swede.
Brassica leaves, borage, spinach, rocket.
Deer and game, fish, farm meats.
Grains and flour.
Dried and fresh beans; dried peas.

As crops come in, they have to be processed, stored, preserved. Unlike supermarket produce, things from outside are covered in soil or dust, with added insects. However, unlike the insidious oily chemicals used by intensive agriculture, all this washes off.

When a community depended on this harvest, work had to be organised. Anything that could be stored outside for the time being was left there. Root vegetables were piled in heaps and covered with soil, which neatly avoided washing them for a while. Look up 'potato clamps'. Apples were left to ripen on the tree, nuts picked but kept in their shells.

The soft fruits had to be dealt with first. There'd be pans of jam simmering on the stove, trays of fruit leather drying in the oven, jars of chutney in the pantry.

Freezers

Today, you can cut short this preserving process. If you're in a hurry, just rinse and freeze your soft fruit in labelled boxes; plastic is fine here. Use it later for syrups, jams and puddings. Lightly stewed fruit, with the juice drained, is less watery when thawed out. Tomatoes are best cooked down into a passata before freezing.

Harder fruits and root vegetables also need to be cooked – don't freeze raw potatoes. If you still have last year's vegetables unused by harvest time, throw them out and revise your storage strategies. Freezers are good short-term ways of storing a glut, but they're not that resilient. The trouble is their dependence on a mains electricity supply, which may be cut off in an emergency.

If a power outage affects your freezer, keep the door shut while you work out a plan. If the freezer is full, the food can last a couple of days; if half-full, only a day. A freezer compartment in a fridge will be compromised after a few hours.

Move your supplies quickly to a working freezer. Prioritise ingredients, such as meat and garden produce, over ready meals. It's harder to tell if the latter have gone off. If this isn't possible, pack them closer together and make sure raw meat is kept separately. As it thaws, juices may drip onto other foods, rendering them all unsafe.

Any frozen food which has been warmer than 4 degrees Centigrade (40 Fahrenheit) – the normal temperature of a fridge – for over 2 hours must be discarded. In a prolonged disruption of services, decaying freezer food can become a serious health hazard.

The process of freezing causes ice to form in plant and animal cells. This expands, breaking the cell walls. When the food defrosts, it becomes soft, even mushy, as this ice turns to water. The nutrients are released from the ruptured cells and are easily accessible to bacteria.

Eggs don't take well to freezing, nor do tins of food. If your winter supplies in the shed get frozen, this is a problem. The expanding ice may burst cans or crack glass jars.

Check your stores carefully if this happens. Throw away anything with a split container. Treat the rest with caution; if the contents look or smell odd, don't taste them. Change accidentally frozen stores for fresh supplies, using a different place.

Preserving

Instead of using a freezer, you could take on the challenge of the season and use traditional methods from the start. Certain vegetables, especially onions and cucumber, can be pickled raw in a jar of vinegar. Chutneys, jams and syrups are easy to make at home.

Such recipes use cooking to destroy the food bacteria, then add vinegar or sugar to create an environment where these micro-organisms can't survive. Finally, the preserved food is put into sterilised jars and kept sealed. If air can't enter, neither can new microbes.

Salting food is another way of keeping it from decay. In the 1950s, fresh allotment produce was often stored in large jars, packed with layers of salt grated from blocks the size of house bricks. There are recipes online for salt pork. It sounds like something you'd only eat if you had to. Large amounts of salt aren't good for you, so this method has fallen out of favour.

Bacteria need water to thrive; without it they can't use the natural sugars in the foods. This is the principle behind dehydration and dried meats. The food to be preserved must be thinly sliced, to ensure it is completely dried all the way through, and stored in a sealed container. If it gets wet, it will keep no longer than if it were fresh.

Learn the principles behind jam making and adapt the recipes. Remember the role of pectin in creating a good firm texture. Does the fruit you're using have enough? Look it up. Find a natural source and don't buy packaged additives. Fortunately, even unripe apples are rich in pectin; add some to the mix.

It requires quite a lot of sugar to preserve fruit. The general rule is a pound of sugar to a pound of fruit (or pint of liquid). Or one kilo per litre. If you'd prefer to store natural fruit juices, you'll need to explore home pasteurising. This involves large pans of boiling water, and is strictly for the adventurous. You need to be confident of your ability to tell when something has gone off.

Do the research first, find some instructions and follow the process. You may need equipment, such as a heat proof thermometer. 'Home canning' is popular in North America – confusingly, it often involves jars – so there's a lot of information online. Maybe your gardening group could form an alliance with a local kitchen to organise an expert demonstration.

Tomato passata makes a good test recipe. The tomato plants themselves are fading fast; all the fruit needs to be used up. Your home-made passata will be okay in the fridge for a short while as long as the jars aren't opened. Pasteurised correctly, it can keep for several weeks. Label jars with the date, including the year, and keep notes.

Having the confidence to deal with a glut of tomatoes might not sound like much, but it's an important survival skill. Another excellent way of using up a large surplus of fruit is winemaking.

Compared to other kitchen preserving activities, brewing is done on an industrial scale. You're working in gallons not pints. It takes four pounds of blackberries to make a single gallon of wine, and you should make more than that for topping up later.

There's a lot to learn about winemaking, but it's very rewarding and popular with the community. If supplies are short, apple cider can be made without added sugar; grapes come with their own yeast. All have food value as well as alcohol content, and keep very well.

Recipes for September

Tomato passata

If you're growing tomatoes, this is when you're likely to have a surplus. Instead of using tinned tomatoes in recipes, make your own passata sauce to add.

Half a kilo (one pound) of well-ripened red tomatoes, chopped
A small onion and two cloves of garlic, finely chopped
A teaspoon of chopped fresh basil, and a few shredded leaves of oregano – or half a teaspoon each of the dried herbs

Sauté the onion and garlic in a little oil, then add the other ingredients and blend until smooth. Simmer for 15 minutes, uncovered, to let the sauce thicken.

If you don't have a blender, cook the sauce first and then press it through a sieve. Use at once, or transfer to a couple of sterilised jars while still hot. This will keep for a few days in the fridge.

Always let cooked food cool right down before putting it in a fridge or freezer.

Pizza

250 grams (8 ounces) of strong (bread) flour
A pinch of salt
A packet of ready to use yeast
150 ml (5 fluid ounces) of warmed milk
1 egg
25 grams (1 ounce) of soft butter or olive oil

Sift the flour into a bowl, add the salt and yeast. Rub in the butter, mix in the milk and egg. Leave the dough to rise in the bowl, covered with a clean damp tea towel, in a warm place. It should double in size over a couple of hours, or the place is not warm enough.

For the topping: -

2 tablespoons oil
1 onion, chopped
1 tin of sieved tomatoes, or a packet of passata, or 500 grams (one pound) of your own passata
Half of a 130 gram tube of tomato puree
1 teaspoon sugar
A bay leaf
A half teaspoon of dried oregano

Lightly fry the onion in the oil, stir in the other ingredients and simmer for 10 minutes or so. It has a tendency to spit as it cooks, but you need to reduce it, so you can't put a lid on the pan. Once the sauce is quite thick, cool slightly, take out the bay leaf and throw it away.

Grease and flour a large baking tray. Pat the risen dough out over it, spread the sauce over the pizza base, then add extras such as anchovies, olives, mushrooms, sweetcorn, pineapple, ham and grated cheese.

Leave to rise for another 15 minutes, uncovered. Bake on the middle shelf of a preheated hot oven (Gas Mark 7; 220C; 425F) for 20 – 25 minutes.

Try using suet and self-raising flour as a base. Adapt the recipe for dumplings, adding less water. Bake this a little first, as with baking pastry blind, then add the toppings and cook. Experiment; this recipe can be made from stores and needs no rising time.

Lasagne

Use the bolognaise recipe from March and the cheese sauce recipe from February
Lasagne sheets
Grated cheese

It's quite a lot of effort to make a lasagne, unless you use it as part of a series of meals. Make extra bolognaise for one meal, then use this the next day in the lasagne. Cook up extra cheese sauce and store some in the fridge; have cheesy pancakes for the third day, as a change from pasta.

Lasagne sheets are used dry. If you try to cook them first, they just stick together. As long as they are well covered with sauce, they'll soften during the baking. Preheat the oven to medium (Gas Mark 5; 190C; 375F).

Use your casserole dish, or a baking tray at least two inches (5 cm) deep. Grease it, then pour in bolognaise mix to make a layer about half an inch thick. Place a single layer of lasagne sheets over this. Keep these whole where possible, avoid too much overlap and break some pieces up to fill in the edges.

Cover this with a thinner layer of cheese sauce, then more lasagne. Add a final layer of bolognaise and scatter grated cheese on top. Bake on a low middle shelf for 45 minutes, until the pasta is soft right through.

The quantities you use depend on the size of your baking dish. If there's room, you can add more layers, though this will increase the cooking time a bit. Making a little too much for a single meal is fine, as lasagne is nice eaten cold as a snack.

Waldorf salad

This salad uses autumn produce. Roughly chop some apple, celery, walnuts, red pepper, grapes and cooked chicken; mix together and serve on a bed of lettuce. You can substitute Stilton cheese or toasted pine kernels for the chicken.

For a salad dressing, mix : -
2 tablespoons natural plain yogurt
2 tablespoons mayonnaise
2 tablespoons of grated cucumber
1 teaspoon of grated onion
Half a teaspoon of fresh tarragon (optional)

Himalayan balsam curry

Himalayan balsam (Impatiens glandulifera) is another accidentally imported edible weed. It likes damp, sheltered ground and has often infested river banks, where water buffalo can be used to keep it in check. The seeds and flowers can be eaten raw, but the rest of the plant is slightly toxic. Blanch young stems (soak briefly in boiling water) and change the water to cook these.

The seeds have a nutty flavour, and have been eaten in India for centuries. Study the plant until you are certain you can identify it. Find a patch which you are sure hasn't been treated with weed killer, and is free of water buffalo.

The ripe seed pods burst as soon as you touch them, spraying seeds over a wide area, so they are quite challenging to harvest. The slightest change of colour from green can indicate that the pod is ready. Slip a wide mouthed glass jar over it, then touch it. The seeds are caught in the jar.

Many pods are too, which you'll need to discard back at the kitchen. They're not inedible, so it doesn't matter if there are a few bits left in. Most of the seeds will be brown; a few unripe ones are fine as well.

For the curry: -

1 medium onion and 2 cloves of garlic, chopped
1 tablespoon of oil, with a dash of tamari added
A tablespoon of curry paste
500 ml (one pint) of vegetable stock
1 small red pepper, 2 sticks of celery and 2 tomatoes, chopped
A good handful of cleaned, raw Himalayan balsam seeds; if you don't have these, cashew or pine nuts will do

Lightly fry the onion in the oil, add the curry paste and stir together over a low heat for a couple of minutes. Stir in the seeds, add the stock and the other vegetables. Simmer for at least half an hour, until the vegetables are all soft. Serve with rice.

Himalayan balsam displaces native plants, so it's illegal to encourage it to grow in the wild in Britain. Make sure you cook all the seeds you bring home. Stray plants are easily cleared from your garden. Himalayan balsam will regrow from cut stems but not root fragments.

Goulash

1 large onion
250 grams (half a pound) of beef – use a cheap cut
1 clove of garlic
A bay leaf
2 teaspoons of sweet paprika
1 teaspoon of cumin seeds
Half a teaspoon of hot paprika (optional)
1 level tablespoon of plain flour
1 pint of stock

Cut the meat into chunks and coat with the flour. Fry the onion, garlic and meat in a little oil, with a dash of tamari for colouring; stir in the cumin seeds as the meat starts to brown.

Add the other spices, tip in the rest of the flour and stir well. Gradually add the hot stock, mixing it as you go to avoid lumps.

Bring to the boil, then turn down the heat, cover the pan and simmer for two to three hours. Remove the bay leaf and serve with boiled potatoes.

Goulash thickens up the next day, but if yours still has too much gravy, just strain it off and serve it separately.

Rissoles

250 grams (half a pound) of cooked mashed potatoes
125 grams (4 ounces) of cooked meat, finely chopped or minced
1 medium onion, grated
2 teaspoons of tamari or Worcester sauce
1 egg, beaten
A tablespoon of flour
A tablespoon of golden breadcrumbs (optional)

Mix everything together well. Divide into burger shapes and dust with flour. Try using the extra crunchy coating described for the chicken nugget recipe in March, with some dried herbs mixed into the breadcrumbs.

Fry the rissoles gently in shallow oil for about 10 minutes on each side, serve with baked beans. This recipe makes four large rissoles for little more than the cost of a bit of ham from the sell-by counter.

Fish and cheese pie

100 grams (4 ounces) of salmon, or white fish
100 grams (4 ounces) of smoked fish
10 grams (half an ounce) of butter
300–450 grams (10–16 ounces) of cooked mashed potatoes, depending on the size of your dish
50 grams (2 ounces) of grated cheese for topping

Lightly fry the flaked fish in the butter for about 10 minutes, until cooked. Stir in the cheese sauce and heat through. Transfer to a greased pie dish and cover with mashed potato; top with grated cheese.

Cook in a preheated medium oven (Gas Mark 5; 190C; 375F) for 30–40 minutes, until the top is turning golden brown.

For the cheese sauce: -
1 medium leek, chopped
1 clove of garlic, finely chopped
25 grams (1 ounce) butter
25 grams (1 ounce) plain flour
200 ml (half a pint) of milk
75 grams (3 ounces) of grated cheese

Sauté the leek and garlic in the butter. Take the pan off the heat and stir in the flour, coating the leeks well. Add a little milk and mix to a paste; keep adding and stirring a bit at a time until all the flour is mixed in, then return the pan to a low heat. Keep stirring gently as it thickens; add any leftover milk, then stir in the cheese and let it melt. Use as above.

Flapjacks

You can find many recipes for ordinary flapjacks online; this one uses survival stores and is suitable for vegans.

4 tablespoons of hemp oil – or whatever clean cooking oil there is to hand
4 rounded tablespoons of white sugar
1 tablespoon golden syrup; this is so uncontrollably sticky that the default measure is a spoonful. You'd never get it back off the scales pan. Add it straight to the mix.
1 rounded tablespoon of soft brown sugar.
6 well rounded tablespoons of oats
1 tablespoon of plain flour

Grease and flour a shallow baking tray, about 20 centimetres (8 inches) across, and preheat the oven to low (Gas Mark 2; 150C; 300F).

Over a gentle heat, mix the sugar, oil and syrup together in a pan. When they've combined and gone liquid, remove from the heat, stir in the oats and flour. Scrape the mix into the tray and pat down. Cook on a lower middle shelf for 40 minutes; check after half an hour.

It'll look quite soft when done, but harden up as it cools. Leave it in the tin to set, but mark out slices after 10 minutes. These are a little oily compared to regular flapjacks, which use butter instead, but make a good survival food. Add raisins or nuts to make a high energy portable snack.

Fruit leathers

These are made from fruit, raw or cooked, turned into a puree and dried. The mix needs to be left in a low oven overnight, or outside all day in the hot sun, covered with a fly-proof mesh. The exact process depends on the fruit you are using; you'll need to do some research.

Fruit leathers are very tasty, full of nutrients and are relatively low in sugar. They still need to be stored in a fridge, but keep longer than most fresh fruits. However, they are a resource-intensive way of using up a surplus.

As with dehydrating, it's a technique to keep in mind to use up excess electrical power from a good off-grid system. Energy can be stored in many ways.

Elderberry wine

2.5 kilos (6 pounds) of elderberries – couple of carrier bags full, with stalks
2.5 kilos (6 pounds) of sugar
9 litres (2 gallons) of water
Wine yeast compound

Elderberries are easy to pick once you've found a couple of good trees, not too near a main road. Use double bags to collect them in; twigs or thorns may tear the outer bag. Once back at home, you have to strip all the berries from the stalks which takes a while. Weigh the berries and empty them into a sterilised and rinsed plastic brewing bin.

These first stages are messy and best done outside. Stray berries, trodden in, will stain a carpet. If you have more or less than the recipe calls for, adjust the other amounts, but don't make more than four gallons in a single bin.

Crush the berries. Boil the water in a stainless-steel pan and pour over the fruit, stirring. You may need to do this in several batches. Have the bin where you plan to leave it during next three days, as it's quite heavy once full. Keep the lid on as it cools.

Prepare the yeast. Into a small jugful of cooled boiled water at blood heat, mix a teaspoon of yeast with a couple of teaspoons of sugar. Using a funnel, pour this into a sterilised glass bottle, plug with cotton wool and leave in a warm place. It should start frothing when it's ready. To check if it's working, give the bottle a shake, then remove the plug and listen carefully. You should be able to hear a faint fizzing sound. If you can't, add another half teaspoon of yeast. The initial water may have been too hot.

The liquid in the brewing bin needs to be warm, but not hot, when you add the yeast. It takes longer to cool down than you might expect. If you're brewing in the evening, reserve some water to boil in the morning and add to the cold wine mix before pouring the yeast in. This'll warm it up again; the yeast doesn't work well in the cold.

Cover the bin and leave for three days, stirring a couple of times a day. You should hear that fizzing noise when you do, as the yeast produces carbon dioxide. Then strain it carefully into another sterilised bucket, discarding the berries. Rinse the first bin clean and measure the wine back into it. Mix the sugar in well; make sure it doesn't all sink to the bottom. Cover while you prepare the demijohns.

Each of these holds about a gallon (4.5 litres). You'll need to make at least two gallons; three is best. Sterilise these, and the three corks and airlocks which go with them. Fill them from the bin, with a funnel, to about six inches (15 cm) from the top. Level some water in the airlocks and seal these with a plug of cotton wool to keep insects out; cork the demijohns.

Elderberry wine is notorious for frothing up when the sugar is added. Top two of the demijohns up over a week, using the third; add a little at a time and wait for the froth to subside the next day. When they have settled down enough to be filled right up to the neck, wrap the demijohns in newspaper and leave in a warm dark place for two months. Make sure the airlock doesn't go dry.

Any left over wine can be added to the next batch, or discarded. Never store home-made wine in screw top bottles.

After a while, stray bits of fruit and dead yeast will settle on the bottom. The wine needs to be siphoned off this sediment into a clean demijohn. This is called 'racking'. The new demijohns will need to be topped up. You need to exclude as much air as possible, or the wine will spoil.

If you don't have any of your own brew for this, commercial wines and fruit juices contain preservatives which may interfere with the yeast. It's better to use local organic pasteurised apple juice from the market, or even cooled boiled water with a few spoonfuls of sugar added. Only a small gap in the narrow neck of the demijohn is left, so that the wine doesn't touch the cork.

Leave until fermentation has stopped. The water in the two halves of the airlock will then be level. Rack once more, adding a crushed Campden tablet to each gallon. Top up with wine only; the last demijohn won't be full. Bottle this one after a couple of days, but leave the rest in a cold place for a week.

As long as the airlocks are still level, siphon into bottles, cork and label. You'll need a small hand-held device to push the corks in; these can be bought at a home brew shop.

Home-made wine doesn't have much preservative in it, so store it in a cool place and keep upright. The yeast may become active again. Often this gives a pleasant fizz to the wine, but it can build up so much pressure that the cork pops out. This is why screw top bottles aren't used; the glass may break before the lid comes off.

Most fruit wines follow these basic principles. There's a lot of information online. However, books are more resilient than electronic devices when it comes to getting wet, and there's a lot of water involved in winemaking. The classic one is 'First Steps in Winemaking' by C. J. J. Berry. Older editions may advise you to filter your wine through asbestos fibres; do not do this. Apart from that, it's full of ancient wisdom.

Chapter Sixteen

October

The flurry of activity slows down as autumn draws to a close. The garden requires little work. You can take time off to hunt for mushrooms in the wild wood. Tourists desert the seashore – go on a day trip to collect seaweed washed up on the beaches while things are quiet. Take extra plastic bags to double wrap in case it's wet.

Meanwhile, fresh food is still coming in. There's a miscellany of vegetables; odds and ends left behind when the main crop was stored need using up. Courgettes will carry on till a cold snap wilts their spreading leaves, then shrivel and die all at once. Squashes are more robust, and can be left to fatten up until the first frost.

The last weeks of autumn are for shutting down the garden before the weather closes in. Pack up your nets and plastic pots to safeguard them from strong winds. Clean and oil garden tools before putting them away; tidy up the greenhouse. Turn over your compost heap, cut the grass one last time, pull up vegetables as they die off. Remember to leave the plants you decided to develop for seed or observation, as you clear away summer and prepare for winter.

Feeding the soil

With harvesting and die-back, empty spaces appear in the garden. Condition the soil while you can get at it easily. Drench it with plant teas from the last of the comfrey leaves mixed with seaweed. Bury the residue, preferably where you were growing hungry crops such as brassicas and tomatoes.

Nettles are seeding at this time of year, so don't use them in a compost tea. Add comfrey leaves and seaweed to them to prepare an anaerobic brew, as described in December. Leave it in your sealed bin for use in the spring; the nettle seeds will have been killed off by then.

Mulch bare soil with finished compost from your own heap, dig in manure. Leaf mould is a good soil conditioner, giving both structure and nourishment. Make a rough enclosure, about a metre square, from chicken wire fastened to wooden posts. Fill it with fallen leaves, packing them down well. They lose a lot of volume as they decay into a rich mulch. Spread this on your garden the following autumn, and make another batch.

The more of these plant foods you can apply to your soil, the better. If you only have a limited amount, some areas will need it more than others. It depends on what you were growing.

Crop rotation

This is an important principle of growing annual food plants. You harvest the fruit, seeds or roots after a single year. The rest of the plant, along with all the nutrients it took out of your soil, ends up on the compost heap. If you grow the same plant there next year, it won't find so much nourishment.

Peas maintain friendly bacteria on their roots – you can see the little nodules where they live – which make soil nitrogen available to the plants. Broccoli is greedy for this mineral and will strip it out. By an amazing coincidence, as you finish picking the florets and clear the old plants away in early spring, it's the right time to prepare for sowing peas. Not only do these come with their own nitrogen, but they'll enrich the soil again.

Pests may be overwintering in the soil ready to pounce on new seedlings. Confuse them by growing something different, something they can't attack. Carrot flies won't eat onions; potatoes are no good to pea moths.

These principles were used centuries ago. A common rotation on a medieval farm was to follow cereals with peas or beans, then leave the field fallow for a year. The more intensive agriculture following the Elizabethan period used a four year rotation, often including a fodder crop, such as clover which also replaces soil nitrogen.

Go for a three or four year rotation in your growing space. This is where your garden notebook comes in handy. Draw a rough plan of where everything was, give some thought to what you'll plant next. Leeks and brassicas will be overwintering where they are, but the courgettes will soon leave bare ground. You could feed this and grow a catch crop of salad rocket, or leave it fallow over the winter.

Tomatoes might thrive in that sunny spot; they'll benefit from a rich soil. Potatoes and other root vegetables don't do well in freshly manured ground. The extra nitrogen encourages them to produce an excess of leaves, even to flower and seed, rather than to create the starchy roots you need. If you're growing in raised beds, you can run your own experiments, trying out various techniques.

Contemplate these as you relax in the autumn sunshine gazing at your vegetable plot. Get to know your plants. Understand what they need in the way of space and feeding. Harvest them with appreciation.

Summing up the year

The end of October brings cold rainy days when a walk in the glorious colours of the forest isn't such an attractive option. The harvest is in, the winter vegetables settling down, the greenhouse empty. Take out your gardening journal and read over your notes.

What plants did you grow? Which ones did you eat? Did you manage to cultivate your favourite herbs or vegetables, or were conditions just not right for these?

Consider how you could use your growing area's microclimate. Rhubarb, sorrel and burdock are woodland margin plants; they droop in full sun. Tomatoes like it hot and dry, but need a lot of watering. Most plants grow slowly in shady areas. A dark corner between high wooden fences is ideal for your wild patch of comfrey and nettles; vegetables won't like it much there.

What pests affected your plants? Did your solutions work? How else could you protect your vegetables? Plants have their own ways of fending off invertebrate predators and disease. Provide them with a healthy, well-structured soil, an abundant supply of the right nutrients, and plenty of room to develop.

Your resilience garden isn't a monoculture. Even in raised beds, there should be a couple of different things growing. Learn about companion planting. Some vegetables make good neighbours; others don't get along well. The wall poster 'Companion Planting Chart' by Michael Littlewood is an excellent guide.

Were your raised beds in the right place? If not, can they be moved? Is there enough space between them? Do nearby bushes need more pruning, or was the shade useful in summer when you were too busy to water often enough? Could you design an irrigation system for next year? Would it be worth getting a greenhouse, or a shed? Creating a wormery, or trying to grow oyster mushrooms?

Write the story of the year in your journal as the Xmas cake is baking, and contemplate your new relationship with food,

Some seasonal foods available on October

Sugar and honey.
Apples; other fresh fruit is getting scarce and you're using preserves now.
Potatoes, onions, carrots, squash, pumpkins, marrows, beans, celery.
The very last tomatoes from the greenhouse; the end of the courgettes.
Meat, offal, lard and fish.
Eggs, milk, butter and cheeses.
Wild game, roots and fungi.
Nuts and seeds.

Wild fungi

The colourful carpet on the forest floor is a bonanza for fungi. The mushrooms you can pick and eat are their fruits. Their tiny seeds – spores – are sent out now with the best chance of alighting on something ready to rot down and feed a new colony. Wild fungi clear the ground ready for spring growth, turning autumn's discarded debris into soluble nutrients. Their association with decay gives them a slightly sinister aspect. Caution is wise. Some are deadly poisonous.

The lurid red cap of fly agaric, with its fairytale white spots, is easily avoided. The more dangerous Death Cap is less distinguished. Exploring the woods around you with a field guide, you notice that none of the mushrooms look exactly like the pictures.

Identifying wild mushrooms is an art. You have to become familiar with the woodland, prepared to take specimens home to study spore patterns, keep notes. A day course or several with an experienced forager is essential.

It's worth recognising field mushrooms, puffballs and ink caps. These are quite common, and cook much like ordinary commercial mushrooms. Only take a few at once, since they don't keep long. Make sure they're not full of maggots. Some species of ink caps react badly with alcohol, so don't drink on evenings when you eat these.

You might wonder whether it's worth the bother. Fungi are a valuable source of protein. If you don't eat meat, this knowledge could be vitally important, and potentially valuable to your community. Our remaining ancient forests need to be protected to safeguard these food reserves.

Fungal networks take years, even centuries, to establish; they can't be replaced from the garden centre.

Winter is coming

It starts to get cold in October. When a real fire was the only way to heat your home, it stayed lit most of the day. An open fireplace loses more than half of its heat up the chimney. Having your fire in a range, like an Aga, made better use of the wood you'd toiled to carry home. Many old cooking and preserving recipes assumed one had an oven which was easy to keep at a low temperature for hours.

Even now, it's the season to begin baking. Pies, pastries and cakes are on the menu. Eggs and milk are beginning to get scarce, but lard is available again. It's not so great in delicate recipes, but there's not much cream or soft fruit about either. Add the final few gleanings to apple-based dishes to vary the flavours.

If you've followed the modern trend and grown pumpkins for Hallowe'en lanterns, rather than the traditional swedes, you'll have a lot of pumpkin. It's good both in soup or in a sweet pie, but you'd have to throw a party to get it all eaten! Unused, they store well in a cool shed. Don't forget about them though, or they'll eventually liquefy all over the shelf.

Consider the blaze of vegetable colour in a Harvest Festival display; compare it to the lurid shelves of labels in the supermarket. Food used to be an adventure; it involved hard work and a sense of triumph as the store cupboard filled up. Buying processed food and eating it without thought is wasting a whole area of fun!

Recipes for October

Stuffed marrow

A marrow that fits in your oven
50–100 grams (2–4 ounces) of brown or white rice, depending on the marrow size
100 grams (4 ounces) of minced meat – optional
1 large onion
1 red pepper
A few mushrooms
Other odds and ends of vegetables which don't need much cooking; not roots
A tablespoon of oil with a dash of tamari

A tablespoon of tomato ketchup

You'll need enough silver foil to wrap the marrow.
Preheat the oven to low medium (Gas Mark 4; 180C; 350F) and cut the washed marrow in half lengthways. Scoop out the seeds from the middle, then prepare the filling.

While the rice is cooking, brown the mince in the oil, then add the vegetables, chopped quite small. Lightly fry for 10 minutes, add the drained cooked rice while it's still hot and mix everything together. Stir in the ketchup. Have a small tin of sweetcorn or peas standing by, to add in case there isn't enough filling.

Pile the rice mixture into both halves. Replace the top half and wrap the whole marrow in silver foil. You can try the old-fashioned way instead; cut the top away and scrape out the insides with a long knife. Replace the top piece after stuffing and hold it in place with a couple of cocktail sticks.

Bake in a roasting tin for an hour and a half, on a low middle shelf. Serve in slices; you don't usually eat the skin.

This dish can be a bit bland; the marrow flesh itself has little taste and is very watery. It's difficult to make for just one or two people; the marrows many gardeners are keen to give away are quite large. Serve with a selection of spicy vegetables to liven it up.

Not many shops sell marrows now. You can use the same filling for stuffing peppers, large courgettes or squashes. It's important not to let the rice cool down before baking, and oven times will be different depending on the size and texture of the raw vegetable being stuffed.

Peppers take around 20 minutes; a butternut squash around 40 minutes.

Pumpkin soup

For each half kilo (one pound) of pumpkin : -
1 medium potato, diced and cooked
1 medium onion, chopped
1 clove of garlic, sliced
1 tablespoon oil
500 ml (one pint) of stock, preferably chicken or vegetable
A teaspoon of fresh thyme leaves (or half that of dried); other herbs to taste

Optional: -
A handful of shredded leaves; you should have spinach, kale and cabbage now
A medium carrot, grated

When you hollow out your Hallowe'en lantern, you'll end up with a big pile of pumpkin – up to a few kilos. If you're very fond of this, you could preserve it; if you're hosting a large party, you could make it into a soup.

Mostly, however, this will end up in the compost. Save enough of it to practise this recipe, just in case you are ever called upon to deal with a whole pumpkin!

Sauté the onions in oil, add small chunks of pumpkin with the garlic and herbs. Stir for 10 minutes till the pumpkin begins to soften. Add the stock, grated carrot and the cooked potatoes, bring to the boil and simmer for 30 minutes.

Stir in the shredded leaves towards the end of cooking.

If you are only cooking for a few, you could make a cream soup. Blend the cooked soup, then reheat to nearly boiling. Remove from the heat and stir in a couple of tablespoons of cream before serving.

Save the pumpkin seeds, wash them and pat dry. Toss them in melted butter with a pinch of salt. Then spread them out on a baking tray and cook for 45 minutes in a very low (Gas Mark 2; 150C; 300F) oven, stirring occasionally.

Tangy braised beef

This recipe for braised beef needs a good casserole dish with a lid. To serve four...

8 slices of beef topside
3 medium onions, chopped
2 tablespoons of made-up English mustard
2 tablespoons of plain flour with a pinch of salt stirred in
Enough stock to cover the meat and onions; use a couple of stock cubes and up to half a litre (1 pint) of hot water

Spread the mustard on both sides of the beef slices. Coat them with the seasoned flour and place in the casserole dish. Cover with the raw onions and pour on the stock. Put the lid on.

Cook in a preheated medium oven (Gas Mark 5; 190C; 375F) for 15 minutes, then turn down to low medium (Gas Mark 3; 170C; 325F) for a further hour and a half.

These lower temperatures aren't good for roasting potatoes, but you can adjust the baking times of softer roots, such as parsnip. A cheesy mashed potato dish would brown nicely on the top shelf too.

This is the sort of meal you could make in a slow cooker or even a hay box.

Devilled kidneys

2 lambs' kidneys
125 grams (4 ounces) of mushrooms, washed and quartered
1 medium onion, chopped
1 clove of garlic, finely chopped
25 grams (an ounce) of butter
1 level tablespoon of plain flour
Half a teaspoon each of cayenne pepper and paprika
1 tablespoon of tomato ketchup
1 tablespoon of Worcester sauce
1 teaspoon of made English mustard
Up to 250 ml (8 fluid ounces) of stock

Cut the kidneys in half and snip out the cores. Cook them cut side down in the hot butter for 2 minutes, then turn over and press the other side down to cook for another 2 minutes. Take them out of the pan and put them aside while you fry the onion, mushrooms and garlic. Add a little more butter if necessary.

Stir the paprika and cayenne pepper into the flour. Remove the pan from the heat, return the kidneys to it and coat everything in the flour mix. Over a gentle heat, add half of the stock slowly to make a thick sauce. Stir in the mustard, ketchup and Worcester sauce as you go.

Cover and simmer the mix for about 15 minutes. Keep an eye on it, as the sauce should be thick but not burnt; it's good to have a thick bottomed, non-stick frying pan for this recipe. Add a little more stock to keep it liquid.

Serve on thick slices of toast. Devilled kidneys were a popular breakfast dish in Victorian times.

The term 'devilling' refers to cooking with any spicy sauce, especially those involving mustard, Worcester sauce and cayenne pepper. Worcester sauce is a modern relation of the fish sauces so popular with ancient Romans; it's not suitable for vegetarians.

Liver and onions

250 grams (8 ounces) of lambs' liver
1 large onion, sliced
A tablespoon of oil with a dash of tamari
2 teaspoons of gravy granules
1 tablespoon of whole grain mustard
Up to 250 ml (half a pint) of stock

Sauté the onion, then add the sliced liver. Fry together, stirring frequently, for about 5 minutes, until the liver pieces are cooked through, stir in the mustard, then add the hot stock until you have enough gravy.

Simmer for another 5 minutes, then thicken the liquid with the gravy granules to taste. Serve on top of mashed potatoes, with seasonal greens.

Make cheesy mashed potato with left over mash. Using a thick-walled casserole dish or similar, make a layer of mash, cover it with grated cheese and repeat. Bake uncovered in a preheated low medium oven (Gas Mark 4; 180C; 350F) for 30 minutes, until the cheese on top begins to brown.

Corned beef shepherd's pie

Tins of corned beef can be an important part of your emergency stores. When using it in recipes instead of fresh meat, remember that it is already cooked and that it has added salt.

1 tin corned beef, cut into chunks
1 tablespoon of dried onions, rehydrated as per packet instructions
A tablespoon of oil with a dash of tamari
Up to 250 ml (8 fluid ounces) of stock
A small tin of peas, sweetcorn or green beans, drained
1 teaspoon of gravy granules
1 tablespoon of tomato ketchup
350 grams (12 ounces) of cooked mashed potato
1 tablespoon of Italian style powdered cheese

Lightly fry the vegetables and corned beef together for 5 minutes, then stir in the ketchup, add the stock and thicken with the granules. Simmer for a few minutes to reduce the liquid. As with the savoury crumble, the filling shouldn't be too wet.

Transfer to a casserole dish, cover with the mashed potato and sprinkle the cheese on top. Bake in a preheated low medium (Gas Mark 4; 180C; 350F) oven for 40 minutes.

The name 'corned beef' comes from the way it was cured using large grains of rock salt, which were called 'corns' of salt.

Braised celery

Half a dozen large sticks of celery, cleaned and cut into finger-length pieces
50 grams (2 ounces) of butter
225 ml (8 fluid ounces) of hot stock – chicken or vegetable

Use a large, thick bottomed frying pan, with a lid. Lay the celery pieces out in a single layer, dot with butter and pour on the stock.

Cover the pan, bring to the boil and simmer for 30 minutes. Serve sprinkled with finely chopped fresh parsley.

Brownies

50 grams (2 ounces) of plain chocolate
100 grams (4 ounces) of butter
100 grams (4 ounces) of self-raising flour, with a pinch of salt and an extra half teaspoon of baking powder
15 grams (half an ounce) of cocoa powder
200 grams (7 ounces) of soft light brown sugar
2 eggs
1 teaspoon of vanilla essence

Grease and flour a 20 centimetre (8 inches) square baking tin. Line it with greaseproof paper, if possible. Preheat the oven to a low medium (Gas Mark 4; 180C; 350F).

Break up the chocolate into a bowl, add the butter and melt them together very gently over a pan of hot water. Some chocolates are designed not to melt properly; use cooking chocolate to be on the safe side. Set this aside to cool a little, while you beat the eggs, sugar and vanilla together in another bowl.

Fold the chocolate into this, then add the sieved flour and cocoa. Fold this in too, until all sign of flour has gone.

Spoon the mix into the baking tin, level it out and cook on a middle shelf for 25 minutes. It's hard to tell when brownies are ready, as the mix is still sticky inside even when fully cooked. You'll just have to trust the timing.

Allow to cool in the tin. Brownies can be very crumbly. Try baking a sweet pastry case blind, and using the brownie mix to make a cake tart.

Gingerbread people

1 tablespoon golden syrup
2 teaspoons of caster sugar
25 grams (1 ounce) butter

125 grams (5 ounces) plain flour
Half a teaspoon of ground ginger
A quarter teaspoon of bicarbonate of soda (baking powder will do)
A pinch of salt

Melt the butter, syrup and sugar, mix them well together.

Cool and add to the dry ingredients. If the dough is too stiff, add a little milk. Roll it out on a floured board and cut the people shapes – you can buy cutters for this now. If you're using the traditional currants for eyes, put them in now.

Transfer to a greased oven tray, with the aid of a thin spatula, and bake in a preheated low medium oven (Gas Mark 4; 180C; 350F) for 7–10 minutes.

Cool on the tray and decorate with plain water icing. Carefully mix a tiny amount of water into a tablespoon of icing sugar until it makes a thick paste. It's nice to make small batches so you can use food colouring and create a palette!

As with flavouring essences, a little food colour goes a very long way. It may stain clothes, but usually washes off fingers with soap.

For Hallowe'en, you don't have to restrict yourself to the classic shapes. Make yourself templates to cut biscuits in the shapes of skulls, witch hats or zombies.

Use the icing to stick other edible decorations to your biscuits, such as thin red liquorice string and green jelly sweets.

Plain biscuits for decorating

150 grams plain flour
50 grams semolina
50 grams of icing sugar, sieved
A pinch of salt
150 grams butter – you can replace up to a third of this with coconut oil for a different flavour

Stir together the dry ingredients, rub in the butter and press the mix into a dough. Roll this out on a floured board to about half a centimetre (a quarter of an inch) thick and cut into shapes. It's a bit stickier than savoury pastry so use plenty of flour and a light touch.

Cook on a greased baking tray in a preheated low medium (Gas Mark 4; 180C; 350F) oven for 10 minutes. This recipe makes about ten biscuits about the size of a Rich Tea biscuit. You can use a pastry cutter, or be inventive.

Cool on the tray, before decorating with plain icing and sweets. Home-made biscuits are often nicer the next day, if they last that long!

The Xmas cake

Traditionally this was made in October, while there was still plenty of butter and eggs. It's a good way to use up the very last of the previous year's dried fruit and nut stocks; there's plenty else to eat and it clears the decks for the new batch being prepared, which can also be added to make up the weight. Flour, which may have got scarce during the summer, is now on the menu again.

The internet abounds with Xmas cake recipes. The basic formula is an ordinary cake mix with as much dried fruit added as this base can hold together; it's a lot. Brandy features prominently; the fruit is soaked well in spirits before adding, then the completed cake is 'fed' at frequent intervals with more.

Most cooks recommend that holes are poked deep into the cake with a skewer just before brushing the top with neat brandy. Do this every fortnight or so, until a week before you plan to ice the cake. If you don't like brandy, or rum, use orange juice. However, as the alcohol is part of the preserving process, you may need to make your cake later in the year.

Wrap the cooked cake well in greaseproof paper, then foil. Store it in an airtight tin in a cool place. If the fruit touches the metal foil directly, it might react and spoil the taste.

Here's a typical recipe. Use a china bowl and a 20 cm (8 inches) round cake tin, twice as deep as the ones used for sandwich cakes. A two-pound loaf tin will do; you need the cake to be thick rather than flat. As you use plain flour, the mix won't rise very much.

For the fruit: -
250 grams (half a pound) of seedless raisins
125 grams (4 ounces) of sultanas
125 grams (4 ounces) of currants
50 grams (2 ounces) of chopped dates
100 grams (4 ounces) of glace cherries, halved
80 ml (3 fluid ounces) of cheap brandy
2 tablespoons of orange juice, and the grated zest of an orange

Mix all these together in the bowl, cover with a plate and leave to soak for a couple of days, stirring occasionally. Put the rest of the brandy away for later.

For the cake mix: -
125 grams (4 ounces) of soft dark brown sugar
125 grams (4 ounces) butter
2 eggs, beaten
125 grams (4 ounces) of plain flour, sieved together with half a teaspoon of cinnamon and a pinch of salt. Add half a teaspoon of ground mixed spice and a pinch of nutmeg, if you have them
50 grams (2 ounces) ground almonds
30 grams (1 ounce) of chopped hazelnuts

Preheat the oven to very low (Gas Mark 2; 150C; 300F), with a shelf at the low middle position. Cream the butter and sugar, mix in the eggs, stir in the flour and add the nuts. Combine this slowly with the fruit mixture, making sure all the fruit is coated in cake.

Grease and flour your cake tin. When you're cooking something in a thin walled tin for a long time, it's easy for the sides to get scorched. Lining your tin with greaseproof paper helps prevent this.

Dollop the cake mix in, level the top and cook for 2–3 hours, until a skewer poked into the middle comes out clean of uncooked cake mix. Cover the top with greaseproof paper after the first hour, or it may burn, and check every 15 minutes after two hours.

Leave the cake in the tin until it has completely cooled. Keep the greaseproof paper lining on it for storing, and trim off any burnt bits on top with a sharp knife. This is a challenging recipe for the amateur cook, but tradition has kindly decreed that it be covered in a thick layer of icing which hides any ragged bits!

Brush the top with a couple of tablespoons of warmed jam, traditionally apricot. Let this set, then wrap and store, adding brandy every fortnight as described above.

About a week before Xmas, you'll need to find somewhere to keep the completed iced cake; a clear space on a cupboard shelf, for example. Roll out some marzipan on greaseproof paper and cover the whole cake. Use jam to stick it on, if necessary.

You leave this to dry for a couple of days – on a plate, not in the tin – so there's plenty time to get more marzipan. You'll need about 500 grams (one pound); leftovers can be coloured with food dye and made into seasonal shapes.

Traditionally, royal icing was used for this cake, which is quite hard. A softer icing, more like a sugar paste, is preferred today. This can be bought ready-made. Roll it out as for the marzipan and stick it to the cake. Carefully smooth over the joins with a knife warmed in hot water. Creative use of seasonal decorations covers patchy bits!

Returned to its tin after the festivities, this cake will keep for a couple of weeks, thanks to its alcohol content and the layers of icing.

Interlude

Samhain

Autumn ends with a feast. The stores are in, there's no more harvest to gather, the work is done. As the nights draw in, travelling becomes difficult, even to the next village. One last party before we huddle around our own fires, listening to the wind in the chimney, the rain hammering on the roof...

Hallowe'en – October 31st – opens the gateway to winter; a celebration of the ancestors, of the dead. Acknowledging death as part of the cycle of life honoured the slaughter of the farm animals and helped people come to terms with it.

In Glastonbury town, there are the Crow Morris. Dressed in ragged black, their feathered head-dresses silhouetted against the lantern light, they clash their cudgels in a complicated dance.

"To Life! To Death! To Life and Death as One!"

Leering and lunging at the onlookers, they stamp out into the darkness, the sound of their eerie chanting fading away.

After this solemn moment, the festivities explode into light with fireworks and extravagant carnival processions. The year is complete, the harvest secured, the seeds for the spring planting safely stored. These celebrations are a glorious defiance of winter!

Conclusion

Remember the serious side of food resilience. You could need those two weeks' worth of stores for a variety of reasons. Having acquired them, they need to be rotated, so your emergency food is always within its use-by date.

You need a small amount of fresh fruit or vegetables every day, ideally provided by a resilience garden. Start planning meals around your own crops. Do you really need to buy something, or have you got a similar ingredient at home which is ready to be used?

Cook your own dinners, puddings, snacks. Avoid the temptations of labels and buy only what you need. The money you save on shopping trips allows you to spend the extra on local produce, to buy organic free-range meats, to invest in community supported agriculture.

Listen to the radio, or an audiobook, in the kitchen; avoid visual distractions. Wash up as you go; it keeps your hands clean and the work area clear.

Practice makes perfect, it's said. When trying something new, a recipe is helpful. The more you make this dish, the easier it becomes to judge 'a bit of this' and 'some of that'. Where you had to keep checking, now you open the oven at exactly the right time.

You learn how to fix a recipe if it's going wrong, how to adapt it to your tastes or food allergies. Make extra and freeze it; have complete control over the ingredients of your ready meals.

A vegetable garden provides a variety of fresh foods; using stored food opens up the concept of bulk buying. You find out what you actually use – plain flour, baked beans, sugar, tea – and can forage for bargains.

Use supermarkets, with their handy car parks, just to stock up on heavy items now and again. Get the bus into market and buy fresh food from local producers the rest of the time. Having an organic vegetable box delivered is another excellent way of getting used to seasonal produce.

Plan ahead, but be flexible; cultivate a resilient attitude to food. You are what you eat!

Afterword

Imagine a community of a hundred households, about two hundred adults. They live in a settlement in the centre of four square miles of productive land. Vegetables grow close to the houses; orchards and animals are further out. Permaculture merges with forest garden, then a belt of wild wood before the next village, a couple of hours' walk away.

Some people work on the farm permanently. They direct the others, who each provide a day's labour a week. Solar panels and windmills power the electric tractor, the smart irrigation systems, the stock fencing, the dairy and the freezers. There's not much need for digging in the rain.

In an emergency, however long, at any season, this community can fall back on its own food, water and power.

Normally there are other jobs. International trade flourishes. This settlement has been going for a long time; its workshops have a reputation for producing excellent precision components. The electronic currency these earn buys in coffee, sugar, foreign holidays. Some people work online as teachers or translators; others make beautiful furniture and trade it with the next village for fine cloth.

Unlike the basic resilience produce, this trade of goods and services is taxed. There's still a need for villages to share infrastructure projects or pool resources for education and medical services. Local decisions – including taxation levels – are the subject of much debate in everyday life. Through the internet, the community is aware of how affairs in the wider world may affect them.

An informed, energetic population who take an active interest in every aspect of their daily lives can create the government they deserve.

Appendix One

Food Types

Most meals contain protein, carbohydrates and fats. Fresh vegetables are an important addition, with their vitamins and minerals. Cakes and puddings have sugar, carbohydrates and fats. When planning your own stores, you need to make sure you have enough of each food type on board.

Proteins

These are found in meat, fish, eggs, dairy products, nuts, pulses and fungi. A lack of protein means you have less energy. Your ability to heal and to fend off illness is also affected.

Many fresh vegetables contain respectable amounts of protein. Unless you have a growing area, you won't have access to these during an emergency. In Britain, your protein stores will often be imported foods. The climate isn't favourable to growing many nuts or edible seeds, hence our reliance on animal products. Peas thrive in a cool climate; note the traditional popularity of mushy peas and pea soup!

The recommended minimum daily intake, depending on your body weight, is 45–55 grams (just under 2 ounces). You certainly don't need to exceed 100 grams a day. This doesn't refer to the weight of the actual food, but to the amount of protein in it. This is helpfully supplied on most labels until you get the hang of it. For example, a medium egg weighs about 60 grams and contains 6 grams of protein. Eggs are easily digestible and useful in a wide range of recipes as a binding agent, but aren't suitable for long term storage.

Animal proteins in general are difficult to store. Without refrigeration, fresh meat and dairy products quickly spoil. You could add canned fish and dried meats, such as biltong, to your list. UHT milk keeps well, though it has a shorter shelf life than most of the stores you'll be using. Parmesan cheese has a very low water content; it's good to keep for adding to pasta dishes.

Nuts, seeds and grains are designed to last. You have to prevent them germinating by keeping them in cool, dry and dark conditions. This is relatively easy – compare it to the infrastructure required to bring you a tin of corned beef!

There are a number of nut roast mixes available. These can be adapted to make pan fried burgers, and have a good shelf life. Whole nuts make good snacks. If you eat 15–25 grams of protein within 30 minutes of hard physical exercise, your body gets the maximum benefit in terms of muscle repair. That's a 100g packet of cashews or a couple of large peanut butter sandwiches.

Survival skills can turn your usual food priorities upside down – you're looking to maximise calories here. It can be hard to balance this with the constant need to use up emergency stores in a regular rotation during everyday life.

A 100g packet of almonds will give you half the protein you need for a day, but also nearly 600 kcal. You'd normally get plenty of protein from other sources, so you wouldn't need to eat them all at once. Use packets of nuts up in a stir fry; once opened, they will keep quite well, especially if you put them in a jar.

If you don't eat meat or dairy products it'd be wise to study edible mushrooms, which are a good protein source. An expert forager is an asset to a community. Some exotic varieties, such as shitake, can be cultivated at home.

Carbohydrates and sugar

These provide your fuel, easily used calories which give you the energy for action. Your body converts them to glucose, a simple sugar found in sweets, and burns them up. Eating actual sweets gives you a quick energy boost, followed by a 'sugar crash' where you feel quite depleted.

It's better to eat a variety of carbohydrates, even if the foods take longer to digest. Starch, as found in grains and root vegetables, is the most important. It's more digestible ground and cooked than eaten raw. Starchy foods, especially whole grains and fruits, are also an important source of dietary fibre, which stimulates digestion.

Carbohydrates are easier to keep than proteins or fats. They're designed to be a storage system for the plant, to feed next year's growth or a sprouting seed. When you're planning your emergency stores, consider that most of your energy supply will have to come from this food type, and that you will need to find a way of cooking it.

If this could be really difficult, then store oat bars with added dried fruit, biscuits, and packets of unsalted nuts. These are useful to carry in your grab bag as well.

Fats and oils

Fats release heat and energy as they are digested, but use up water in the process. They're not great as a body fuel supply where drinking water is very limited. Fats and oils supply essential nutrients though, so they have to be part of your resilience store.

At least two fats – linoleic and alpha-linolenic – are essential to health. They used to be called 'vitamin F' but were reclassified as 'essential fatty acids' for technical reasons. In your body, these are used to build specialised long chain polyunsaturated fats called omega-3 and omega-6.

There are two main types of fats – saturated and unsaturated. Saturated fats are solid at room temperature and keep well, while unsaturated are liquid and go rancid on exposure to air. An industrialised food distribution network favours the former for ease of transport. Hence saturated fats, which mainly come from land animals, became a larger part of our diet while the unsaturated fish and plant oils were neglected.

Fats and oils are the hardest food type to store, and the sell-by dates often mean it. If you ever have to make survival choices about eating out-of-date tins, contents with a lot of oil will generally have spoiled fastest. It's also difficult to produce in a British resilience garden as the climate is too cool and wet for many oil rich plants to flourish.

Here, in the old days, flax and hemp seeds – rich in the omega fats – were a by-product of growing for 'homespun' textiles and supplemented a diet dependant on animal fats from eggs, milk and meat. Fish – another good source of unsaturated fats – was also a key food. During Lent and certain other holy days, the population was obliged to eat it.

Some tins of oily fish are a useful addition to your survival stores, as are nuts and seeds. If you have a cool, dark place where bottles of liquid can be stored upright, keep some cold pressed plant oils such as olive or hemp. Coconut oil, although very good for you and one of the easiest fats to store, doesn't contain the essential omega fatty acids.

Vitamins

These are vital nutrients which your body requires in order to work properly. Currently, thirteen are recognised and most of these are obtained from food. You only need to eat a small amount of each, but it has to be regular.

You'll need to do some research to be sure of keeping a good supply of these vitamins in your stores. I add dried and evaporated milks, porridge oats and nuts to mine. Vitamin B12 is another one that isn't found in plants, only in animal foods; a jar of yeast extract covers that one.

The deficiency disorders take a while to develop. Generally, a shortage of key elements in your diet for a limited time will just weaken you. However, being more susceptible to illness, slower to heal injuries and lacking energy are not survival traits!

There are two different sorts of vitamin –

Fat soluble

These are mainly found in animal products. Vitamins A, D, E and K belong to this type. Your body can store them, so you can last awhile without having them in your diet. It can even be harmful to eat too much of them, as Arctic explorers found when sampling polar bear liver – very rich in Vitamin A! Your stores should include tinned oily fish and some nuts. Use your saved seed to get those leafy green vegetables going in your resilience garden.

If you don't eat animals, you'll need mushrooms for Vitamin D. It's not found in other plants, but exposing your bare skin to sunlight allows your own body to synthesise this vitamin. People in the northern lands, with long dark winters, tend to eat more meat, fish and dairy than those living in places with more sunshine.

Vitamin A – found in liver, orange, ripe yellow fruits, leafy vegetables, carrots, pumpkin, squash, spinach, fish, soya milk, milk. A deficiency can cause night blindness.

Vitamin D – found in fish, eggs, liver, mushrooms, sunlight. A deficiency can cause rickets, especially in children.

Vitamin E – found in many fruits and vegetables, nuts and seeds. A deficiency can cause reproductive problems.

Vitamin K – found in leafy green vegetables such as spinach, also egg yolks and liver. A deficiency leads to the slow healing of wounds.

Water soluble

Most of these are found in a wide range of foods, which is handy as you can't store them in your body. You must have a small amount of each every day. Vitamin C and the B vitamins are in this category. As they're easily washed out of food, the best sources are those fresh leaves from your garden. Processed foods will lose a large percentage of their original vitamin content.

Vitamin B1 (thiamine) – found in pork, oatmeal, brown rice, vegetables, potatoes, liver, eggs. Deficiency can lead to beri-beri.

Vitamin B2 (riboflavin) – found in dairy products, bananas, popcorn, green beans, asparagus. A deficiency can cause inflammation of the mouth, anaemia and weakness.

Vitamin B3 (niacin) – found in meat, fish, eggs, many vegetables, mushrooms, tree nuts. Deficiency can result in pellagra.

Vitamin B5 (pantothenic acid) – found in meat, broccoli, avocados. A deficiency can cause an unpleasant sensation of pins and needles to develop.

Vitamin B6 (pyridoxamine) – found in meat, vegetables, tree nuts, bananas. Deficiency leads to anaemia.

Vitamin B7 (biotin) – found in raw egg yolk, liver, peanuts, leafy green vegetables. A deficiency can cause dermatitis, and inflammation of the small intestine.

Vitamin B9 (folic acid) – found in leafy vegetables, pasta, bread, cereal, liver. Deficiency can lead to birth defects, and pregnant women are often given supplements of this vitamin.

Vitamin B12 (cobalamin) – found in meat, fish, dairy, yeast extract – low in plant foods. Humans can store a little of this in their livers. A deficiency leads to pernicious anaemia and nerve damage.

Vitamin C (ascorbic acid) – found in many fruits and vegetables. Deficiency causes scurvy, a notorious problem on sailing ships in the olden days. It was cured by dosing the sailors with lime juice, hence the name 'Limeys' for British seamen.

Minerals and trace elements

These are simpler chemicals than the vitamins, mere elements broken right down and incorporated into the complex molecules used by the cells of your body to do stuff. Many of them are only needed in tiny amounts.

Potassium

Important for the balancing of body fluids and cardiac health; an adult needs about 4 grams of potassium each day. It's found in fruit, especially dried bananas. Meat, nuts and pulses such as lentils, peas and beans supply potassium too.

Without enough of this element in your diet, you can feel faint and dizzy as well as overtired. Muscle cramps and even heart spasms can result.

Sodium Chloride

Common salt. Dietary advice tends to focus on the sodium content – which is just under half by weight – but we need chlorine too. It's an essential part of the hydrochloric acid we use in our stomachs, and helps with general fluid balance. Most foods contain potassium chloride. Although you need around 2 grams per day, it's very difficult to acquire a chlorine deficiency.

Sodium controls blood pressure and is crucial in sending nerve impulses around the body. Due to the high levels of hidden salt in processed foods, most people are eating too much sodium. You only need 500 milligrams a day to get by, and shouldn't eat more than 2400 mg, the equivalent of a teaspoon of salt.

Too much sodium causes you to automatically dilute your blood with water, so raising your blood pressure as there is more liquid in the same space. Cooking from raw ingredients means you can control the amount of sodium in your diet.

Salt doesn't go off, though it can get damp. A small plastic packet with a few teaspoons full can be slipped into your stores box, or even your grab bag. Try to get tinned foods without added salt though; you may need to use the water in recipes.

Calcium

Calcium is used to build bones and teeth. You need vitamin D to be able to absorb it from food. Children raised in the old factory towns with little access to sunlight and dairy foods often developed rickets, a condition where their bones were too soft to bear their weight and became bent.

An adult needs about 0.7 grams (700 milligrams) a day. Milk products, nuts and seeds supply calcium. Seaweeds and some plants – notably broccoli and dandelion – can be a source, but other leafy vegetables may contain binding agents which won't let you absorb it. The oxalic acid which holds the iron in spinach and chard also keeps their calcium away from you.

An unusual source of calcium is powdered eggshell. You may not fancy it yourself, but your dog might appreciate the extra nutritional value if you're eating from stores. I find the shells easier to grind if they're baked a little first.

Phosphorus

Another ingredient of bones and teeth. Phosphorus also helps release energy from food. You need about 0.5 grams (500 milligrams) daily. It's found in protein rich foods such as meat and dairy products. Grains contain phosphorus too, but a lot of it is in the form of 'phytates' which aren't easily absorbed by us.

These can also interfere with the take up of other nutrients. Sprouting and fermenting grains gets rid of a lot of the troublesome phytic acid. Sourdough bread is a particularly good way of getting the best value from rye flour.

Usually, you don't need to extract the maximum possible nutritional value from food, because there's plenty of it. Our ancestors weren't so well off, and modern science can explain many traditional customs around food preparation.

Magnesium

Magnesium is involved in many essential chemical reactions in the body. It works with enzymes to break down food, regulate cholesterol levels and produce proteins. It's important in growing new cells, protecting the DNA which determines how they develop. The levels and balances of other minerals in your body are controlled by magnesium.

An adult needs 0.3 grams (300 milligrams) a day from meat, grains, nuts or green leafy vegetables. As refining removes a great deal of magnesium from food, a modern diet can fall short of the recommended daily intake. Lightly cooked garden leaves are a good source, as this mineral is part of the chlorophyll which gives plants their green colour.

Iron

This has several important roles. Iron gives the red colour to blood, and is crucial in transporting oxygen around the body. Without enough iron, you become easily tired and can develop anaemia. Men need about 9 milligrams (mg) a day, while women have to have nearly twice that.

Iron deficiency is quite common compared to other dietary disorders. However, a slight deficiency can provide protection against some illnesses which affect the blood, such as malaria and tuberculosis. This is because the disease agents need iron themselves, and cannot flourish without it. Blood, human milk and egg white all contain proteins which hold iron tightly, away from hostile bacteria.

Meat is, of course, a good source of iron. It's difficult to store, so consider nuts, lentils, dried fruits and chocolate as well. Your leafy green vegetables – not chard or spinach – can provide this element. So can cooking in a cast iron pan.

There are two types of dietary iron. Heme iron comes from animal sources and is easily absorbed. Non-heme iron is from plants and is harder for our bodies to use. Adding vitamin C to the meal – a squeeze of lemon juice, some fresh leaves – helps the uptake of plant iron. Other foods, such as tea, coffee and milk, can block your ability to absorb iron. A dilemma for the survivalist!

Zinc

Zinc is important to the body's immune system. It's involved with cell growth and repair, especially in healing wounds. Children need zinc in their diet. It's also important in breaking down carbohydrates, in smell and taste, and aids the action of insulin. Deficiency is associated with post-natal depression, ulcers, skin conditions and apathy.

Dark meat is the best source of zinc, but nuts and seeds are fine in normal circumstances; seaweed too. If crops are grown on soil poor in zinc though, they have a much lower content of the mineral. This is a serious issue; there could be up to 2 billion people worldwide suffering from zinc deficiency. It's a complex problem as zinc tends to interfere with the uptake of iron and copper. You need to deal with several problems at once.

If you're interested in creating plans for a permanent resilient diet, it's worth studying nutrition for these little ambushes!

An adult needs a mere 4–13 milligrams per day, depending on body weight. Without it, you become vulnerable to infections. Too much and its highly toxic effects kick in, so don't overdo supplements – 20mg a day is more than enough.

Copper

Along with iron, which it helps the body to absorb from food, copper is important in forming red blood cells. It stimulates the immune system and neutralises harmful 'free radicals' as well as being involved with key metabolic processes. Copper is particularly essential for pregnant women and children, to ensure normal development.

An adult needs between 1 and 1.3 milligrams daily, which is easy to obtain from a balanced diet. Be careful with supplements; too much iron or zinc makes copper unavailable to the body. Eat nuts, potatoes, shellfish, beans and those dark leafy greens from your resilience garden. Liver, cocoa, olive oil, barley and yeast are also good sources of copper.

Studies are going on around a maximum recommended dose of 10 milligrams a day; excess copper, like many of these minerals, is toxic. It's not usually a problem unless there is copper in your drinking water supply.

Iodine

This is important in the thyroid gland, which produces hormones affecting the entire body. A lack of iodine can stunt mental and physical growth in children; it causes a variety of symptoms in adults. Goitres – where the neck is swollen from an enlarged thyroid gland – used to be common in certain parts of the world.

The provision of iodised table salt in areas at risk has helped eliminate this uncomfortable problem. British salt is no longer iodised; instead, milk and dairy products are the main sources of iodine for most people. Soya milk may have iodine added to it.

Sea-foods are another classic source, with white fish having more iodine than oily fish. Some seaweeds, especially brown ones, contain so much that you could exceed the recommended dose. In Japan, where the diet is full of iodine-rich sea-foods, people can be eating up to three milligrams a day. One milligram a day is generally considered excessive.

However, tea – especially the green tea popular in Japan – interferes with the absorption of iodine, due to its fluoride content.

The thyroid is a temperamental part of your body. It can be overactive; this makes you ill as well, and can be brought on by too much iodine. The USA recommends a daily intake of 0.15 milligrams (150 micrograms) for adults. Most people in developed countries take in more than this RDA, around 0.25 to 0.4 mg.

The effects of an excess of iodine are most pronounced when suddenly increasing your dose. This was observed in the salt supplement programme, and is a danger if taking iodine as protection against radioactive fallout. You should have a pack of the right type of iodine tablets in your emergency stores as speed is crucial to protect your thyroid, and they are quite hard to come by in Britain. 'Thyrosafe' is recommended by some prepper sites.

Don't drink the sort of iodine you dab on wounds. This is tincture of iodine and not meant to be swallowed, though it can be used in tiny amounts to purify water for drinking, in a similar way to bleach. Do some serious research before you try out any of these emergency life savers!

Trace elements

The minerals described above are often referred to as trace elements, or micronutrients. Compared to the amount of food you eat, the quantities needed are very tiny. You require even less of the key minerals below, but you do need them. They often form part of complicated molecules involved with enzymes and hormones.

Boron – Green vegetables, fruit, nuts
Chromium – Meat, whole grains, lentils, broccoli, potatoes, spices
Cobalt – Fish, nuts, green leafy vegetables, cereals
Manganese – Tea, bread, nuts, cereals, peas and runner beans
Molybdenum – Nuts, tinned and leafy vegetables, cereals, peas, cauliflower
Nickel – Nuts, lentils, oats
Selenium – Brazil nuts, fish, eggs, meat

Silicon – Grains, fruit, vegetables
Sulphur – In many foods and as additive in some processed foods
Vanadium – Mushrooms, shellfish, beer, wine, grain, black pepper, parsley

Appendix Two

Fourteen days on stored food

The menus below are based on the contents of a 32 litre plastic box which will fit under many beds, even in a wardrobe and certainly in a loft. If you store food in an outside shed, put it in a metal box placed on wooden runners. Check your tins for freezing in cold weather, as described in the September chapter.

The amounts used provide reasonable meals for one, and slightly skimpy portions for two. The wide range of recipes gives the best chance to incorporate kitchen supplies and garden produce, which you should use in preference to longer lasting stores.

You can cook them on a single cooker ring. If you have the use of an oven, you could turn some recipes into pies; if not, make pan breads with the flour.

It's not necessary to wait for an emergency to test these menus. An adventurous way of rotating your survival stores would be to actually practise living on them once a year. Was it enough? What else might you need? This exercise really increases your practical resilience!

Why keep stores?

In a serious emergency, there may be problems with the water supply. Sourcing fuel could be difficult. You might need to cook on an open fire, measuring out ingredients with a flat piece of wood. More probably, you'll be in an evacuation centre faced with an unfamiliar cooker, a drawer of odd cutlery and a random assortment of food.

This idea of an emergency is an extreme case, but if you make some preparations for this, you'll find them useful in much smaller disruptions. If traffic is particularly bad, you can delay that shopping trip because you are certain there is enough food in the house. Recovering from an unexpected injury? Get someone to bring your box into the kitchen, and you have all your cooking essentials to hand, including tea.

Depending on your normal kitchen stock to see you through isn't very organised. You could be caught unawares with low supplies. Having a good selection of stored food to hand is easy to achieve, and has many collateral benefits.

Even if you have a loft, or other convenient place to keep larger amounts, it's good to know how to pack the sort of stack box described in this chapter. As outlined in 'The Resilience Handbook – How to Survive in the 21st Century', you are typically either isolated or evacuated in an emergency.

If essential services can't reach you, at least you have your own kitchen and garden to help tide you over. Occasionally, however, your local area may become too dangerous to stay in. In Britain, this is mainly due to flooding. You may have to stay elsewhere on a temporary basis.

It's very likely that you could drive to safety, as long as you left in a hurry. Along with your grab bags, this box of stores can be brought with you. Familiar food is an important morale booster in this kind of situation.

Better yet is the confidence which comes from having a plan, with the resources to carry it out. Having a good selection of stored food to hand is easy to achieve, and has many collateral benefits.

A reminder about water

As I have a floored loft, I can keep a good supply of clean water. I have twenty of the two litre bottles of sparkling water, which is the sort of bulky purchase you would continue to get from supermarkets. I use these to make fizzy drinks with home-made fruit syrups, so they're easy to rotate.

That gives me 40 litres of drinking water; enough for nearly three weeks, so I can afford to share. In addition, I keep some of the larger, five litre containers of still water, which provides 25 litres for cooking and cleaning. Don't skimp on washing up even if water if short – you can soon get food poisoning from dirty utensils. At worst, wipe them completely clean with newspaper, then scald with a little boiling water.

These recipes assume you have the basic minimum of water and at least one cooking ring, but no fridge or access to fresh food from outside your immediate area. This could be due to a local or national emergency, but a sudden unexpected gap in your household budget might have a similar effect.

Suggested recipe list

Day one – Lentil soup and bread

Have porridge for breakfast each morning. Add jam, honey, tinned or foraged fruit. Use up the UHT milk while it lasts. The dried milk will taste much better when you're hungry.
Make a loaf of bread (see the November recipe). I store a tin of bread yeast, but if you have trouble using this up in rotation, save space by keeping three sachets instead. Cook up a lentil soup, using the December recipe for chicken and lentil soup. You can make a good stock by boiling clean vegetable peelings with some garden herbs.

Pan bread

Make the bread mix, knead the risen dough lightly, form it into flat buns about half an inch (just over a centimetre) thick, and let these rise a little before cooking on a griddle or thick frying pan. Don't use oil; sprinkle a layer of dry flour on the pan.

Turn the buns often; cook for 20–30 minutes. Keep the griddle well warmed, but not sizzling. Scrape off the loose flour before serving.

Day Two

Toast the rest of the bread and have it with baked beans and sardines (August recipe). This is nice with home-made chutney and a salad of foraged leaves.

Put the peas for tomorrow's meal on to soak overnight; there will be instructions on the packet. Use a quarter of the pack for each of the meals.

Day Three

Make stew using corned beef and the soaked, cooked dried peas, flavoured with a stock cube.

Add fresh vegetables from your resilience garden, some sprigs of herbs from pots. You need to keep up those trace elements.

Use plain flour to make dumplings (January recipe), raising them with lemon juice and bicarbonate of soda. Plain flour is more versatile in stores than self-raising flour. Lemon juice and bicarb have many other uses; look them up.

Day Four

Drain some tinned chickpeas, reserving the juice. If you know how to use this as an egg substitute, there's a little extra sugar, plain flour and coconut oil in the stores for making a cake of sorts.
Heat the chickpeas with two thirds of a jar of curry sauce, add any fresh vegetables you might have, stir in some chutney. Serve with rice.

Day Five

Reserve some of the curry sauce and have it with falafels, made with the dried mix. Serve with fresh rice; reheated rice carries a high risk of food poisoning.

Day Six

Have pasta with tomato passata. Sprinkle on a powdered cheese, like Parmesan. This stores well, and is a good flavouring for otherwise bland dishes. Try it on some shredded, steamed cabbage leaves.

Soak the peas for the next day.

Day Seven

Make another loaf of bread, or some more pan bread; soak some more peas. Serve with nut burgers from dried mix, tomato ketchup and mushy peas.

Day Eight

You've got enough bread flour for three loaves. Have toast for breakfast, spread with coconut oil or yeast extract, as a change from porridge.

Tonight's meal is lentil stew with rice. Your pound of rice will do for four meals; there's enough left for one more.

Day Nine

Make your last loaf, have beans and sardines again. Put another quarter packet of peas on to soak.

If you really are in a survival situation, you need to give serious thought to your next move. Talk to other people affected. Even if the food transportation system was badly damaged, plans to deliver basic rations would be moving into place by now.

Your community should have an emergency plan, held by town or parish councils. Make sure you know how to contact relevant authorities for progress reports. Use the Resilience Handbook to help identify goals, barriers and strategies; think around the wheel, as described in this book.

Rations are usually more stored food. Fresh vegetables may not be available for a while. Is it appropriate to organise a community growing space and use your saved vegetable seeds? A crop of fresh leaves can be produced by cress or rocket within a few weeks, at most times of the year.

Day Ten

Use some tomato passata to make a sauce with tinned tuna and cooked dried peas. Serve with pasta.

Day Eleven

Cook up the last of the pasta with the rest of the passata. There should be plenty of dried cheese left. Soak the last of the peas.

Day Twelve

Stew with dried peas and dumplings. Keep adding fresh herbs to these recipes, towards the end of cooking to preserve the vitamin C. If you can't keep a pot of these at home, and have no growing space, add some vitamin tablets to your store box.

Day Thirteen

Mix plain flour and water into a dough, roll this out into thin rounds, rather like pancakes. Cook gently in a dry frying pan, turning often. Serve these chapatis with lentil soup.

Day Fourteen

Celebrate the end of your stores with a Thai curry. Lightly cook the sachet of curry mix with the unsalted cashews for a few minutes, stir in the coconut milk, add the drained tin of butter beans and simmer attentively for about 20 minutes. Serve with the last of the rice.

A sample checklist for this fourteen day store

Porridge oats (500g)
Bread flour (1.5 kg)
Tin of dried bread yeast
Plain flour (500g)
Red lentils (500g)
Tube of tomato puree
Half a dozen stock cubes
Baked beans x 2 medium sized tins
Sardine tins x 2
Jar of coconut oil
Dried peas (250g)
Gravy granules
Suet packet
Lemon juice
Bicarbonate of soda
Tin of chickpeas
Jar of curry sauce
Rice (500g)
Falafels (dried mix)
Tomato passata packets x 2
Italian style powdered cheese (small tub)
Pasta (500g)
Nut roast or burger mix (dried)
Tomato ketchup
Small jar of yeast extract
Tin of tuna
Sachet of Thai curry paste
Tin of butter beans
Tin of coconut milk
Small packet of unsalted cashew nuts
Peanut butter
Coffee (100g tin)
Tea bags (packet of 40)
Soft brown sugar (500g)
UHT milk (2 x 500ml)
Dried milk (to make 6 pints)
Small tin of evaporated milk

Customising your food store

This very basic food store, which can serve for two people, cost around £50 (2019 prices). It includes tea, coffee, sugar and milk. If your community became isolated, you would need to confer with your neighbours. Having tea is a good start.

The supplies fit in a box which is easily stored – and portable, should you need to evacuate by car. For people with allergies, a personal food supply could be a lifesaver. Design your own, taking into account the principles outlined in this book, around the foods you prefer to eat. Only put away food with over three months of shelf life, and remember you have to use it up in everyday cooking.

Some other useful supplies

If you've got the space, keep a larger store for home use. Extra carbohydrates – pasta, rice, oats, flour – are always handy, as are sugar, oils and UHT milk. The list below gives some more suggestions.

Drinking chocolate or cocoa, herb teas, squashes
Coffee whitener (to conserve milk for cooking)
Water purifying tablets
Tins of vegetables (unsalted)
Tins of fruit, cream, custard, golden syrup
Jams, packets of jelly
Biscuits, oatcakes, crispbreads
Mustard, vinegar, sachets of salt and sauces
Raisins, dried fruit, prunes, sealed packets of nuts
Dried seaweed, beans, potato
Biltong and jerky
Ration packs and other survival foods, vitamin C tablets

You can cut down on general food costs by 'harvesting' bargains which you know you're going to use; with the money saved, you can buy better quality, locally produced fresh food to go with these stored basics.

Recommended Reading

Beer, Gunter and Jaros, Patrik: Waste Not, Want Not – you call it leftovers we call it ingredients, Parragon Books Ltd, Bath 2008

Berry, C.J.J: First Steps in Winemaking, Holmes and Sons (Printers) Ltd, Andover, Hants 1960

Dartnell, Lewis: The Knowledge – How to Rebuild our World from Scratch, The Bodley Head, London 2014

Davies, Barry: The Encyclopaedia of Outdoor Survival, Lewis International Inc, Miami 2002

Diamond, Jared: Collapse – How Societies Choose to Fail or Survive, Penguin Books Ltd, London 2005

Dowding, Charles: Organic Gardening, the natural no-dig way, Green Books Ltd, Totnes 2007

Fairlie, Simon: Meat; a Benign Extravagance, Permanent Publications, Hampshire 2010. Nobody should comment on food production until they've read this book.

Fern, Ken: Plants for a Future – edible and useful plants for a healthier world, Permanent Publications, Hampshire 1997

Foley, Caroline: The Allotment Handbook, New Holland Publishers (UK) Ltd., London 2004

Jones, Terry and Ereira, Alan: Barbarians – an alternative Roman history, BBC Books 2007

Jordan, Peter: The Mushroom Guide and Identifier – the ultimate guide to identifying, picking and using mushrooms, Hermes House (an imprint of Anness Publishing Ltd) London 2010

Larkcom, Joy: Grow Your Own Vegetables, Frances Lincoln Ltd., London 2002

Littlewood, Michael: The Companion Planting Chart

Mars, Ross and Willis, Simone: How to Permaculture Your Life – strategies, skills and techniques for the transition to a greener world, Candlelight Trust, Australia 2015

McNab, Chris: The SAS Handbook of Living off the Land, Silverdale Books, Leicester 2002

Rowbotham, Michael: The Grip of Death – a study of modern money, debt slavery and destructive economics, Jon Carpenter Publishing, Oxford 1998. Essential to understand the global debt-based economy.

Rowse, A.L: The England of Elizabeth, Macmillan and Co. Ltd 1950

Segnit, Niki: The Flavour Thesaurus – Pairings, recipes and ideas for the creative cook, Bloomsbury, London 2010

Staments, Paul: Mycelium Running – how mushrooms can help save the world, Ten Speed Press (a division of Random House Inc) USA 2005

Walker, Elizabeth Jane: The Resilience Handbook – How to Survive in the 21st Century, Magic Oxygen, Lyme Regis 2015. You need this book.

Whitefield, Patrick: How to Read the Landscape, Permanent Publications, Hampshire 2014

Wiseman, John: SAS Survival Guide, Collins, London 2010 (4th Edition)

About the Author

Elizabeth J Walker is a teacher and writer with many years of experience in living 'off the grid'.

She gained an Honours degree in Psychology from Edinburgh University in 1977, while restoring an old tenement flat, and rebuilding a car engine to see how it worked. Having failed to prevent the demolition of her street, she bought a camper van and began a career in event management.

With this lifestyle, it was rare to have access to mains services. Water had to be carried from a standing tap, sometimes over a mile away. She used solar panels in the days when you had to solder your own diodes, and cooked with bottled gas.

At the end of the Nineties, Elizabeth moved into a house near Glastonbury, Somerset. There, she began a business in steward training, specialising in off grid events. She wrote a Steward Handbook and ran large teams of volunteers.

With the introduction of the 2006 Licensing Act, Elizabeth branched out into event welfare work. With industry colleagues she formed a charitable organisation – Medical Welfare – to act as an umbrella group, and worked with emergency services at Silver Command level.

Crisis management at events gave Elizabeth direct experience of how situations can develop and plans must be adapted. She became involved with the local Town Council's emergency planners, where she realised that many of the key elements for a resilient community were not in place.

Working with colleague Linda Benfield, they set about analysing the complex interaction of resources, networks and barriers involved in achieving community resilience. Surrounded by flow charts and spider diagrams, they had a sudden inspiration and reinvented the wheel. Using the Resilience Wheel concept, Elizabeth wrote a training manual for their event volunteers, which evolved into 'The Resilience Handbook – How to Survive in the 21st Century', and associated resources.

'Recipes for Resilience' is an instruction manual for your personal food security, and answers the riddle in the Handbook.

Visit elizabethjwalker.com to learn more about practical resilience.